GREATER WASHINGTON AREA BICYCLE ATLAS

Fifth Edition

Edited by
Jim McCarthy
Sharon Gang

Photography by
Martha Tabor

Cover design by Monica Snellings
Maps by Bob Flanagan
Typeset by Bill Silverman
Printed by Banta Company, Harrisonburg, Virginia

Photos by Martha Tabor except p. 231 by Ruddy Aukschum

The publishers, editors and authors have done their best to ensure the accuracy of all the information in the *Greater Washington Area Bicycle Atlas*. However, they accept no responsibility for any loss, injury or inconvenience sustained as a result of information or advice contained in the book.

ISBN 0-9614892-4-3
Washington Area Bicyclist Association
Potomac Area Council of Hostelling International

Library of Congress Catalog Card Number 97-061653

This book is printed on recycled paper.

Printing History	Editor(s)
1st Edition, 1974	Alan Berkowitz
2nd Edition, 1977	Dave Gilbert
3rd Edition, 1985	Ken Moskowitz
3rd Edition Revised, 1987	Sharon Gang
4th Edition, 1992	Charles Baughman, Bonnie Nevel and Bill Silverman
5th Edition, 1998	Jim McCarthy and Sharon Gang

There is more to life than increasing its speed.

— Mahatma Gandhi

Table of Contents

Introduction

This atlas invites you outdoors. It encourages you to discover your surroundings at a more leisurely pace than the mad dash to the office. It entices you to explore the Washington area — from the Blue Ridge Mountains to the Eastern Shore — under your own steam.

Each tour in the atlas offers something special, whether natural, cultural or historical. Spectacular, diverse and interesting, the tours in this atlas are worth exploring without a bike, but are even more special on one.

And what is so special about bicycling? As a sport, it is healthier than most, with aerobic stimulation of the heart, lungs and muscles. Bicycling is also an aesthetic experience: a means of transportation so simple and energy-efficient that the rest of the world seems comparatively busy, noisy and intense. The bicycle allows us to experience the beauty and simplicity of our environment in a clean, economical way. And most of all, it is *fun!*

What Is In This Atlas

Now in its fifth edition, the *Greater Washington Area Bicycle Atlas* includes everything you need to know about bicycling in the mid-Atlantic region. The Introduction describes climate, topography and history, provides safety tips, and explains how the tours are organized and described. It suggests equipment and other essentials to help make your trip trouble-free, and provides suggestions for obtaining information on current road and trail conditions.

The main part of the book consists of 67 tours, ranging from 10 to 184 miles in length. Most are 20-50 miles — two to five hours for the average recreational cyclist. We've organized the tours in three groups:

- *In Your Backyard*, 12 rides that begin within the Capital Beltway, and for the most part, stay there;

- *Not Too Far Away*, 30 rides that start within an hour's drive of Washington; and

- *Farther Afield*, 25 rides that start one to three hours' drive from Washington, including 11 rides on the Eastern Shore of the Chesapeake Bay.

Route locator maps at the end of this Introduction show the general location of each ride. These maps follow the organization of the book, except that for readability we have separated Eastern Shore rides from the others in the Farther Afield section.

For many riders, we realize, the *length* of the ride may be more important than where it is located. For this group, we've listed the rides in order by length, on the next page.

Each tour listing includes a cue sheet, detailing exact directions, and a map of the ride showing the route in the context of other local roads. Tour descriptions provide information on getting to the starting point, length of route (including options), terrain, points of interest, food, lodging and additional maps. Rides that start near Metro stations are identified by a Metro or 🅜 symbol, and directions from Metro to the starting point are provided. New in this edition are nearly 50 photos by Martha Tabor. We hope the photos will whet your appetite by showing some of the interesting sites along the way.

The Appendix contains useful information on bike organizations (many of which sponsor rides or tours); where to obtain additional touring information (both sources of additional tours and maps); a list of Hostelling International (HI) hostels, several of which are starting or ending points for tours in this book; a section on car-free bike touring, which describes Metro's Bike-on-Rail program (14 rides are accessible by Metrorail), crossing the Chesapeake Bay without a car, and, for out-of-area visitors, bicycle access to Amtrak and commercial airline flights; and bicycle access to Washington's three major airports.

The Index catalogues the routes, points of interest, and geographic locations of each tour in an easy-to-use format.

The Mid-Atlantic Region

Mountainous to the west and flat to the east, the mid-Atlantic region includes a variety of terrain that will interest cyclists of every skill level. Maryland's western panhandle has lush forest, steep mountains and broad valleys, while its Eastern Shore features flat farmland and sleepy fishing villages on the spectacular Chesapeake Bay. Virginia's topography ranges from the majestic Blue Ridge Mountains and the historic Shenandoah Valley in the west to the Piedmont region, an elevated rolling plain south and west of Washington. East of the Piedmont, the flat Tidewater area extends 100 miles inland from the Atlantic Ocean.

Rides by Length

UNDER 20 MILES

2. Monuments and Museums [M]
3. Capital Crescent Trail [M]
5. Mount Vernon Trail [M]
11. Alexandria Loop [M]
17. Seneca Mini-Tour

22. Triadelphia Reservoir
27. Baltimore and Annapolis Trail/BWI Trail
29. Geese Galore
32. Prince William Park

33. Hill Haters Half Hundred Kilometers (alternate)
57. Loch Raven Loop (alternate)

20-30 MILES

1. National Capital Bike Tour [M]
3. Capital Crescent Trail [M] (alternate finish)
4. Rock Creek Trail [M]
10. Arlington History Ride [M]
12. Anacostia Headwaters Loop [M]
13. Monocacy Aqueduct Ride
15. Back of Sugarloaf (alternate)

20. Three Covered Bridges (alternate)
23. Ellicott City Loop
46. St. Michaels - Oxford Loop
53. Bethany Beach Backroads
54. Amish Country Ride
55. St. Mary's City to Point Lookout
56. Northern Central Railroad Trail

58. Prettyboy Reservoir Challenge (alternate)
62. Shenandoah Valley Venture (northern loop)
62. Shenandoah Valley Venture (southern loop)
63. Bear's Den to Harpers Ferry
67. Williamsburg - Jamestown Loop

30-40 MILES

8. Glen Echo to Seneca Loop
9. Georgetown to Great Falls [M] (alternate)
16. Seneca - Poolesville Loop
21. Gaithersburg Getaway
24. Howard's Hills (alternate)
25. Washington to Baltimore [M] (alternate)
28. Anne Arundel Adventure
30. Portside Pacer
33. Hill Haters Half Hundred Kilometers

34. Vineyard Visit
40. Leesburg-Waterford-Hamilton Trek
41. Mount Gilead to Hamilton Trek
42. Point of Rocks Explorer
44. Rock Hall Ramble (alternate)
45. Chestertown to Betterton Loop
48. Bridges of Dorchester County
51. Princess Anne to Deal Island
52. Ghost Town Gambol

57. Loch Raven Loop
58. Prettyboy Reservoir Challenge
60. South Mountain - Sharpsburg Tour
61. Antietam Battlefield Loop
62. Shenandoah Valley Venture (alternate)
65. Berkeley Springs Loop

40-50 MILES

6. W&OD Trail [M]
9. Georgetown to Great Falls [M]
14. Poolesville - Leesburg Loop
20. Three Covered Bridges
24. Howard's Hills
25. Washington to Baltimore [M]
31. Chesapeake to Patuxent

36. Virginia Hunt Country
43. Chesapeake & Delaware Canal Ride
47. Ride to Wye Oak
49. Blackwater Wildlife Refuge Ride
50. Princess Anne/Snow Hill

62. Shenandoah Valley Venture
64. Penn Dutch Treat
66. Charlottesville Circuit (alternate)

OVER 50 MILES

6. W&OD Trail [M] (alternate finish)
7. C&O Canal Towpath [M]
15. Back of Sugarloaf
18. Lilypons Loop

19. Washington to Harpers Ferry [M]
26. Capital to Capital (and Back!) [M]
35. Pedaling the Piedmont
37. The Resplendent Rappahannock

38. Warrenton Wanderlust
39. Front Royal Hills
44. Rock Hall Ramble
59. Westminster to Gettysburg Loop
66. Charlottesville Circuit

Across the region, the spring and fall months are ideal for bicycling. Most bicyclists break out of their winter doldrums and hit the road in March. The region is famous for its spring seasons with cherry blossoms in late March or early April, followed by dogwood and azaleas in late April and early May. Summer temperatures reach well into the 90s, often with heavy humidity. Cycling is best early in the day during the peak summer months. In September, the heat of summer gives way to a long, gentle autumn. Touring is often comfortable into November.

The region is steeped in history and includes many important Civil War sites. Barely 100 miles separate Richmond and Washington, the two capitals of the divided nation. Dozens of decisive battles were fought on the Piedmont plain at places like Bull Run, Chancellorsville and Fredericksburg. The fertile Shenandoah Valley was ravaged time after time by numerous campaigns from both sides. In the Tidewater region, the Confederate Army gave ground inch by inch when more than 120,000 Union troops landed near Norfolk to march on Richmond. Sharpsburg, northwest of Washington in Maryland, was the site of America's bloodiest day at the Battle of Antietam. And the Maryland flatland southeast of Washington provided John Wilkes Booth his famous escape route after he shot President Abraham Lincoln at Ford's Theater. Tours in the atlas include many of these Civil War points of interest — some famous, some obscure.

RIDES OF CIVIL WAR INTEREST

7.	C&O Canal Towpath Ⓜ
10.	Arlington History Ride Ⓜ
19.	Washington to Harpers Ferry Ⓜ
30.	Portside Pacer
38.	Warrenton Wanderlust
39.	Front Royal Hills
42.	Point of Rocks Explorer
59.	Westminster to Gettysburg Loop
60.	South Mountain - Sharpsburg Tour
61.	Antietam Battlefield Loop
62.	Shenandoah Valley Venture
63.	Bear's Den to Harpers Ferry

Bicycle Safety

When riding the routes in this atlas, you will in most cases be on public roads along with other, larger vehicles. We've made an effort to pick roads that minimize traffic, but no matter where you cycle, it is crucial that you pay attention to safety.

All rules of bicycle safety can be generalized under two rules of thumb: 1) use cautious, defensive bicycling skills, and 2) wear a good bicycle. helmet. The hazards of the road for bicyclists are greater than those for car drivers. In addition to other, larger vehicles, cyclists must look out for sewer grates, railroad tracks, road debris, potholes and uneven pavement. In a crash, a bicyclist has less protection than a motorist. The cyclist's objective must be to avoid crashes by biking defensively. On bike paths, many cyclists erroneously discount the danger of collisions with other cyclists or pedestrians. Caution is called for here, as well.

Besides exercising caution, the single most important thing you can do to protect yourself is to wear a helmet. Each year more than 800 people in the United States — more than two per day — are killed while riding bicycles. About 75 percent of these fatalities result from head injuries. A bicycle helmet can protect your head from serious injury, and is required by law in a growing number of jurisdictions. Wear a helmet that is well-ventilated, fits securely on your head and meets safety standards. The Washington Area Bicyclist Association (WABA) publishes a *Consumer's Guide to Bicycle Helmets*. Send a self-addressed stamped envelope to WABA, 1511 K Street NW #1015, Washington, DC 20005-1401, for a copy of the brochure.

Using the Atlas

As noted earlier, each tour description in this atlas consists of a general overview, specific information on starting point, terrain, distance, food, lodging and points of interest, a map or maps, and a set of directional cues. While en route, bicyclists generally follow the cue sheet, using the map as a back-up reference.

The directions in the cues are presented in a simplified, easy-to-read format, as follows:

START: The location, address or landmark of the beginning of the tour with explicit directions to the starting point from the Capital Beltway or another well-known location. Car parking is generally available. Approximate mileage from the Capital Beltway is given where applicable. Alternate starts and Metro stations near the start or along the tour also are noted.

LENGTH: Total mileage of the tour from start to finish. The lengths of alternate routes, starts and side trips also are included. Directions for the alternate routes and side trips are found at the end of the tour cues.

TERRAIN: Steepness, hilliness and road surface conditions along the tour. For example, "level" indicates flat or nearly flat for most of the tour; "rolling hills" denotes small hills along the route; "hilly" means at least some steep and difficult hills or mountains.

POINTS OF INTEREST: Highlights, including cultural and historical landmarks, recreational facilities, unique local attractions and natural amenities such as lakes, mountain views and rivers.

FOOD: Restaurants, fast food, cafes, markets and general stores, with mileage to help plan meal stops. Generally, these are grouped into "markets" and "restaurants." Food stops also are listed in the ride cues.

LODGING: Hostels, campgrounds, inns, bed-and-breakfasts and motels.

MAPS (AND INFORMATION): Suggested road and bike maps to supplement the maps in this atlas. Where applicable, this listing also contains additional sources of information, such as local Chambers of Commerce and visitor centers.

The cue sheets contain abbreviations and symbols to improve readability. For example, the T symbol refers to an intersection where one road dead-ends into a cross street at a right angle. In cases where a road has more than one name, the most common is listed first, with the alternative name listed parenthetically. Only the names of streets *bicycled on the tours* appear in **boldface**. State route references and U.S. highways are delineated (e.g., VA 28, US 13). Note that "BUS" denotes a *business* route, usually an alternative to a bypass, as in BUS VA 7.

Two or more turns within 0.1-miles are indicated within a single mileage cue.

Each map contains symbols indicating the points of interest, food stops, hostels, Metro stations and bicycle shops.

Touring Tips and Gear

Before starting your bike tour, you should quickly check that your bicycle is in good order. Use these helpful steps suggested by the League of American Bicyclists:

- Check tires for proper inflation. They should compress slightly on the sides, and feel very hard on the treads. If possible, use a pump with a pressure gauge to pump your tires to proper inflation.

- Spread a light oil or lubricant on the chain if it squeaks.

- Squeeze your front brakes and push forward (on bikes equipped with front and rear brakes): the rear wheel should rise. Squeeze the rear brakes and push forward: the rear tire should skid. Your brake levers should not touch the handlebars when squeezed with full force.

- Make sure brake pads are in the correct position (contacting only the rim and not the tire when engaged), and brake cables are not frayed.

- Check that quick release wheels are on securely, and that the levers point to the rear of the bicycle to prevent accidental release.

- Spin the wheels. They should rotate evenly and not touch the frame, brakes, or fenders.

- Handlebars, seat, cranks, racks and pedals should be securely fastened.

- Let the bicycle fall from 3-4 inches off the ground, and listen for rattles or loose parts. Check your baggage for loose ends that might enter spokes or other moving parts.

Remember the bicyclists' adage: eat before you're hungry and drink before you're thirsty. Always take a water bottle. Especially in the warm, humid conditions of summer in the mid-Atlantic region, it is absolutely necessary to keep yourself hydrated.

It's a good idea to take bike tools with you, as well. If you don't need them, someone else will. Tire irons, a patch kit or a spare tube, and a frame pump will handle the most common emergency — a flat tire. New stick-on patches make changing a tire easier than ever. Other useful tools include a small adjustable wrench, pliers, small flathead and Phillips screwdrivers, and various-sized Allen wrenches. If you have tires with Presta valve heads (rather than Schrader), carry an adapter so that you can use conventional air pumps at gas stations or so that you can borrow a pump from another cyclist.

In addition to the maps and cues from the atlas, consider carrying a detailed county-level road map. County road maps generally show all roads in the area in which you'll be traveling, a particularly useful feature if you get lost. The Appendix contains a complete listing of map sources for the region.

Bicyclists carry a variety of bags. Small handlebar bags with plastic sleeves for cue sheets and maps are handy. For longer tours, panniers that attach to front and rear racks provide a way to carry clothes and other essentials. Look for panniers that are made from rain-resistant material with large openings to various compartments, covered zippers and reinforced seams. Avoid backpacks, which become uncomfortable on long trips.

Bike gloves are also useful. They absorb much of the road shock that you will inevitably feel and they protect your hands and wrists from nerve damage.

Many cyclists use rear view mirrors that attach to handlebars, glasses or helmets. Others find them distracting. Do whatever works best for you.

A bicycle bell warns traffic ahead of you that you are coming (especially useful on trails). Bells are required in some jurisdictions.

Many cyclists use odometers, which simplify following cue sheets and help track distance and speed (and even altitude) on long tours.

Clothes for biking should not restrict leg and arm movements. Clothes can also be a safety device. Wear bright colors or white to increase your visibility. Bicycle shorts are comfortable and constructed to maximize padding where you need it the most.

Bike shoes distribute foot pressure evenly over the pedal, but any sneaker with a firm sole is adequate and usually less expensive. Make sure your shoes have a flat bottom if your bicycle has toe clips. Some cyclists buy shoes that fit into clipless pedals.

It's a good idea to carry rain gear, no matter what the weather looks like when you start your ride. There are several miracle fabrics on the market that will keep you warm and dry — consider getting a waterproof jacket and pants. (Ponchos are less useful: they tend to flap around in the wind.) Fenders on your bike add weight, but they keep the rain off of you and off of anyone behind you.

If you own a lightweight cellular telephone, take it along too, for use in emergencies. Most of the tours in this atlas are through areas covered by cellular telecommunications.

Bicycle Groups

Washington is the home to many active bicycle organizations, from touring clubs to advocacy groups to racing clubs to mountain bike clubs. These groups — and the larger bicycling community — benefit from the membership, support and involvement of individuals like you. Many of these groups, particularly the touring clubs, sponsor rides — a good way to get to know the area in the presence of other cyclists. The Appendix lists more than two dozen local and regional bicycling groups, with information on how to contact them.

In addition, several national bicycle organizations, such as the League of American Bicyclists, the Rails-to-Trails Conservancy and Adventure Cycling Association, work on a broader scale to improve and support bicycling. These groups can provide information on tour routes outside the Washington area. The Appendix provides information on how to contact these groups, as well.

Checking Current Conditions / Improving the Atlas

While every effort was made to assure the accuracy and utility of the information in this atlas, road conditions and traffic levels change from year to year. Even off-road conditions may be affected — for example, in 1996, the C&O Canal and its Towpath were severely damaged by two floods, which left portions impassable for much of the year. You can check current conditions of the routes in this atlas by contacting bicycle organizations listed in the Appendix, or by posting an inquiry on "dcbike," the mid-Atlantic area's bicycling Internet discussion group (Usenet newsgroup dc.biking or listserver dcbike@igc.apc.org).

In addition, we would love to hear from you about ways to make future editions of the atlas better. Send your comments, corrections and suggestions about the tours to GWABA, c/o Washington Area Bicyclist Association, 1511 K Street NW #1015, Washington, DC 20005-1401. Alternatively, you can send them to us via internet to: gwaba@waba.org.

Finally...

It was Proust who said, "The real voyage of discovery consists not in seeking new landscapes, but in having new eyes." This book — and a bicycle — can give you new eyes, starting you on the path of discovery. Bon voyage!

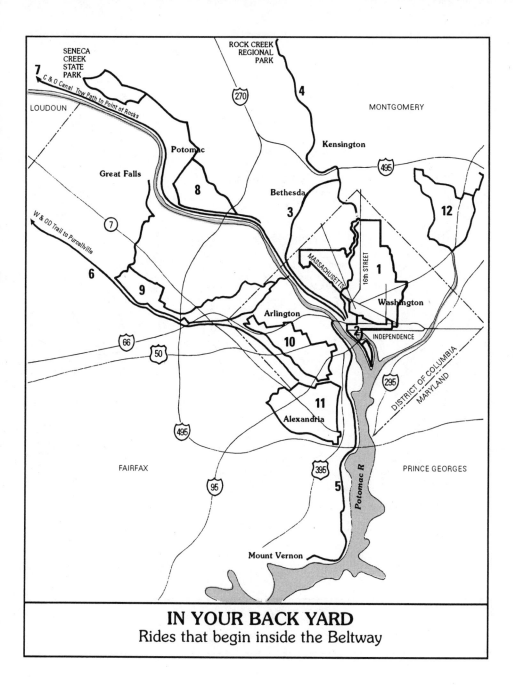

IN YOUR BACK YARD
Rides that begin inside the Beltway

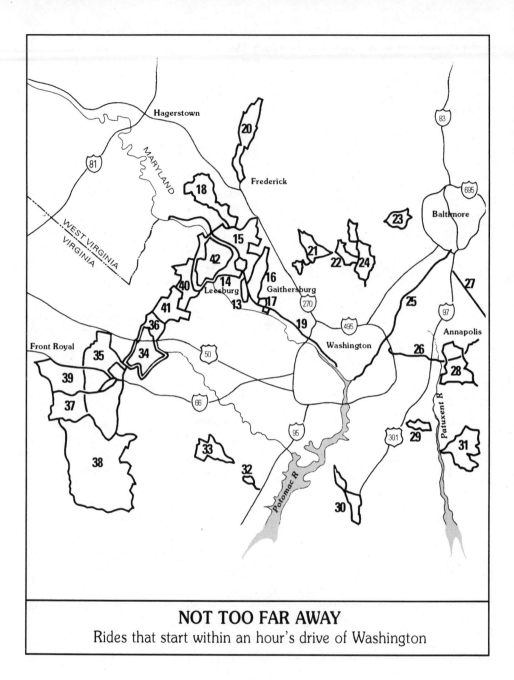

NOT TOO FAR AWAY
Rides that start within an hour's drive of Washington

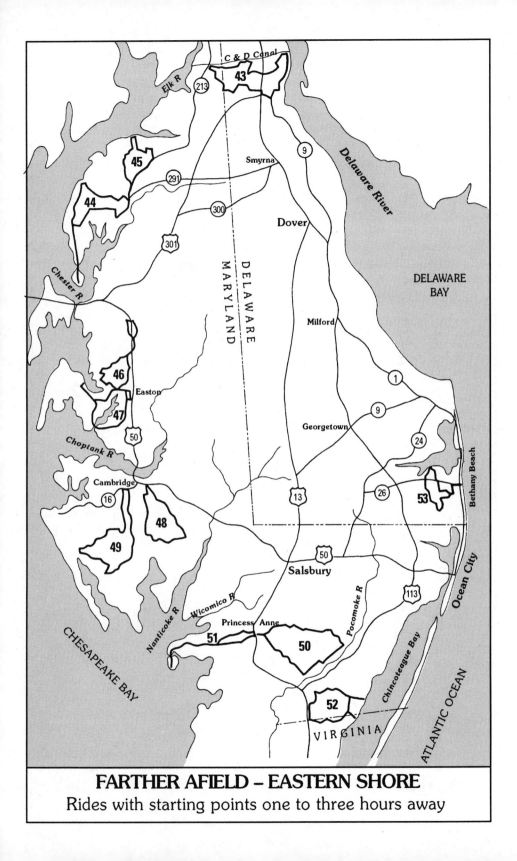

FARTHER AFIELD – EASTERN SHORE
Rides with starting points one to three hours away

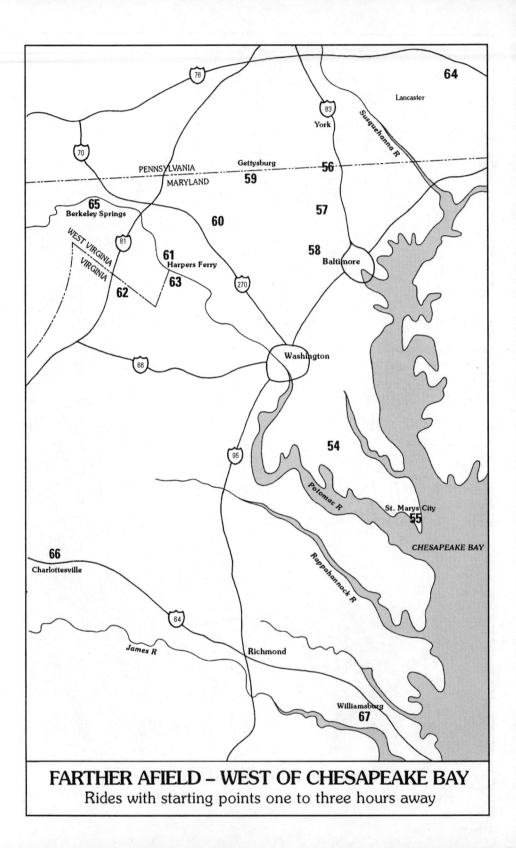

FARTHER AFIELD – WEST OF CHESAPEAKE BAY
Rides with starting points one to three hours away

In Your Backyard

1. NATIONAL CAPITAL BIKE TOUR

A comprehensive tour of the nation's capital, this ride offers views of Embassy Row, the White House, Capitol Hill with the U.S. Capitol and Supreme Court, the National Cathedral and the Shrine of the Immaculate Conception, American University and Catholic University, Rock Creek Park and a cross-section of city neighborhoods.

Because of heavy traffic on many parts of the route, this ride is best taken on a Sunday morning. An organized ride on the route attracts hundreds of riders each fall (for information, call the Washington Area Bicyclist Association at 202-628-2500).

START: American University, at the northwest corner of Massachusetts and Nebraska Avenues NW. Visitor parking available on weekends in the Commuter/Student Parking Lot, on the south side of Nebraska Avenue NW, just west of Ward Circle. The starting point is within the Capital Beltway. **METRO START:** Tenleytown Metro station (Red Line), at Wisconsin Avenue NW and Albemarle Street NW is 0.8 miles northeast of the start. Go south on Wisconsin Avenue NW 0.1 miles to Tenley Circle, go one-third of the way around the circle to a right turn on Nebraska Avenue NW and proceed 0.7 miles to Ward Circle and American University campus. Numerous other Metro stations are along or near the route, including most stations between Dupont Circle and Fort Totten on the Red Line, most stations between Farragut West and Eastern Market on the Blue and Orange Lines, and the Archives station on the Yellow and Green Lines.

LENGTH: 22.5 miles.

TERRAIN: Hilly.

POINTS OF INTEREST: American University at start; National Cathedral (one block north at 1.0 miles); Vice President's Mansion and Naval Observatory at 1.5 miles; Embassy Row, with more than a dozen foreign embassies (1.4 to 2.9 miles); White House at 4.1 miles; National Archives at 5.2 miles; National Gallery of Art at 5.4 miles; Supreme Court and U.S. Capitol at 6.0 miles; Catholic University and Shrine of the Immaculate Conception at 10.5 miles; Rock Creek Park at 14.9 miles.

FOOD: Numerous restaurants and food/drink options are available on or near the route in downtown D.C., between 2.9 and 5.4 miles; a good place to stop mid-way is Colonel Brooks' Tavern at 901 Monroe Street NE.

MAPS: *ADC's Washington Area Bike Map.*

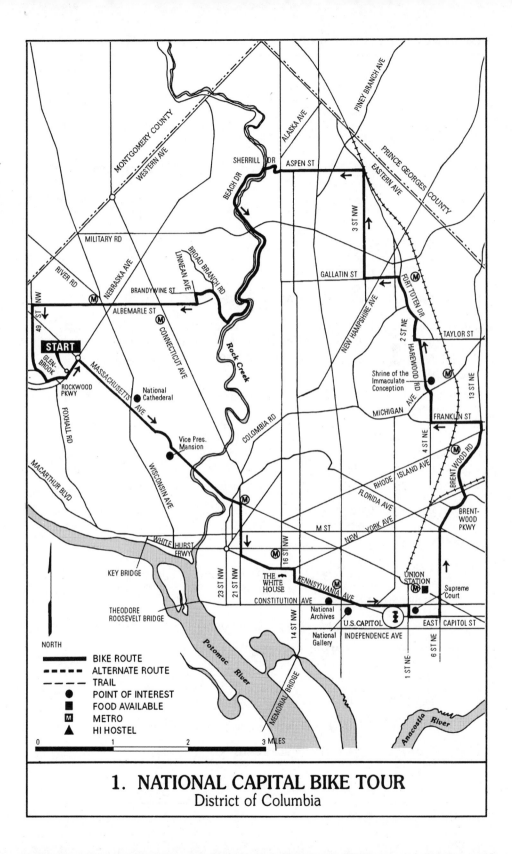

1. NATIONAL CAPITAL BIKE TOUR
District of Columbia

MILES   DIRECTIONS & COMMENTS

0.0   From American University campus, exit **left** on **NEBRASKA AVENUE NW.** (Turn **right** if exiting parking lot.) Follow Nebraska Avenue NW to Ward Circle.

0.1   **Right** at Ward Circle on **MASSACHUSETTS AVENUE NW.** (Sidewalk is also a bikeway.)

1.0   Cross Wisconsin Avenue NW. National Cathedral visible to left, one block north.

1.5   Naval Observatory and Vice President's Mansion on right.

2.9   **Right** on **21ST STREET NW.**

3.6   **Left** on **PENNSYLVANIA AVENUE NW.**

4.0   Straight on Pennsylvania Avenue NW, crossing barriers. (This portion of Pennsylvania Avenue NW is closed to motor vehicle traffic.) Old Executive Office Building, White House and Treasury Department on right.

4.3   Cross barriers in front of Treasury Department, then go **right** on **15TH STREET NW.**

4.6   **Left** on **PENNSYLVANIA AVENUE NW.** *(Note: two streets are marked Pennsylvania Avenue NW at 15th Street NW. The first is one-way westbound. Do not enter. Take left on the second street marked Pennsylvania Avenue NW.)*

5.2   National Archives, home of the Declaration of Independence, the Constitution, and much more, on right.

5.4   National Gallery of Art on right.

5.5   **Soft left** on **CONSTITUTION AVENUE NW.** *Caution: traffic.*

5.9   **Right** on **1ST STREET NE.**

6.0   U.S. Capitol on right, Supreme Court on left.

6.1   **Left** on **EAST CAPITOL STREET.**

6.5   **Left** on **6TH STREET NE.**

7.8   **Bear right** on **BRENTWOOD PARKWAY NE.**

8.1   **Bear left** on **9TH STREET NE.** Pass over New York Avenue NE.

8.5   **Bear right** on **BRENTWOOD ROAD NE.**

9.1   **Straight** on **13TH STREET NE** after crossing Rhode Island Avenue NE.

9.2   **Left** on **FRANKLIN STREET NE** at traffic light.

9.9   **Right** on **4TH STREET NE.**

10.3 **Left** on **MICHIGAN AVENUE NE.** National Shrine and Catholic University on right. (For Colonel Brooks' Tavern, take right on Michigan Avenue NE 0.2 miles to Monroe Street NE, then right on Monroe Street NE three blocks to 9th Street NE.)

10.4 **Right** on **HAREWOOD ROAD NE.**

11.2 **Left** on **TAYLOR STREET NE.**

11.3 **Right** on **2ND STREET NE.**

11.6 **Soft left** on **FORT TOTTEN DRIVE NE.**

12.2 **Left** on **GALLATIN STREET NE** at stop sign.

12.6 **Right** on **3RD STREET NW** at stop sign.

13.9 **Left** on **ASPEN STREET NW.**

14.9 Cross 16th Street NW and **enter Rock Creek Park** on **SHERRILL DRIVE.** Note: Sherrill Drive is closed to motor vehicles on weekends. *If Sherrill Drive is closed to motor vehicles, watch out for gates at the bottom of the hill!*

15.3 **Left** on **BEACH DRIVE.**

16.4 Cross Joyce Road. Continue straight on Beach Drive. Park Police Headquarters on left.

18.0 **Right** on **BROAD BRANCH ROAD.**

18.5 **Left** on **BRANDYWINE STREET NW.**

18.7 **Left** on **LINNEAN AVENUE NW.**

18.8 **Right** on **ALBEMARLE STREET NW.**

21.0 **Left** on **49TH STREET NW.**

21.8 **Left** on **GLENBROOK ROAD NW** at T.

22.0 **Left** on **ROCKWOOD PARKWAY NW** at T.

22.3 **Left** on **NEBRASKA AVENUE NW.** Take sidewalk.

22.5 **Arrive** at **AMERICAN UNIVERSITY.**

The Capitol.

2. MONUMENTS AND MUSEUMS

With the Washington Mall as its centerpiece, this short tour passes many of the major parks, monuments, museums, government buildings and national landmarks in downtown Washington. The only hill you will climb is Capitol Hill.

The Washington Mall accentuates the grand design of the city laid out by the French engineer Pierre Charles L'Enfant in 1791. The dozens of museums, monuments and statues tell their own stories. In addition, the headquarters of many federal agencies and departments are located on this route. Consult a tourist guidebook for detailed information about the Mall sites and surrounding attractions.

The second half of the tour predominantly follows busy city streets. Watch out for both vehicular and pedestrian traffic. Try to schedule your trip on a weekend and avoid the bustle of federal workers. Bring a good lock so you can leave your bike and explore the sites.

Washington is famous for its springtime cherry blossoms, which make a fleeting but memorable appearance in late March or early April. They most notably grace the Tidal Basin with their fragile blossoms.

START: East side of Lincoln Memorial (between the Memorial and the Reflecting Pool) on 23rd Street NW between Constitution Avenue and Independence Avenue, in Washington, D.C. This point is near the southern terminus of the Rock Creek Trail, and is just across the Potomac River (via Memorial Bridge) from the Mount Vernon Trail. Parking nearby in Potomac Park. The starting point is within the Capital Beltway. **METRO STARTS:** Foggy Bottom Metro station (Blue and Orange Lines) is the closest to the starting point, six blocks north of start on 23rd Street NW. The route passes or is close to most downtown D.C. Metro stations, including Federal Triangle, Smithsonian, L'Enfant Plaza, Federal Center SW and Capitol South on the Blue and Orange Lines, Union Station on the Red Line, and Archives and L'Enfant Plaza on the Yellow and Green Lines.

LENGTH: 11.7 miles.

TERRAIN: Level. Surface includes bike paths, city streets and sidewalks.

POINTS OF INTEREST: Lincoln Memorial and Korean War Memorial at start; Tidal Basin, cherry trees and Franklin Delano Roosevelt Memorial at 0.8 miles; Potomac Park at 1.7 miles; Hains Point and "The Awakening" sculpture at 3.1 miles; Jefferson Memorial at 5.2 miles; Bureau of Engraving and Printing and Holocaust Museum at 5.6 miles; Washington Monument at 5.7 miles; Smithsonian Castle and Hirshhorn Museum with Sculpture Garden at 6.4

miles; National Air and Space Museum at 6.7 miles; Botanical Garden at 6.9 miles; U.S. Capitol, Taft Memorial, and Garfield and Peace statues at 7.1 miles; Postal Museum and Union Station at 7.7 miles; Senate Office Buildings at 8.0 miles; Supreme Court and Library of Congress at 8.1 miles; House Office Buildings at 8.3 miles; National Gallery of Art (East and West Wings) at 9.2 miles; National Archives, J. Edgar Hoover Building (FBI Headquarters), Ford's Theater, site of President Abraham Lincoln's assassination, and National Museum of American History at 9.5 miles; Old Post Office Pavilion and Wilson Building (D.C. City Hall) at 9.8 miles; Treasury Building, White House, Lafayette Park, Renwick Gallery, Old Executive Office Building, Corcoran Gallery of Art and Organization of American States building between 10.2 and 10.6 miles; and Vietnam Veterans Memorial at 11.1 miles.

FOOD: Many choices at Union Station (7.7 miles) and Old Post Office Pavilion (9.8 miles). Hot dog vendors along route. Cafeterias at Air and Space Museum (6.7 miles) and National Gallery of Art (9.2 miles). On weekdays, the cafeterias of many government buildings are also open to the public.

MAPS: *ADC's Washington Area Bike Map.*

MILES   DIRECTIONS & COMMENTS

0.0   Go clockwise one-fourth of the way around Lincoln Memorial, to go **left** (south) on **23RD STREET SW.**

0.2   **Straight** on **OHIO DRIVE SW** (West Potomac Park). Use sidewalk or street. Franklin Delano Roosevelt Memorial on left across fields.

0.8   **Right** over **INLET BRIDGE,** then **right** again, to stay on **OHIO DRIVE SW** (East Potomac Park). Tidal Basin on left.

1.3   **Left** on **BUCKEYE DRIVE SW** (mandatory).

1.7   **Right** on **OHIO DRIVE SW** at T. Miniature golf, swimming pool, refreshments, restrooms, on right.

3.1   End of East Potomac Park at Hains Point. "The Awakening" sculpture. Round point and pass cherry trees. **Do not cross** Inlet Bridge again. Restrooms. Hains Point is closed to cars 3 p.m. - 6 a.m. Saturday, Sunday and holidays, from Memorial Day to Labor Day.

5.2   **Cross left** over to **bike path** in front of Jefferson Memorial. *Use crosswalk.*

5.4   **Bear left** over **OUTLET BRIDGE.**

5.6   Cross with traffic light on **15TH STREET SW.** Use sidewalk. Bureau of Engraving and Printing and Holocaust Museum on right.

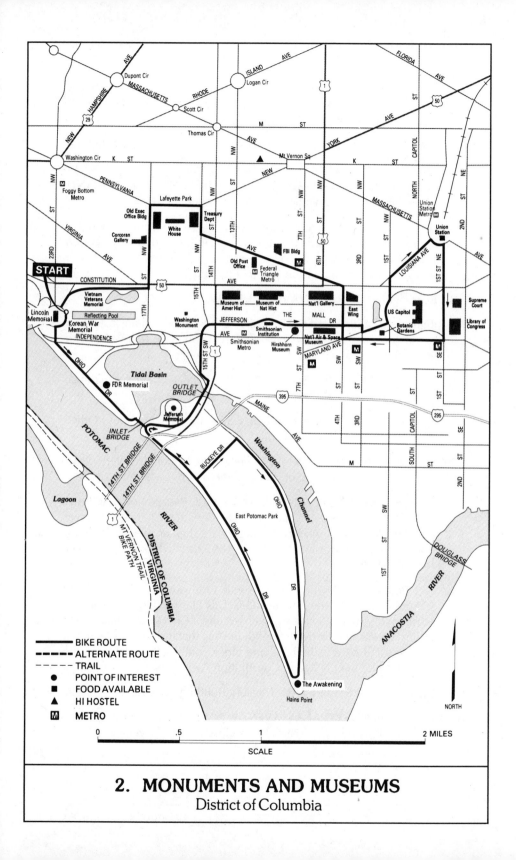

2. MONUMENTS AND MUSEUMS
District of Columbia

5.7   Cross Independence Avenue SW and travel diagonally across park. Washington Monument on left. **Bear right** on **JEFFERSON DRIVE SW** path. Smithsonian Castle and Hirshhorn Museum.

6.7   National Air and Space Museum with cafeteria (often crowded) on right.

6.9   **Right** on **3RD STREET SW** at T, then **first left** on **MARYLAND AVENUE SW.** Pass Botanical Garden on right.

7.1   **Left** on **1ST STREET SW,** by going counter-clockwise three-quarters of the way around Garfield statue. U.S. Capitol on right. **Straight** on **1ST STREET NW** by going counter-clockwise half-way around Peace statue. Taft Memorial visible on right (carillon).

7.4   **Bear right** on **LOUISIANA AVENUE NW.**

7.7   **Right** on **MASSACHUSETTS AVENUE NE.** Smithsonian Institution Postal Museum on left. Union Station, beautifully renovated with restaurants, food court, shops and Metro on left.

7.8   **Second right** on **1ST STREET NE.** Pass Senate Office Buildings, Supreme Court, U.S. Capitol, Library of Congress.

8.3   **Right** on **INDEPENDENCE AVENUE SE** at traffic light. House Office Buildings on left. Steep downhill.

8.9   **Right** on **4TH STREET SW.** Cross Mall, pass National Gallery of Art on left, and its East Wing on right. Cafeteria on lower level.

9.2   **Bear left** on **PENNSYLVANIA AVENUE NW.** Pass National Archives on left at 7th Street NW and FBI Headquarters (J. Edgar Hoover Building) on right at 9th Street NW. Ford's Theater, where President Abraham Lincoln was assassinated in 1865, is one block north at 511 10th Street NW.

9.8   Old Post Office Pavilion on left with food court, restaurants and souvenir shops. Wilson Building (D.C. City Hall) on left. The National Museum of American History, with excellent Civil War artifacts, First Ladies' gowns, the Hope Diamond, the flag that inspired the National Anthem, and other exhibits is one block south (left) of route on the Mall at 14th Street NW and Constitution Avenue NW.

10.2   **Right** on **15TH STREET NW.** Treasury Building on left.

10.3   **Left** on **PENNSYLVANIA AVENUE NW.** White House on left, Lafayette Park on right. (This area is closed to motor vehicles.)

10.6 **Left** on **17TH STREET NW.** Renwick Gallery on right, Old Executive Office Building on left. Corcoran Gallery of Art two blocks south on right. Organization of American States building with indoor garden and museum next to Corcoran on south side.

11.1 **Right** on **SERVICE ROAD** after crossing Constitution Avenue NW. Pass Constitution Gardens on left. Vietnam Veterans Memorial on right. [Note: bicycling through the Vietnam Memorial grounds is *strictly* prohibited. Lock your bicycle beyond the memorial grounds and walk.]

11.6 **Bear left** on **HENRY BACON DRIVE.**

11.7 **Arrive** at **LINCOLN MEMORIAL.**

Vietnam Veterans Memorial.

3. CAPITAL CRESCENT TRAIL

The Washington area's newest and best trail, the Capital Crescent, combines wonderful views, memorable bridges, a tunnel and a thick green forest environment with the area's smoothest surface. Built on the corridor of the old Georgetown Branch railroad, the Capital Crescent Trail climbs from the level of the Potomac River in Georgetown to downtown Bethesda (elevation 300 feet) at a imperceptible grade easy enough for even young children to handle.

Initiated by the Washington Area Bicyclist Association, the effort to create the trail required ten years of collaboration between the Coalition for the Capital Crescent Trail, the National Park Service, Montgomery County, the Maryland Department of Transportation and the U.S. Army Corps of Engineers. Land acquisition and trail construction cost more than $25 million.

From its southern terminus, the Capital Crescent links with the Rock Creek Trail by traveling 0.9 miles east on K Street NW. It also links with Virginia's Mount Vernon and Custis Trails by traveling 0.5 miles south over Key Bridge to Rosslyn Circle. Although the paved trail currently terminates in Bethesda, a crushed stone interim trail (called the Georgetown Branch Trail), suitable for bikes, opened early in 1997, extending the trail east across Rock Creek Park and on to Silver Spring.

Because of its outstanding design and surfacing, the paved portion of the Capital Crescent Trail is heavily used not only by skilled cyclists but also by walkers, rollerskaters, children, parents with strollers, dogs and others. Excellent sight distance reduces the danger, but care, courtesy, defensive driving and respect are in order. During heavy-use times, DO NOT SPEED.

STARTS: (Southern end) Georgetown, extreme western end of K Street NW (under Whitehurst Freeway and under Key Bridge). **(Bethesda)** Bethesda Avenue near Woodmont Avenue (adjoining Ourisman Honda). **(Silver Spring)** Stewart Avenue, one-half block south of Brookville Road. All starting points are within the Capital Beltway. **METRO STARTS: (Southern end)** Trail start is equidistant from Rosslyn and Foggy Bottom Metro stations (Blue and Orange Lines). *From Rosslyn,* go one block east to North Lynn Street, north on North Lynn Street to Key Bridge. Cross bridge on east (downstream) sidewalk, take sharp right immediately at end of bridge, descend asphalt trail, and cross C&O Canal on small bridge. Make U-turn onto Towpath at end of bridge ramp. After about 100 feet turn right and descend long flight of stairs to K Street NW. Turn right towards Key Bridge. Trail begins 0.2 miles west. *From Foggy Bottom,* go north on 23rd Street NW to Washington Circle, then left (west) on Pennsylvania Avenue NW by traveling counterclockwise two-thirds of the way around Washington Circle. At 29th Street NW, turn left (south), cross over C&O Canal, and continue to bottom of hill. At K Street NW, turn right (west).

Trail begins in 0.8 miles. **(Bethesda)** *From Bethesda Metro, travel south on* Wisconsin Avenue to Bethesda Avenue. Turn right. Trail is one-and-a-half blocks west. To interim (Georgetown Branch) trail go south on Wisconsin Avenue 0.1 miles. Turn left on Elm Street. After one block enter Elm Street Park. Trail entrance is on left, just beyond tennis courts. **(Silver Spring)** *From Silver Spring Metro, take right on Colesville Road. After one block, go left on* 2nd Avenue and continue 0.7 miles, then turn left on Grace Church Road. After 0.2 miles, turn right on 4th Avenue, then immediately left on Talbot Avenue. Continue 0.5 miles to Brookville Road. Turn left. After 0.2 miles, turn left on Stewart Avenue. Entrance to trail is one block downhill, on right.

LENGTH: 11.2 miles. **ALTERNATE FINISH:** 21.4 miles.

TERRAIN: Level, smooth asphalt surface. Interim (Georgetown Branch) trail is crushed stone, suitable for bicycles.

POINTS OF INTEREST: Outstanding views of the Potomac River, Key Bridge, the Rosslyn skyline, the Virginia shoreline and Palisades, and the Three Sisters Islands, all within first 0.5 miles of trail; numerous fishing opportunities on first 2.0 miles of trail; Fletcher's Boathouse at 2.4 miles; Dalecarlia Tunnel at 4.0 miles; Bethesda Pool at 6.4 miles; Rock Creek trestle at 9.8 miles.

FOOD: There are numerous restaurants near the Georgetown and Bethesda endpoints of the paved trail. Fletcher's Boathouse (mile 2.4) has snacks. Fast food and a supermarket are available at River Road (mile 5.8); deli, pizza, Starbucks and a supermarket on Connecticut Avenue, just north of the interim trail (mile 8.5).

MAPS: An excellent map of the trail is available from selected bicycle shops or for $2 from the Washington Area Bicyclist Association, 1511 K Street NW #1015, Washington, DC 20005-1401.

MILES   DIRECTIONS & COMMENTS

0.0   From Georgetown (southern) terminus, **go west on trail**. Pass Washington Canoe Club (private) on left. Potomac River views and Three Sisters Islands on left.

0.4   On right are two connections: steps/ramp up to C&O Canal Towpath; and tunnel under Towpath and Canal Road NW to Glover-Archibald Park, Glover Park neighborhood and Georgetown University.

2.4   Fletcher's Boathouse. Parking. Bicycle, canoe and rowboat rental. Telephone, restroom, snack bar. Picnic tables, fishing access. [*Note: This is the last easy access from the trail to the C&O Canal Towpath. Bear right here for points west along the canal and for Chain Bridge and all points in Virginia.*]

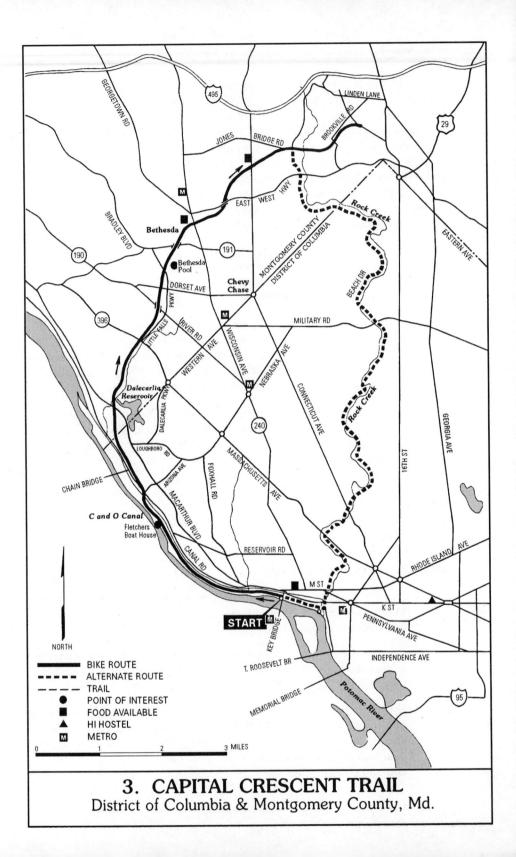

3. CAPITAL CRESCENT TRAIL
District of Columbia & Montgomery County, Md.

2.8   Arizona Avenue Bridge over C&O Canal and Canal Road NW.

3.6   Access on right (informal trail alongside fence) to Potomac Avenue NW, Norton Street NW and MacArthur Boulevard NW. Sibley Hospital is four blocks to the right on Norton Street NW.

3.7   Leave D.C., enter Maryland. Enter U.S. Army Corps of Engineers property (Dalecarlia Reservoir).

4.0   Dalecarlia Tunnel under MacArthur Boulevard, built 1910, with intricate brickwork.

4.3   Little Falls Park; connection to Little Falls Trail.

5.2   Former railroad bridge over Massachusetts Avenue.

5.8   Bicycle bridge over River Road. Many food choices on River Road. Telephone. Limited parking.

6.1   Cross Dorset Avenue at grade *[use caution]*.

6.4   Cross Little Falls Parkway *[use caution—busy road]*. Bethesda Pool (public — open Memorial Day to Labor Day).

6.8   Former railroad bridge over Bradley Boulevard.

7.0   Bethesda Avenue. Parking, telephone. Numerous food and other shops. At trailhead, turn **right** on **BETHESDA AVENUE** to continue on **Georgetown Branch Trail.**

7.1   **Left** on **WISCONSIN AVENUE**, then **immediate right** on **WILLOW LANE.**

7.2   After one short block, turn **left** on **47TH STREET**.

7.3   After one short block, turn **right** on pedestrian entrance to **ELM STREET PARK.** Ramp access to **GEORGETOWN BRANCH TRAIL** on **left** just past tennis court.

8.0   Trail passes through Columbia Country Club.

8.5   **Jog right** to cross Connecticut Avenue at traffic light. Pizza, deli and Starbucks are one-half block north of trail on west side of street. Supermarket on east side one-half block north. **Continue on trail** on east side of Connecticut Avenue.

Note: The remainder of the cues assume a detour around the Rock Creek Trestle. The trestle, which will afford spectacular views of the Rock Creek Valley when open to cyclists, needed extensive repairs at the date of publication. If the trestle and the remainder of the Capital Crescent Trail are open, continue on the trail to its terminus at mile 11.2.

The cues that follow are required if you want to use the Alternate Finish.

9.2 Rock Creek trestle detour. **Left** on **JONES MILL ROAD.** *Caution: at grade crossing — watch for traffic, or cross at the traffic light to your left.* After traffic light, take **immediate right** on **SUSANNA LANE.** Follow Susanna Lane around to left.

9.4 At end of Susanna Lane, **continue** on paved **TRAIL** into Rock Creek Park.

9.6 **Right** on **ROCK CREEK TRAIL.** Cross footbridge.

9.8 Rock Creek trestle, future path of Capital Crescent Trail.

10.2 To continue on the Georgetown Branch Trail, turn **left** on **MEADOWBROOK LANE**, before East-West Highway. To return to the starting point in Georgetown by a different route, see Alternate Finish.

10.3 **Left** on **FREYMAN DRIVE.** Hill.

10.7 **Left** on **TERRACE DRIVE.** To resume trail, **continue straight** on **TRAIL** where Terrace Drive swings right to become Grubb Road.

11.2 **End** of trail on Stewart Avenue.

The bridge over the C&O Canal and Canal Road NW.

ALTERNATE FINISH

10.2   Cross East-West Highway. Proceed **straight** on **MEADOWBROOK LANE.** Pass stables on right.

10.5   **Right** to remain on **MEADOWBROOK LANE** at T. Follow trail to the left through parking area.

10.8   At Candy Cane City, **cross bridge** over Rock Creek, then turn **left** on **BEACH DRIVE.** Continue on Beach Drive, or Rock Creek Trail parallel to it, for 9.7 miles. (Major portions of this route are on a paved bicycle trail. On weekends, motor vehicles are prohibited on many sections of Beach Drive. For detailed information concerning the Rock Creek Trail, see Tour 4.)

20.5   **Right** on **K STREET RAMP** under Whitehurst Freeway. Follow K Street NW.

21.4   **Arrive** at **CAPITAL CRESCENT TRAILHEAD.**

4. ROCK CREEK TRAIL

The scenic and popular Rock Creek Trail winds 25 miles from the Lincoln Memorial in Washington, D.C. to Lake Needwood Park in Montgomery County, Md. The Algonquin Indians, the area's original settlers, fished from Rock Creek, hunted bison and deer, raised crops and quarried quartzite for weapons and tools in what is now Rock Creek Park. Later, European settlers built grist mills and a saw mill on the creek, where farmers brought corn, wheat, buckwheat and rye to be ground into flour or meal.

Today the park and trail provide a refreshing escape to a more natural setting without leaving the city. The trail's popularity and narrow width, however, make the Washington section highly congested, especially in fair weather and on weekends. Cyclists should observe caution, particularly at the dangerous car ramp intersections and the many sharp turns with short sight distances. On weekends and holidays, the National Park Service closes Beach Drive to through motor vehicle traffic from Broad Branch Road to the Maryland line (a few stretches remain open to shared use with cars).

The Montgomery County section is less congested, wider and better maintained. It winds through woods, parks and residential neighborhoods, generally buffered from traffic and suburban sprawl. As on the Washington portion of the route, cyclists should expect toddlers, pets and other users along the path.

The beginning of this route connects to the Mount Vernon Trail (Tour 5) just across the Memorial Bridge. Together, the two trails provide a tri-state 44-mile bicycling artery through the heart of the Washington area, with additional connections into Virginia via Arlington's Custis Trail to the north and Four Mile Run Trail to the south, both of which connect further west to the W&OD Trail (Tour 6). Also, the C&O Canal Towpath (Tour 7) starts at 1.2 miles; the Capital Crescent Trail (Tour 3) can be accessed from the Towpath, or by following K Street NW west (at mile 1.1) for approximately one mile under the Whitehurst Freeway. Finally, Rock Creek Regional Park, at the end of the trail, provides a mountain bike route around Lake Needwood.

START: Lincoln Memorial in Washington, D.C. Parking in Potomac Park, south of start. The starting point is within the Capital Beltway. **METRO STARTS:** Foggy Bottom Metro station (Blue and Orange Lines) is near start, at 23rd and I Streets NW (go south on 23rd Street NW to the Mall and the Lincoln Memorial); Woodley Park-Zoo Metro station (Red Line) is near the 3.1-mile cue (from the elevator, go south one block [about 100 feet] on Connecticut Avenue NW, take soft right on 24th Street NW, cross Calvert Street NW, and proceed down steep hill on entrance road; the trail crosses the entrance road toward the bottom of the hill); Grosvenor Metro station (Red Line) is at 17.1 miles (go south one block on Rockville Pike, then left on Grosvenor Lane,

then bear right on Beach Drive to intersection of trail and Franklin Street).
ALTERNATE START: At 10.8 miles. Meadowbrook Recreation Center (Candy
Cane City), Silver Spring, Md. From the Capital Beltway, take Connecticut
Avenue south for one mile and turn left on East-West Highway (MD 410). Go
one mile, then turn right on Beach Drive. Center is on left, at traffic light.

LENGTH: 25.0 miles. From **ALTERNATE START:** 14.2 miles.

TERRAIN: Level with minor hills. 6-8 feet wide asphalt trail, some roadway.

POINTS OF INTEREST: Lincoln Memorial near start; Kennedy Center at 0.6
miles (bike racks located on front plaza); Thompson's Boat House (202-333-
4861) at 1.0 miles, with bike and boat rentals; Old Stone House, 3051 M
Street NW, three blocks off the trail at 1.2 miles in Georgetown (open
Wednesday-Sunday); Mount Zion Cemetery (oldest African-American burial
ground in D.C.) at 2.1 miles; National Zoo at 3.7 miles, with more than 2,000
animals from around the world, including a panda bear from China; Pierce
Mill at 5.4 miles, a restored 18th-century grist mill; Art Barn at 5.4 miles, an
old carriage house exhibiting local art (closed Mondays, Tuesdays and
holidays); Miller's Cabin at 7.5 miles; Meadowbrook Recreation Center and
Candy Cane City playground at 10.8 miles; riding stable at 11.1 miles;
Mormon Temple at 12.9 miles; and Lake Needwood Park at end.

FOOD: Your best food stops, in terms of convenience, are at the Zoo, at 3.7
miles, or at the numerous markets, fast food stops and restaurants in Georgetown (take Pennsylvania Avenue NW exit at 1.2 miles and head west). Food
also available at 3.1 miles (Calvert Street NW exit, up steep hill), 4.2 miles
(Porter Road NW exit, turn right up long hill to Connecticut Avenue NW) and
22.8 miles (turn right on Baltimore Road to Bauer Drive). Water fountains
along trail. Snack vendors (seasonal) near start.

MAPS AND INFORMATION: *Rock Creek Park Official Guide* available from
National Park Service Rock Creek Park Headquarters, 5000 Glover Road NW,
Washington, DC 20015-1098 (202-282-1063); *Rock Creek Hiker-Biker Trail*
available from MD-NCPPC Community Relations, 8787 Georgia Avenue,
Silver Spring, MD 20910-3760 (301-495-4600); ADC's *Washington Area Bike
Map; Lower Montgomery County Bicycle Route Map.*

MILES   DIRECTIONS & COMMENTS

0.0   From underneath Memorial Bridge, go **north** (upriver) on **TRAIL.** The
      trail is accessible by sidewalk from the Mall by following
      Independence Avenue SW west to its junction with Ohio Drive SW
      and Rock Creek and Potomac Parkway (southwest side of Lincoln
      Memorial). Sidewalk on the river side of the parkway passing under
      Memorial Bridge becomes the trail.

0.3   Cross Parkway Drive.

0.6   Pass Kennedy Center for the Performing Arts.

0.8   Watergate complex, site of the 1972 break-in that unraveled the Nixon Presidency, on right.

1.0   Thompson's Boat House on left. *Use caution crossing car ramps.*

1.1   Pass under K Street NW overpass. [To connect to Capital Crescent Trail (Tour 3), go under overpass, take sharp left onto auto ramp, then follow K Street NW approximately one mile.]

1.2   C&O Canal Towpath (Tour 7) begins on left. Cross Pennsylvania Avenue NW car ramp. (Exit here to Georgetown eateries and Old Stone House.)

2.4   Exercise course begins on left.

3.1   Cross Calvert Street NW ramp. *Caution: motor vehicles do not slow for bicycles.* Choose trail to right after crossing road.

3.4   **Left** around tunnel (you may also walk bicycle through tunnel on narrow sidewalk).

3.7   Intersection with road to National Zoo on left. Food, toilets, bike parking. *Note: bicycle riding is prohibited within Zoo grounds except on the Rock Creek Trail.*

4.2   Bike ramp on left to Porter Street NW, Connecticut Avenue NW groceries and restaurants just after bike bridge.

5.4   Pierce Mill and Art Barn on left, mill spillway on right. Public restrooms at Pierce Mill.

5.7   **Straight** on **BEACH DRIVE** (closed to motor vehicles on weekends and holidays). *Caution crossing Broad Branch Road.* Parallel bike path to left after street crossing.

7.3   Park Police Substation on right.

7.4   **Straight** on **BEACH DRIVE**. Alternate on signed bike trail. (Another trail goes left on Joyce Road. Do not take it!)

7.5   Miller's Cabin on left.

8.1   **Straight** on **BEACH DRIVE**. Do not take bike path which goes left on Bingham Drive. Path becomes steep and poorly maintained, and is not a good alternate route.

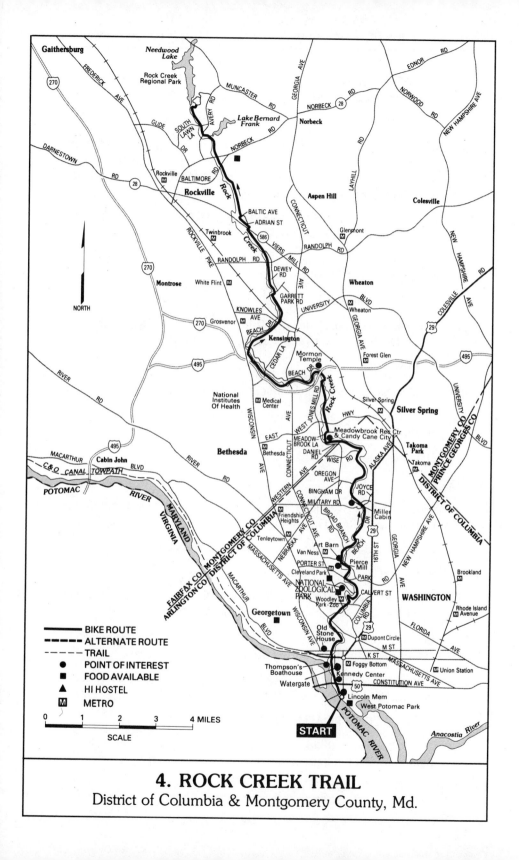

4. ROCK CREEK TRAIL
District of Columbia & Montgomery County, Md.

Map labels:

Gaithersburg

Needwood Lake

Rock Creek Regional Park

270 · FREDERICK AVE

MUNCASTER RD

GEORGIA AVE

EDNOR RD

NORBECK 28 RD

NORWOOD RD

NEW HAMPSHIRE AVE

GUDE · SOUTH LAWN LA · DR · AVERY RD

Lake Bernard Frank

Norbeck

NORBECK RD

DARNESTOWN RD

28

Rockville M · BALTIMORE · Rockville

BALTIC AVE

ADRIAN ST

Aspen Hill

LAYHILL RD

Colesville

ROCKVILLE PIKE

Rock Creek

586

CONNECTICUT

Glenmont

NEW HAMPSHIRE RD

270

Twinbrook M

RANDOLPH RD

VIERS MILL RD · RANDOLPH RD

DEWEY RD

Wheaton M

COLESVILLE AVE

NORTH

Montrose

White Flint M

GARRETT PARK RD · UNIVERSITY

BLVD

Wheaton · GEORGIA AVE

29

270 · Grosvenor M

KNOWLES AVE · BEACH DR

Kensington

Forest Glen

495

495

RIVER RD

National Institutes Of Health

CEDAR LA

Mormon Temple

BEACH DR

Rock Creek

Silver Spring · Silver Spring

UNIVERSITY BLVD

Medical Center M

WISCONSIN AVE · EAST AVE · WEST JONES MILL RD

HWY

Takoma Park

MONTGOMERY CO · PRINCE GEORGES CO

MACARTHUR BLVD

Cabin John

C&O CANAL TOWPATH

Bethesda

Bethesda M · CONNECTICUT AVE

Meadowbrook Rec Ctr & Candy Cane City

MEADOW-BROOK LA · DANIEL RD · WISE AVE

ALASKA AVE

Takoma M

DISTRICT OF COLUMBIA

POTOMAC RIVER

RIVER RD

OREGON AVE

JOYCE RD

Miller Cabin

BROAD BRANCH RD

MILITARY RD

BINGHAM DR

29

16TH ST

GEORGIA AVE

NEW HAMPSHIRE AVE

Brookland M

MARYLAND · VIRGINIA

MACARTHUR BLVD

FAIRFAX CO · MONTGOMERY CO · ARLINGTON CO · DISTRICT OF COLUMBIA

MASSACHUSETTS AVE

Friendship Heights M

Tenleytown M

NEBRASKA AVE · CONNECTICUT AVE

Art Barn

Van Ness M

PORTER ST

Pierce Mill

BEACH DR · PARK

WASHINGTON

Rhode Island Avenue M

FLORIDA AVE

WISCONSIN AVE

Cleveland Park M

NATIONAL ZOOLOGICAL PARK

Woodley Park-Zoo M

CALVERT ST

COLUMBIA RD

29

Georgetown

Old Stone House

Dupont Circle M

M ST

Union Station M

Thompson's Boathouse

K ST

Foggy Bottom M

MASSACHUSETTS AVE

Watergate

Kennedy Center

CONSTITUTION AVE

50

Lincoln Mem

West Potomac Park

START

POTOMAC RIVER

Anacostia River

Legend:

— BIKE ROUTE
--- ALTERNATE ROUTE
- - - TRAIL
● POINT OF INTEREST
■ FOOD AVAILABLE
▲ HI HOSTEL
Ⓜ METRO

0 1 2 3 4 MILES

SCALE

9.4   Pass Wise Road on left. Share road with motor vehicles for 0.1 miles on weekends. **Bear left** to stay on **BEACH DRIVE.**

10.2   Maryland line. Motor vehicles, even on weekends.

10.8   **Right** over bridge at traffic light to enter **MEADOWBROOK RECREATION CENTER** and Candy Cane City. Go **north** through recreation center parking lot on **MEADOWBROOK LANE. ALTERNATE START** begins here.

11.1   **First left** to stay on **MEADOWBROOK LANE.** Riding stable on left. Trail is two-way on road shoulder.

11.4   Cross East-West Highway at traffic light to return to off-road portion of trail. **Bear left** on **TRAIL.**

12.7   Cross Jones Mill Road.

12.9   Trail shares shoulder briefly. **Left** to stay on **ROCK CREEK TRAIL** at Beach Drive. Mormon Temple to right after turn.

13.3   Pass exercise course.

14.2   Cross under Connecticut Avenue. Alternate at-grade crossing to right.

15.0   Cross Cedar Lane at traffic light. Bike route to National Institutes of Health goes left.

16.4   **Stay left** at fork.

16.7   **Stay left** at fork.

17.1   Cross Knowles Avenue at traffic light. (Grosvenor Metro station 0.9 miles away: left on Grosvenor Lane, then right on Rockville Pike.)

18.1   Cross Garrett Park Road. Veirs Mill Park offices on right.

18.8   **Bear right** to stay on **TRAIL** at fork.

19.1   Trail forks. **Bear right** and follow sidewalk to traffic light at Randall Road. Cross Dewey Road and **continue** on **TRAIL.**

19.5   **Bear left** to stay on **TRAIL** at fork with drinking fountain. Immediately cross bridge, then **sharp right** up hill.

21.0   Cross Veirs Mill Road at Aspen Hill Road. **Left** on **ADRIAN STREET,** then **right** on **BALTIC AVENUE.**

21.1   **Left** on **ACCESS ROAD** to **TRAIL.**

22.8   Cross Baltimore Road. (For pizzeria and market, turn right on Baltimore Road to Bauer Drive.)

23.1   Trail junction with Norbeck Road.

23.9   Cross parking lot and Avery Road.

24.3   Cross South Lawn Lane.

25.0   **Arrive** at Rock Creek Regional Park, **LAKE NEEDWOOD.**

Pierce Mill in Rock Creek Park.

5. MOUNT VERNON TRAIL

A well-traveled route along the Potomac River, the Mount Vernon Trail takes bicyclists, joggers and hikers from Roosevelt Island near Key Bridge to George Washington's home in Mount Vernon (now Fairfax County), Va. The route affords riders beautiful vistas of the Potomac River and of the national memorials, the U.S. Capitol and the National Cathedral.

Intrinsic to Washington, D.C.'s premier trail system, the Mount Vernon Trail receives heavy usage, especially on weekends. It takes bicycle commuters into the city from the south and also provides an escape from downtown Washington. By crossing Memorial Bridge, riders can connect from the Mount Vernon Trail to the Rock Creek Trail (Tour 4) to the north and the C&O Canal Towpath (Tour 7) and Capital Crescent Trail (Tour 3) to the northwest. The trail is also linked to the W&OD Trail (Tour 6) to the west via Arlington's Custis Trail or Four Mile Run Trail.

This is a beautiful and interesting ride, but use caution: highway ramp crossings and weekend congestion from a variety of trail users require attentive cycling. The best times to ride are early in the morning on weekends, or on weekdays.

START: Theodore Roosevelt Island on the Potomac River in Rosslyn, Va. By car, Roosevelt Island is accessible only by traveling north on the George Washington Memorial Parkway from Roosevelt Bridge (I-66/US 50) or points further south. Accessible from downtown Washington, D.C. via the Roosevelt Bridge. Rosslyn is within the Capital Beltway. **METRO STARTS:** Rosslyn Metro station (Orange and Blue Lines) is near start. Go one block east then turn left on North Lynn Street. Turn right onto bike trail immediately after highway exit ramp. (If you see the National Park Service depot on your right, you've missed your turn.) Cross over the George Washington Memorial Parkway on a bicycle bridge to the Roosevelt Island parking lot. National Airport Metro station (Blue and Yellow Lines), Arlington Cemetery Metro station (Blue Line), King Street Metro station (Yellow Line) and Braddock Road Metro station (Yellow Line) are on or near the trail.

LENGTH: 18.5 miles.

TERRAIN: Level with three hills. Well-maintained asphalt; boardwalk in swamp areas. Narrow in some places.

POINTS OF INTEREST: Navy and Marine Memorial (1934) at 2.0 miles, dedicated to Americans who served at sea; Gravelly Point at 3.0 miles, with good view of the Potomac River and spectacular view of National Airport's busy main runway; Daingerfield Island at 5.8 miles, with Washington Sailing Marina, food, bike shop (open every day), sailing and fishing facilities; Old

Town Alexandria at 7.6 miles, with Torpedo Factory art galleries, parks, shops, food, museums; Jones Point Lighthouse at 9.7 miles, once southernmost tip of the District of Columbia; Belle Haven at 11.2 miles, a 1730s tobacco warehouse that is now a picnic area; Dyke Marsh at 11.2 miles, a 240- acre wetland with more than 250 bird species; Fort Hunt Park at 15.7 miles, with 156 acres; and Mount Vernon (703-780-2000) at end, historic home of George Washington (fee charged for tour).

FOOD: Old Town Alexandria, at 7.6 miles, has a wide range of markets and restaurants. Additional restaurants at 5.8 and 18.5 miles. Picnic areas at 5.8 and 10.6 miles.

MAPS AND INFORMATION: *Mount Vernon Trail Official Guide* available from the National Park Service, Turkey Run Park, McLean, VA 22101 (703-285-2601).

MILES   DIRECTIONS & COMMENTS

0.0   Theodore Roosevelt Island. Restrooms, water. (Bicycles are prohibited on the island itself; park at the bike rack near the footbridge if you're interested in exploring the island.) Go **south** (downriver) on **TRAIL.** Note connection with Arlington's Custis Trail to the north (upriver) via the bicycle bridge over the George Washington Memorial Parkway into Rosslyn.

1.0   Pass under Memorial Bridge. *Caution: narrow crossing!*

2.0   Navy and Marine Memorial on left. *Caution: narrow passage over "Humpback Bridge" with poor protection from cars.*

3.0   Gravelly Point. Phones. Restroom facilities. Soccer field. Noisy but spectacular view of jet operations on National Airport's busy main runway. Pass National Airport. *Caution: dangerous intersections with airport ramps.*

4.1   Crystal City Connector. Crystal City is 0.3 miles from here with Waterfront Park, shopping, restaurants and connections to a bike route to Pentagon City.

4.9   Connection to W&OD Trail via Arlington's Four Mile Run Trail, by bearing left through underpass under highway and railroad tracks. **Keep right** to remain on **MOUNT VERNON TRAIL**.

5.8   Daingerfield Island (Washington Sailing Marina). Restaurant, water, bike shop, toilets, picnic facilities.

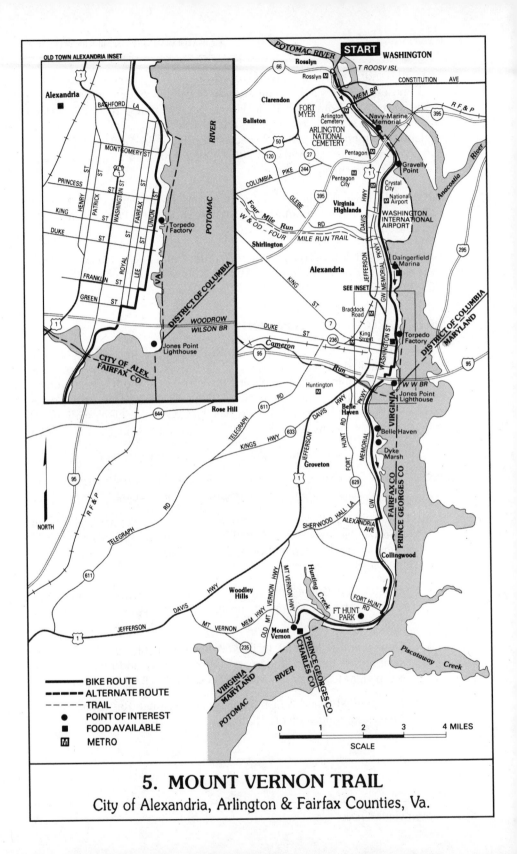

OLD TOWN ALEXANDRIA INSET

Alexandria

BASHFORD LA
MONTGOMERY ST
PRINCESS ST
KING ST
DUKE ST
FRANKLIN ST
GREEN ST

HENRY ST
PATRICK ST
WASHINGTON ST
ALT 1
ST
FAIRFAX ST
UNION ST
ROYAL ST
LEE ST
VA

POTOMAC RIVER

Torpedo Factory

WOODROW WILSON BR

CITY OF ALEX
FAIRFAX CO

Jones Point Lighthouse

DISTRICT OF COLUMBIA

POTOMAC RIVER

START WASHINGTON
T ROOSV ISL
66 Rosslyn
Rosslyn
CONSTITUTION AVE
MEM BR
R F & P
395
Clarendon
FORT MYER
Arlington Cemetery
Navy-Marine Memorial
Ballston
ARLINGTON NATIONAL CEMETERY
Pentagon
Gravelly Point
50
120
27
244
Pentagon City
Crystal City
COLUMBIA PIKE
395
Virginia Highlands
National Airport
WASHINGTON INTERNATIONAL AIRPORT
Anacostia River
Four Mile Run
W & OD — FOUR
MILE RUN TRAIL
RD
Shirlington
295
DAVIS HWY
Alexandria
JEFFERSON
GW MEMORIAL PKWY
Daingerfield Marina
SEE INSET
DISTRICT OF COLUMBIA
MARYLAND
7
KING ST
Braddock Road
WASHINGTON ST
Torpedo Factory
King Street
DUKE ST
236
Cameron
95
Run
95
W W BR
VIRGINIA
Jones Point Lighthouse
Huntington
Rose Hill
611
RD
644
Belle Haven
TELEGRAPH
KINGS HWY
633
Belle Haven
Dyke Marsh
DAVIS HWY
HUNT RD
FAIRFAX CO
PRINCE GEORGES CO
GW MEMORIAL PKWY
JEFFERSON
Groveton
1
629
R F & P
95
611
SHERWOOD HALL LA
ALEXANDRIA AVE
NORTH
TELEGRAPH
Collingwood
611
Woodley Hills
MT VERNON HWY
Hunting Creek
FORT HUNT RD
FT HUNT PARK
DAVIS HWY
MT VERNON MEM HWY
OLD MT VERNON HWY
Mount Vernon
Piscataway Creek
JEFFERSON
1
235
PRINCE GEORGES CO
CHARLES CO
VIRGINIA
MARYLAND
POTOMAC RIVER

—— BIKE ROUTE
– – – ALTERNATE ROUTE
- - - TRAIL
● POINT OF INTEREST
■ FOOD AVAILABLE
Ⓜ METRO

0   1   2   3   4 MILES
SCALE

5. MOUNT VERNON TRAIL
City of Alexandria, Arlington & Fairfax Counties, Va.

7.6   Enter Alexandria. Alternate routes through the city (mostly on-road) — just keep heading south. Torpedo Factory, museums, restaurants, markets, shops.

9.7   Jones Point Lighthouse. Cross under Wilson Bridge (Capital Beltway).

11.2   Belle Haven picnic area. Separate trail to Dyke Marsh.

15.7   Fort Hunt Park on right. View of Fort Washington, an early 19th century fortification, across river.

18.5   **Arrive** at **MOUNT VERNON** parking lot and bike racks.

Jones Point Lighthouse in Alexandria.

6. W&OD TRAIL

One of the Washington area's great bicycling resources, the Washington and Old Dominion (W&OD) Railroad Regional Park takes bicyclists through Northern Virginia west from Shirlington Village in Arlington to Purcellville, just nine miles east of the Blue Ridge Mountains.

The W&OD Trail takes its name from the railroad that ran along the right-of-way for nearly 100 years. Also named the "Virginia Creeper" after the pervasive vine growing along the corridor (and because of its reputed slow service!), the train transported residents of Washington to the Northern Virginia countryside, where they escaped the hot city summers in country resorts established along the rail line. The corridor was abandoned for train travel in 1968, and later put to new use by the Northern Virginia Regional Park Authority. Today the W&OD Trail is one of the country's most popular and successful rail-trails and one of the most heavily used parks in Virginia.

The town of Purcellville, a business center for surrounding cattle farms and villages, was incorporated in 1908. In its early days, a bicyclist was fined a hefty $2.50 for riding on the wooden sidewalks.

For a rewarding westward extension to this tour, you can continue on country roads from Purcellville to the HI-Bear's Den Lodge. From the terminus of the W&OD Trail in Purcellville, this short but challenging extension explores the rural community of Bluemont before ending at Bear's Den.

Bear's Den Lodge is a mountaintop mansion built in the 1930s by Wagnerian diva Francesca Caspar Lawson. It offers a sweeping view of the Shenandoah Valley and serves as a hiking and bicycling stopover on the way to Front Royal and Shenandoah National Park.

For a trip to Harpers Ferry, and return to Washington by a different route, combine this tour with Bear's Den to Harpers Ferry (Tour 63), and take either the C&O Canal Towpath (Tour 7) or the Washington to Harpers Ferry route (Tour 19), reversing the directions given.

START: Shirlington Village, eastern terminus of the W&OD Trail at the intersection with Four Mile Run Drive and Shirlington Road in Arlington, Va. Shirlington Village is north of the Shirlington exit of I-395. The W&OD Trail is also accessible from the Mount Vernon Trail (Tour 5), at the southern tip of National Airport, by way of the Four Mile Run Trail to the intersection of South Glebe Road and West Glebe Road, then reverse cues in Arlington History Ride (Tour 10) from 20.7 miles to 19.6 miles. The starting point is within the Capital Beltway. **METRO STARTS:** From Ballston Metro station (Orange Line), take North Fairfax Drive west (to the right from the Metro elevator) to the I-66 Custis Trail, then go left (west) two miles to the W&OD Trail at Bon Air Park at mile

3.6; the East Falls Church Metro station (Orange Line) is adjacent to the W&OD Trail, at the Arlington line; West Falls Church Metro station (Orange Line) is near mile 7.6.

LENGTH: 45.0 miles; 59.1 miles with continuation to Bear's Den.

TERRAIN: Level, smooth asphalt surface. Continuation from Purcellville to Bear's Den is rolling, with extended and steep uphill climb to the hostel.

POINTS OF INTEREST: Glencarlyn Park at 1.7 miles; Bon Air Park at 3.5 miles, with beautiful rose garden; Falls Church Community Center at 5.7 miles; Historic Freeman House at 11.8 miles; Vienna railroad station and train museum at 12.0 miles; Lake Fairfax Park at 17.0 miles; Sunset Hills railroad station at 18.0 miles; Herndon railroad station at 20.0 miles; Leesburg Community Center at 33.7 miles; Leesburg train station at 34.5 miles; Work Horse Museum at 39.5 miles; Hamilton train station at 41.1 miles; and Purcellville train station at 44.4 miles. Bluemont at 56.5 miles, with fall fair and picnic grounds; Bear's Den at end (59.1 miles), with scenic overlook. Many bicycle shops on or near the trail.

FOOD: Generally available. Markets at 5.6, 11.8, 17.5, 18.1, 27.7, 35.0, 45.0, 45.5 and 54.5 miles. Fast food at 7.2, 11.8, 17.0, 20.0, 23.6 and 34.5 miles. Restaurants in Arlington, Falls Church, Vienna, Herndon, Reston, Leesburg and Purcellville. Water on trail at 2.5, 3.3, 3.9, 11.6, 16.6, 20.0, 22.5 and 34.0 miles.

LODGING: In Leesburg, Laurel Brigade Inn (703-777-1010) at 20 West Market Street, three blocks north of the trail, near intersection with US 15 at 35.8 miles. In Purcellville, Purcellville Inn (540-338-2075) on Main Street (VA 7). Near Bluemont, HI-Bear's Den Lodge (540-554-8708) on Blue Ridge Mountain Road (VA 601).

MAPS: *W&OD Railroad Regional Park Trail Guide,* a detailed book of strip maps and information available for $5.75 postpaid from W&OD Trail, 21293 Smith Switch Road, Ashburn, VA 20147-6016 (703-729-0596); Loudoun County, Va. road map.

MILES DIRECTIONS & COMMENTS

0.0 Go **west** on **TRAIL** from Shirlington Road and Four Mile Run Drive. Bike shop in Shirlington Village. Arlington Community Center is northwest of start, on South Monroe Street.

1.0 Pass through Arlington County parks.

1.7 Glencarlyn Park on right. Restrooms available.

3.5 Bon Air Park with rose garden.

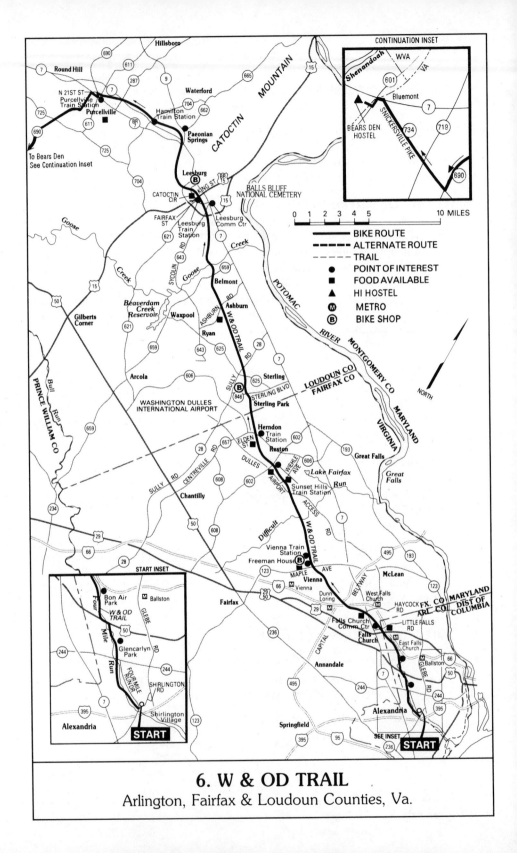

6. W & OD TRAIL
Arlington, Fairfax & Loudoun Counties, Va.

3.6   Junction with I-66/Custis Trail. Water fountain. **Bear left** at fork.

5.6   East Falls Church Metro station on right. Convenience store near Lee Highway (US 29) crossing.

5.7   Falls Church Community Center is two blocks south of here, on Little Falls Road.

7.2   City of Falls Church. Bicycle overpass at West Broad Street (VA 7). Fast food and bike shop on West Broad Street to left.

7.6   West Falls Church Metro station (off trail) north on Haycock Road, approximately 0.5 miles.

9.0   Cross over Capital Beltway.

11.8   Town of Vienna. Whole Foods on right. Fast food on Maple Avenue (VA 123) to left. Historic Freeman House beside the trail on Church Street.

11.9   Bike shop on left.

12.0   Vienna railroad station and train museum on left. Note bright red caboose.

17.0   Fast food on right at Wiehle Avenue. Lake Fairfax Park is one block north.

17.5   Fresh Fields market on left.

18.0   Sunset Hills railroad station and ranger station, in Reston, on right. Convenience store on left. Bike shop in Reston Town Center (toward back, left corner).

20.0   Herndon railroad station and fast food. Bike shop is four blocks northeast, on Elden Street. Restroom at Bready Park (go right on Elden Street).

21.4   Enter Loudoun County.

22.5   Bike shop on left. Water available.

23.6   Church Road. Deli on right.

27.7   Convenience store on Ashburn Road on left.

30.3   Cross over Goose Creek.

33.7   Leesburg Community Center on Sycolin Road on right.

34.0   Water. Restrooms.

34.5 Leesburg Train Station. Bike shop on Fairview Street in Leesburg on right (right on Catoctin Circle, cross VA 7, shop on right).

35.8 Laurel Brigade Inn three blocks north of trail, near intersection with US 15.

38.5 Historic stone arch.

39.5 Residential hamlet of Paeonian Springs, location of the Work Horse Museum.

41.1 Hamilton train station on right.

44.4 Purcellville train station on left.

45.0 Trail ends in Purcellville at North 21st Street. Inn, restaurants and groceries in Purcellville.

CONTINUATION TO BEAR'S DEN

45.0 **Left** at trail terminus to go south on **VA 690** (North 21st Street).

45.1 **Right** on **MAIN STREET** (BUS VA 7). Purcellville. Markets, fast food, restaurants, inn.

45.5 **Left** on **VA 690** (South 32nd Street). 7-Eleven on corner. *Caution: narrow, winding road with no shoulder.*

51.1 **Right** on **VA 734** (Snickersville Turnpike).

56.5 Bluemont. General store with ice cream and food. Continue on VA 734, climbing hill.

57.6 **Left** on **VA 7.**

58.3 **Left** on **VA 601** at Snickers Gap, on crest of Blue Ridge.

58.7 **Right** on **GRAVEL DRIVEWAY.**

59.1 **Arrive** at **HI-BEAR'S DEN LODGE**, elevation 1,300 feet.

Making hay while the sun shines.

7. C&O CANAL TOWPATH

(Note: The C&O Canal experienced two disastrous floods in 1996 that washed out large portions of the Towpath. Check with the National Park Service at 301-432-2231 concerning current Towpath conditions.)

Paralleling the Chesapeake and Ohio (C&O) Canal amidst woodland and wildlife, the 184-mile C&O Canal Towpath serves both cycling and hiking interests in the Washington area. The C&O Canal played a part in the history of the national competition to open the western frontier (in the early 19th century the "frontier" was Wheeling, W.Va. on the Ohio River). On the same day that the C&O Canal Company began construction of its water route to Cumberland (which would then connect to Wheeling by road), the B&O Railroad began its westward push. The railroad ultimately won the race to the West.

The canal-building industry suffered from high land costs and persistent trouble in obtaining land titles. The B&O Railroad obtained land rights at Point of Rocks, Md., and secured an injunction against canal passage there for four years. The canal finally reached Cumberland in 1850, eight years after the railroad. Plans for further extensions to the west were abandoned.

The C&O Canal contains 74 lift locks and 11 stone aqueducts over Potomac tributaries. It was used until 1924, when a flood destroyed it for the second time. The Towpath is now surfaced with earth and crushed stone and ribbed with tree roots. Heavy rains can cause temporary washouts. Most of the Towpath is impassable on light touring or racing bicycles; a mountain bike or one-speed clunker with heavy-duty tires is recommended.

For additional rides from Harpers Ferry, see Bear's Den to Harpers Ferry (Tour 63), and Washington to Harpers Ferry (Tour 19).

START: Rock Creek Trail at the corner of Pennsylvania Avenue NW ramp and Rock Creek Parkway near Georgetown in Washington, D.C. The starting point is within the Capital Beltway. **METRO START:** From Foggy Bottom Metro station (Orange and Blue Lines), go north one block on 23rd Street NW to Washington Circle, and go 270 degrees counterclockwise around Washington Circle to Pennsylvania Avenue NW toward Georgetown. Go three blocks to Rock Creek Parkway ramp, on left, before the Four Seasons Hotel.

LENGTH: 184.5 miles.

TERRAIN: Level. Packed dirt and crushed stone surface, 6-8 feet wide. The surface may not be suitable for thin bicycle tires, particularly outside of the Capital Beltway.

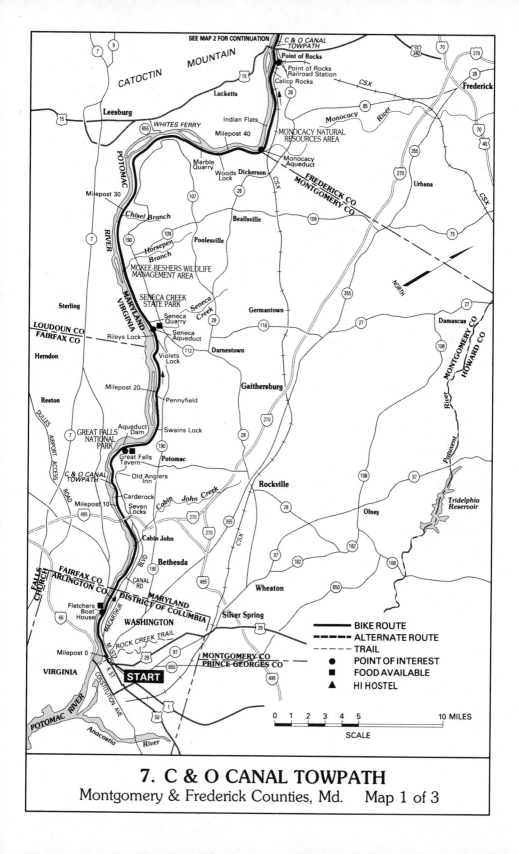

SEE MAP 2 FOR CONTINUATION

7. C & O CANAL TOWPATH
Montgomery & Frederick Counties, Md.   Map 1 of 3

Legend:
— BIKE ROUTE
--- ALTERNATE ROUTE
- - - TRAIL
● POINT OF INTEREST
■ FOOD AVAILABLE
▲ HI HOSTEL

0 1 2 3 4 5 — 10 MILES
SCALE

START

POINTS OF INTEREST: Thompson's Boat House (202-333-4861) and Tidal Lock 0.3 miles south of start (on Rock Creek Trail), with bike rentals; old locks and gate houses at 0.3 through 14.3 miles; Fletcher's Boat House (202-244-0461) at 3.1 miles, with canoe and bike rentals; Great Falls Tavern and C&O Canal Museum and visitor center at 14.3 miles; Point of Rocks at 47.8 miles, with restored 19th century railroad station; Harpers Ferry at 60.7 miles; C&O Canal Park Headquarters (301-739-4200) at 76.6 miles in Sharpsburg; Williamsport (301-223-7711) at 99.0 miles, a classic C&O Canal town; Fort Frederick State Park (301-842-2155) at 112.5 miles, including the last remaining British stone fort in the United States; Paw Paw Tunnel at 155.2 miles; and Cumberland at 180.7 miles, featuring a scenic steam-powered train ride round-trip from Cumberland to Frostburg.

FOOD: Markets and restaurants along the route.

LODGING: On the Towpath, campsites are located every five miles, with pit toilets, picnic tables, fire grills and water in most cases. Near Harpers Ferry, HI-Harpers Ferry Lodge, 19123 Sandy Hook Road, Knoxville, Md. (301-834-7652); and Hilltop House (800-338-8319), on Ridge Street, 10 blocks from C&O Canal Towpath. In Cumberland area, bed-and-breakfasts include the Inn at Walnut Bottom, 120 Green Street (301-777-0003) and the Casselman Inn in Grantsville (301-895-5055).

MAPS AND INFORMATION: *C&O Canal Official Guide* available from the National Park Service at C&O Canal, P.O. Box 4, Sharpsburg, MD 21782-0004 (301-739-4200). *Chesapeake and Ohio Canal*, a detailed handbook on the history of the canal, is available at a few visitor centers along the trail. The Allegany County, Md. Visitors Bureau can supply local information for the areas near the western portion of the route (800-508-4748).

MILES   DIRECTIONS & COMMENTS

0.3   Go **west** from Rock Creek Trail on **TOWPATH.** [Note: C&O Canal mileage is traditionally measured from Tidal Lock, 0.3 miles south of here.]

3.1   Fletcher's Boat House on left, through tunnel.

14.3   Great Falls Tavern (C&O Canal Museum) on right.

22.8   Seneca Aqueduct. Stonemill ruins.

42.2   Monocacy Aqueduct. [See Monocacy Aqueduct Ride (Tour 13) for connections.]

47.8   Point of Rocks railroad station. [End of Map 1 instructions.]

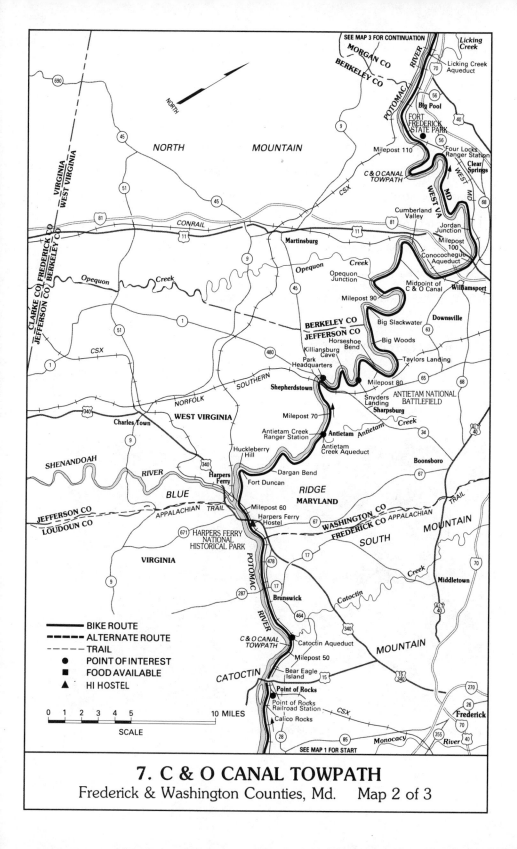

NORTH

Licking Creek

MORGAN CO

BERKELEY CO

Licking Creek Aqueduct

POTOMAC RIVER

70

56

Big Pool

FORT FREDERICK STATE PARK

40

690

9

NORTH MOUNTAIN

Milepost 110

56

Four Locks Ranger Station

45

C & O CANAL TOWPATH

WEST MD

Clear Springs

51

68

45

CSX

Cumberland Valley

WEST VA

Jordan Junction

81

CONRAIL

11

11

81

Milepost 100

Conococheague Aqueduct

Martinsburg

9

Opequon Junction

Midpoint of C & O Canal

Williamsport

Opequon Creek

Opequon Creek

45

Milepost 90

Big Slackwater

Downsville

CLARKE CO / FREDERICK CO
JEFFERSON CO / BERKELEY CO

1

51

CSX

1

Horseshoe Bend

Killiansburg Cave

Park Headquarters

480

BERKELEY CO

JEFFERSON CO

Big Woods

63

Taylors Landing

65

68

SOUTHERN

Shepherdstown

Milepost 80

ANTIETAM NATIONAL BATTLEFIELD

NORFOLK

WEST VIRGINIA

340

Charles Town

9

Milepost 70

Snyders Landing

Sharpsburg

Antietam Creek Ranger Station

Antietam

Antietam Creek

34

Huckleberry Hill

Antietam

Antietam Creek Aqueduct

Boonsboro

SHENANDOAH

RIVER

BLUE

Harpers Ferry

Dargan Bend

Fort Duncan

RIDGE

MARYLAND

67

APPALACHIAN TRAIL

TRAIL

JEFFERSON CO

LOUDOUN CO

340

Milepost 60

Harpers Ferry Hostel

67

WASHINGTON CO

FREDERICK CO

APPALACHIAN

SOUTH

MOUNTAIN

671

HARPERS FERRY NATIONAL HISTORICAL PARK

478

17

VIRGINIA

9

POTOMAC

17

70

Middletown

287

464

Brunswick

Catoctin Creek

ALT 40

MOUNTAIN

15

340

270

C & O CANAL TOWPATH

Catoctin Aqueduct

RIVER

Milepost 50

Bear Eagle Island

15

CATOCTIN

Point of Rocks

Frederick

70

40

Point of Rocks Railroad Station

CSX

Calico Rocks

355

Monocacy River

26

28

85

SEE MAP 1 FOR START

—— BIKE ROUTE
---- ALTERNATE ROUTE
- - - TRAIL
● POINT OF INTEREST
■ FOOD AVAILABLE
▲ HI HOSTEL

0 1 2 3 4 5   10 MILES

SCALE

7. C & O CANAL TOWPATH
Frederick & Washington Counties, Md.   Map 2 of 3

51.3   Catoctin Aqueduct.

60.7   Cross Appalachian Trail. HI-Harpers Ferry Lodge to right. Harpers Ferry to left.

69.4   Antietam Creek Aqueduct. *Caution: walk bike.*

76.6   Snyders Landing. Road north to Sharpsburg and Park Headquarters.

99.0   Pass Williamsport, a classic C&O Canal town.

112.5   Fort Frederick State Park on right.

118.0   [End of Map 2 instructions.]

155.2   Paw Paw Tunnel.

176.0   C&O Canal boat replica at North Branch.

180.7   Evitts Creek Aqueduct, entering Cumberland area.

184.5   **End** of **TOWPATH**.

The C&O Canal and the competition that drove it out of business.

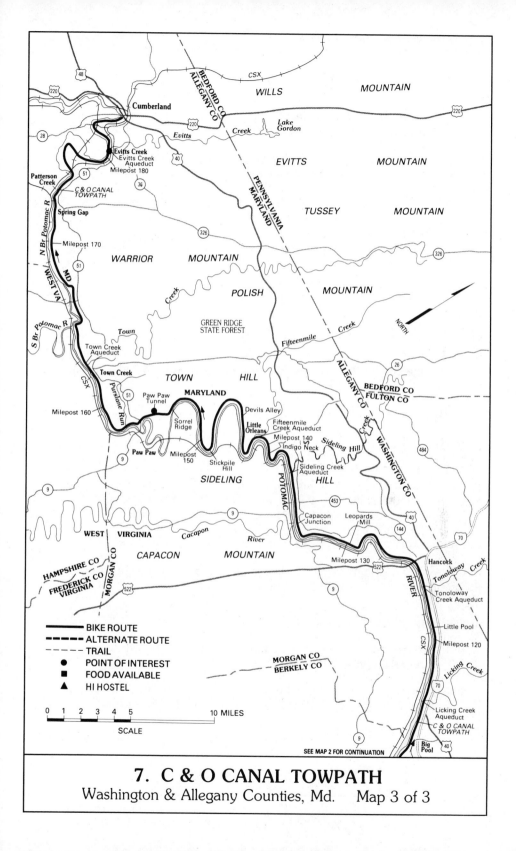

7. C & O CANAL TOWPATH

Washington & Allegany Counties, Md.   Map 3 of 3

8. GLEN ECHO TO SENECA LOOP

Taking you from Glen Echo Park in Bethesda, Md. to Seneca Creek State Park, this tour passes rolling horse country and the stylish community of Potomac.

Glen Echo Park preserves the site of the once-popular amusement park and gathering place. For 60 years, the Glen Echo amusement park hosted thousands of Washingtonians, who explored the Midway, rode the hand-carved Dentzel Carousel, danced in the Spanish ballroom and swam in the gigantic pool which held 3,000 people. When the amusement park closed in 1968 due to poor attendance, a joint effort by the local community and the federal government preserved the site as a national cultural arts park, dedicated in 1971. Today the antique Dentzel Carousel still entertains children and adults alike, and the park hosts live bands and dances in the large ballroom and arts and community affairs classes in the other refurbished buildings.

START: Glen Echo Park at the corner of Goldsborough Road and MacArthur Boulevard in Bethesda, Md. The park is 2.5 miles northwest of the Washington, D.C. line and just north of the Potomac River. Glen Echo Park is within the Capital Beltway.

LENGTH: 33.1 miles.

TERRAIN: Hilly. Final six miles are all either level or downhill.

POINTS OF INTEREST: Glen Echo Park with antique carousel, and Clara Barton House at start; Cabin John Bridge at 0.5 miles; Great Falls Park at 6.2 miles; Blockhouse Point Park at 15.1 miles; and Seneca Creek State Park at 18.2 miles. Horse stables and Potomac mansions along the route.

FOOD: Food at start, 1.3, 7.8, 13.5 and 22.0 miles.

MAPS: *ADC's Washington Area Bike Map; Lower Montgomery County Bicycle Route Map;* Montgomery County, Md. road map.

MILES   DIRECTIONS & COMMENTS

0.0   **Left** to go north out of Glen Echo Park (Oxford Lane) on **MACARTHUR BOULEVARD.**

0.5   Cross single-lane Cabin John Bridge, once the world's largest stone arch (220 feet). *Note: bicycles are required to use the trail on the left when crossing the bridge.*

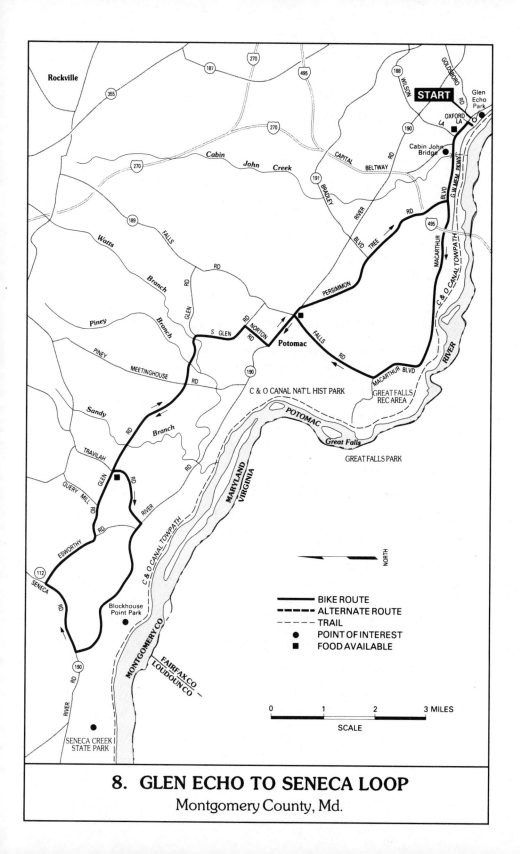

8. GLEN ECHO TO SENECA LOOP
Montgomery County, Md.

1.3   Bethesda Co-op market.

6.0   **Right** on **FALLS ROAD.** Great Falls Park is southwest of the intersection.

7.8   Shopping center on right. Ice cream at end of parking lot in corner.

7.9   **Left** on **RIVER ROAD** (MD 190). *Caution: heavy traffic.*

8.7   **Right** on **NORTON ROAD.**

9.2   **Left** on **SOUTH GLEN ROAD.** Horse stables along road.

10.3   **Left** on **GLEN ROAD,** over bridge, then **left** again to stay on **GLEN ROAD.**

13.5   **Left** on **TRAVILAH ROAD.** Food at corner.

14.8   **Right** on **RIVER ROAD** (MD 190), through Blockhouse Point Park.

17.8   **Right** on **SENECA ROAD** at T. (Seneca Creek State Park is 0.5 miles to left on continuation of River Road.)

19.3   **Right** on **ESWORTHY ROAD.**

20.6   **Left** on **QUERY MILL ROAD.** *Caution: poor road surface.*

21.2   **First right** on **GLEN ROAD** (unmarked).

22.0   Cross Travilah Road. Food on right.

24.2   Cross Piney Meetinghouse Road.

25.1   **Right** across bridge, then **right** on **SOUTH GLEN ROAD.**

26.3   **Right** on **NORTON ROAD.**

26.8   **Left** on **RIVER ROAD** (MD 190). *Caution: heavy traffic.*

27.8   Cross Falls Road.

28.0   **Right** on **PERSIMMON TREE ROAD.**

31.5   **Left** on **MACARTHUR BOULEVARD.**

33.1   **Right** into **GLEN ECHO PARK.**

9. GEORGETOWN TO GREAT FALLS

Passing by posh homes, small parks and historical landmarks, this route takes you across the Potomac on Chain Bridge and on to Great Falls Park on the Virginia side of the river. CAUTION: Traffic can be heavy on some of these roads. The roads are curvy and often have no shoulder. As a result, this route is probably not for the beginning cyclist or the squeamish.

START: Capital Crescent Trailhead in Georgetown, at the extreme west end of K Street NW (under Whitehurst Freeway and under Key Bridge). The starting point is within the Capital Beltway. **ALTERNATE START:** Virginia side of Chain Bridge in Arlington at North Glebe Road and 41st Street North. **METRO STARTS:** Trail start is equidistant from Rosslyn and Foggy Bottom Metro stations (Blue and Orange Lines). *From Rosslyn,* go one block east to North Lynn Street, north on North Lynn Street to Key Bridge. Cross bridge on east (downstream) sidewalk, take sharp right immediately at end of bridge, descend asphalt trail, and cross C&O Canal on small bridge. Make U-turn on Towpath at end of bridge ramp. After about 100 feet turn right and descend long flight of stairs to K Street NW. Turn right. Trail begins 0.2 miles west. *From Foggy Bottom,* go north on 23rd Street NW to Washington Circle, then head west on Pennsylvania Avenue NW to 29th Street NW. Turn left (south) on 29th Street NW, cross over C&O Canal, and continue to bottom of hill. At K Street NW, turn right (west). Tour begins at trailhead, just past Key Bridge, in 0.8 miles.

LENGTH: 42.6 miles. From **ALTERNATE START:** 35.6 miles.

TERRAIN: Hilly. Some narrow and winding roads with some heavy traffic and fast-moving cars.

POINTS OF INTEREST: Fletcher's Boathouse at 2.4 and 40.2 miles; Chain Bridge, with spectacular view of the Potomac River at 3.3 and 39.1 miles; Kirby Park at 7.4 miles; Fairfax County Courthouse at 12.6 miles; Freedom Hill Fort Park at 12.9 miles; Wolf Trap Barns at 15.5 miles; Filene Center at 15.6 miles; Wolf Trap Performing Arts Center at 15.7 miles; Great Falls Park at 19.9 miles; W&OD Trail at 27.3 miles; Freeman House Museum at 29.2 miles; Fort Ethan Allen Civil War site and Gulf Branch Nature Center at 38.0 miles.

FOOD: Frequent along the route. Markets at 33.8 and 35.5 miles. Fast food restaurants at 12.9 miles. Buy or bring food for a picnic at Great Falls Park or Freedom Hill Fort Park.

MAPS: *Bikeway Map* (Arlington County, Va.); Arlington and Fairfax Counties, Va. road maps.

Winding road, typical of the Great Falls area.

MILES   DIRECTIONS & COMMENTS

0.0   From Capital Crescent Trailhead, **go west** on **TRAIL**. Pass Washington Canoe Club (private) on left.

0.4   On right are two connections: steps/ramp up to C&O Canal Towpath; and tunnel under Towpath and Canal Road NW to Glover-Archibald Park, Glover Park neighborhood and Georgetown University.

2.3   Fletcher's Boathouse. Parking. Bicycle, canoe and rowboat rental. Telephone, restroom, snack bar. Picnic tables, fishing access. **Bear right** on **C&O CANAL TOWPATH**.

3.2   **Left** to ascend concrete ramp and go **south** on **CHAIN BRIDGE** across Potomac River into Virginia.

3.5   [ALTERNATE START] **Bear left** on **NORTH GLEBE ROAD** at bridge end. **Immediate right** on **41ST STREET NORTH.** Climb steep hill.

3.6   At top of hill, take short switchback uphill. *Caution: Very steep, and usually unrideable due to grade and road surface.*

3.7   **Left** on **NORTH RANDOLPH STREET** after leaving switchback.

3.8   **Right** on **OLD GLEBE ROAD. Bear left** over bridge. Then **bear right** at Military Road to stay on **OLD GLEBE ROAD.**

4.2   **Left** on **NORTH GLEBE ROAD** at stop sign.

4.3   **Right** on **CHESTERBROOK ROAD** at traffic light.

5.6   **Left** on **KIRBY ROAD** (VA 695).

7.1   Cross Westmoreland Road at traffic light. Pass Kirby Park at 7.4 miles.

7.8   Cross Great Falls Road and proceed **straight** on **IDYLWOOD ROAD.**

8.9   Cross Leesburg Pike (VA 7). To reach West Falls Church Metro station (Orange Line), go 0.6 miles east on VA 7, turn left on Haycock Road, go 0.2 miles to Metro station.

10.4   Cross Gallows Road at traffic light. *Caution: traffic.*

10.9   Cross Cedar Lane. *Caution: traffic.*

11.1   **Right** on **WILLIAMS AVENUE** (VA 896).

11.3   **Left** on **VA 697** (Electric Avenue). This road follows an old trolley route to Vienna.

11.6   **Right** on **WOODFORD ROAD** (VA 697).

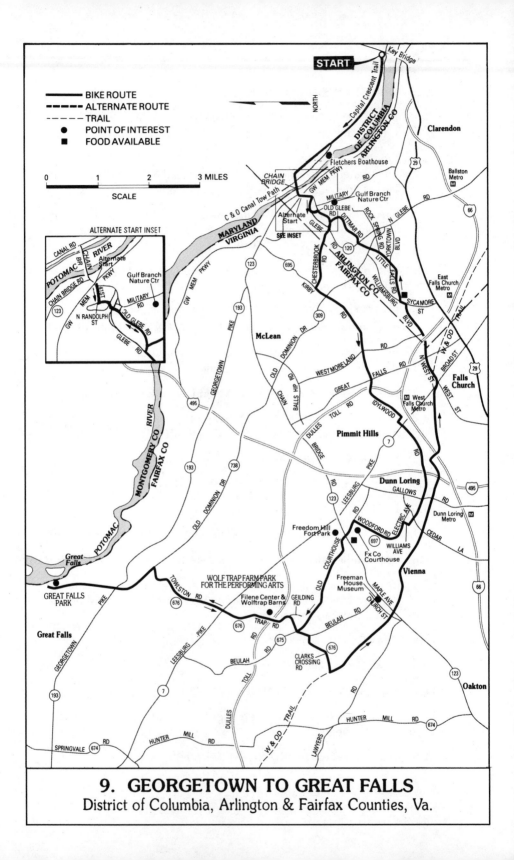

9. GEORGETOWN TO GREAT FALLS
District of Columbia, Arlington & Fairfax Counties, Va.

12.6   **Left** on **OLD COURTHOUSE ROAD** at T. Pass Fairfax County Courthouse.

12.9   Cross Chain Bridge Road (VA 123). Fast food, traffic. Buy food here for a picnic in one of the parks.

13.0   **First left** to stay on **OLD COURTHOUSE ROAD.**

13.1   Freedom Hill Fort Park on left. Picnic areas.

15.2   **Right** on **TRAP ROAD** (VA 676).

15.5   **Left** to remain on **TRAP ROAD** at T. Pass Wolf Trap Barns, then Filene Center and Wolf Trap Performing Arts Center, on right.

16.5   **Straight** on **TOWLSTON ROAD.** Do not take Trap Road as it veers off to the right. Continue climbing hill through residential area.

16.9   Cross Leesburg Pike (VA 7). Beautiful homes.

18.9   **Left** on **OLD DOMINION DRIVE** at T.

19.9   Cross Georgetown Pike (VA 193) into Great Falls Park.

20.9   Parking and picnic area. **Reverse direction.**

21.9   Cross Georgetown Pike (VA 193), staying on **OLD DOMINION DRIVE.**

23.0   **Right** on **TOWLSTON ROAD.**

24.8   **Straight** on **TRAP ROAD**. Pass theaters. **Right** to stay on **TRAP ROAD** and avoid Geilding Road.

26.2   **Straight** on **BEULAH ROAD** (VA 675), crossing Old Courthouse Road.

26.4   **Right** on **CLARKS CROSSING ROAD,** passing horse farm.

27.3   Road narrows to parking lot. **Left** (east) on **W&OD TRAIL.**

29.2   Town of Vienna. Freeman House Museum on left, between Church Street and Maple Avenue (VA 123). Food in Vienna.

33.8   City of Falls Church. Cross West Broad Street (VA 7) on bicycle overpass bridge. (For food in Falls Church, exit trail immediately before bridge.)

34.0   **Left** on **NORTH WEST STREET.**

34.5   North West Street becomes **WILLIAMSBURG BOULEVARD,** before I-66 overpass.

35.5   **Left** on **NORTH SYCAMORE STREET** at CVS Drug Store (food available on North Sycamore Street). **Bear right** on **LITTLE FALLS ROAD,** following signed bike route.

35.8   **Bear right** to stay on **LITTLE FALLS ROAD** at Yorktown Boulevard.

36.3   Cross Yorktown Boulevard, leaving bike route, to stay on **LITTLE FALLS ROAD.**

36.6   **Bear left** to stay on **LITTLE FALLS ROAD** at Rock Spring Road.

36.8   Cross Old Dominion Drive. *Caution: traffic.*

37.1   **Straight** to cross North Glebe Road. Little Falls Road becomes **NORTH DITTMAR ROAD.**

38.0   **Right** on **OLD GLEBE ROAD.** Pass Fort Ethan Allen Civil War site on right.

38.5   **Bear left** at stop sign to stay on **OLD GLEBE ROAD.** *Note: follow Bike Route signs to Chain Bridge. Do not obey automobile instructions to Chain Bridge.* If you want to visit the Gulf Branch Nature Center, it is 0.3 miles to right on Military Road.

38.6   **Left** on **NORTH RANDOLPH STREET.**

38.7   **Right** on switchback marked by Bicycle Route sign. *Caution:* very steep grade downhill with sharp turns. At the end of the switchback, proceed down VERY steep hill on **41st STREET NORTH.** *Caution!*

38.9   At bottom of hill, bear left onto sidewalk before North Glebe Road intersection.

39.0   Cross intersection with VA 123 at traffic light, then **cross CHAIN BRIDGE** on upriver sidewalk.

39.4   Just before end of bridge, **descend ramp** on left to **C&O CANAL TOWPATH.** Note: sign says ramp and area beyond are open to FOOT traffic only. **Right** (downstream) on **TOWPATH** at bottom of ramp.

40.3   Fletcher's Boathouse. **Bear right** to continue in same direction on **CAPITAL CRESCENT TRAIL.**

42.6   **Arrive** at **CAPITAL CRESCENT TRAILHEAD.**

10. ARLINGTON HISTORY RIDE

Some of Arlington's best and least-known trails form the spine of this urban tour, which traces the county's rich history and takes you by interesting historic spots.

A pamphlet available at the Arlington Historical Museum provides a map with historical background for each stop. Historical markers at the sites also furnish general information.

[Note: This route takes you through Fort Myer, an active military base. Identification (such as a driver's license) is required for entry. Fort Myer also may restrict civilian bicycle access without notice. Call the Fort Myer Welcome Center (703-696-3025) for current regulations.]

START: Arlington Historical Museum at 1805 South Arlington Ridge Road in Pentagon City, Arlington, Va. The starting point is within the Capital Beltway. **METRO STARTS:** From the Pentagon City Metro station (Blue and Yellow Lines), go north on South Hayes Street, left on Army-Navy Drive, then turn left on North Lynn Street, which becomes South Arlington Ridge Road. Arlington Cemetery Metro station (Blue Line) is near the route at 2.5 miles; Virginia Square Metro station (Orange Line) at 6.0 miles; Ballston Metro station (Orange Line) is one block west of route at 6.4 miles.

LENGTH: 22.8 miles.

TERRAIN: Level with a few steep but short hills. Some gravel on the bike trails. Traffic is generally not heavy, but riders should exercise appropriate caution as this is an urban area.

POINTS OF INTEREST: Arlington Historical Museum (703-892-4204) at start (open Fridays and Saturdays from 11 a.m. to 3 p.m. and Sundays from 2 p.m. to 5 p.m.); Arlington National Cemetery with Tomb of the Unknown Soldier, John Fitzgerald Kennedy and Robert Kennedy memorial grounds and U.S.S. Maine memorial at 2.5 miles; Arlington House at 2.8 miles, home of the Custis family and Robert E. Lee; Arlington Arts Center at 5.9 miles; the Glebe House at 7.2 miles, a colonial parson's farmhouse; Maple Shade Mansion at 9.5 miles; original western cornerstone of the District of Columbia at 11.6 miles; Bon Air Park Rose Garden at 14.6 miles; Ball-Sellers house at 16.5 miles, an early working-class settler's home; George Washington's survey marker at 17.2 miles; and Prospect Hill overlook at 22.4 miles.

FOOD: Frequent along the route. Picnic area at 14.6 miles.

MAPS: *Bikeway Map* (Arlington County, Va.).

MILES   DIRECTIONS & COMMENTS

0.0   **Right** out of museum to go north on **SOUTH ARLINGTON RIDGE ROAD.**

0.2   **First right** on **SOUTH LYNN STREET**.

0.6   **First right** on **ARMY-NAVY DRIVE.**

0.7   **First left** on **SOUTH JOYCE STREET,** under I-395.

1.0   **Straight** on **SOUTHGATE ROAD.**

1.3   **Bear right** through **HENDERSON HALL GATE.**

1.6   **Right** through **PEDESTRIAN GATE** into Fort Myer. **Straight** on **CARPENTER ROAD,** along stone wall.

2.0   **Right** on **McNAIR ROAD.**

2.5   **Right** on **LEE DRIVE,** through Arlington Cemetery gate. Becomes **MEIGS DRIVE.**

2.8   **Arrive** at **ARLINGTON HOUSE. Reverse direction.**

3.1   **Left** on **McNAIR ROAD.**

3.7   **Right** on **CARPENTER ROAD**. This becomes **2ND STREET SOUTH** outside Fort Myer.

4.6   **Right** on **NORTH IRVING STREET**.

5.3   **Left** on **6TH STREET NORTH**.

5.6   **Right** on **NORTH MONROE STREET**.

6.0   **Left** on **NORTH FAIRFAX DRIVE**.

6.4   **Right** on **NORTH STAFFORD STREET.** Ballston historic marker. Ballston Metro station ahead on left. (To reach Ballston Metro station and Ballston Common Shopping Center with restaurants and fast food, continue one block on North Fairfax Street then turn left on North Stuart Street.)

6.7   **Left** on **13TH STREET NORTH.**

6.8   **Right** on **NORTH UTAH STREET.**

7.2   **Left** on **17TH STREET NORTH.** Pass the Glebe House on right, at 4727 North Glebe Road. Cross North Glebe Road.

7.6   **Left** on **NORTH ABINGDON STREET** at T.

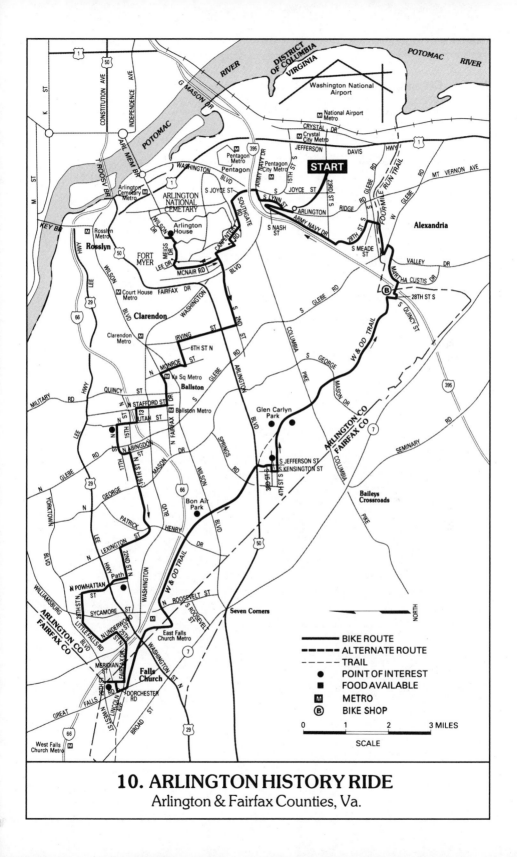

10. ARLINGTON HISTORY RIDE
Arlington & Fairfax Counties, Va.

7.7   **Second right** on **16TH STREET NORTH.** *Caution: heavy traffic.*

8.5   **Bear right** on **NORTH LEXINGTON STREET.**

9.1   **Left** on **22ND STREET NORTH.**

9.5   **Right** on **TRAIL at 6125 22th Street North.** Maple Shade Mansion on left, at 2230 North Powhatan Street. **Straight** on **NORTH POWHATAN STREET.**

10.0   **Left** on **28TH STREET NORTH.** Cross North Sycamore Street. Becomes **LITTLE FALLS ROAD.**

10.7   **Left** on **NORTH UNDERWOOD STREET.**

10.9   **Right** on **25TH STREET NORTH,** which becomes **NORTH FAIRFAX DRIVE,** crossing I-66. Victorian houses on left.

11.6   **Right** on **MERIDIAN STREET.**

11.8   Western Boundary Stone on left. **Reverse direction.**

Military funerals are a common sight at Arlington National Cemetery.

11.9   **Right** on **DORCHESTER ROAD.**

12.0   **Left** on **GREAT FALLS ROAD.**

12.1   **Left** on **W&OD TRAIL.**

14.3   Water available.

14.6   Pass Bon Air Park Rose Garden and picnic area to left.

16.3   Pass under Arlington Boulevard (US 50) bridge high overhead, and **immediate right** on **PAVED TRAIL** straight up hill.

16.5   **Left** on **SOUTH JEFFERSON STREET. Right** on **3RD STREET SOUTH.** Ball-Sellers house on left at 5620 3rd Street South.

16.6   **Left** on **SOUTH KENSINGTON STREET. Left** on **4TH STREET SOUTH** into Glencarlyn Park. Hill.

17.2   Pass bridge. **Right** on **W&OD TRAIL.** George Washington's survey marker on right.

19.6   **Right** on **SOUTH QUINCY STREET. First left** on **28TH STREET SOUTH.** Bike shop and food in Shirlington Village. Follow bike route signs to ramp and pedestrian overpass crossing I-395.

19.9   **Left** on **MARTHA CUSTIS DRIVE** at bottom of ramp.

20.5   **Left** on **WEST GLEBE ROAD** at T.

20.7   **Right** on **FOUR MILE RUN BIKE TRAIL** at traffic light (South Glebe Road in Arlington).

21.1   **Left** on **SOUTH MEADE STREET.** [Trail continues to National Airport and Mount Vernon Trail (Tour 5).]

21.2   **First left** on **28TH STREET SOUTH.**

21.7   **Right** on **ARMY-NAVY DRIVE** at T.

22.1   **Straight** on **SOUTH NASH STREET** where Army-Navy Drive curves left.

22.4   **Follow U-turn** on **SOUTH ARLINGTON RIDGE ROAD** at Prospect Hill, a hairpin turn. View Washington skyline.

22.8   **Left** into **ARLINGTON HISTORICAL MUSEUM.**

11. ALEXANDRIA LOOP

A close-in ride, almost perfectly flat, with little traffic, the Alexandria Loop is an ideal ride for beginners. About two-thirds of the route is on off-road trails that follow three tributaries of the Potomac (Cameron Run, Holmes Run and Four Mile Run). These trails are less traveled than better-known trails such as the Mount Vernon or W&OD.

START/METRO START: King Street Metro station (Blue and Yellow Lines) at King Street and Diagonal Road in Alexandria, Va. (Parking is limited weekdays during business hours, but plentiful on weekends and weekday evenings.) Eisenhower Avenue Metro station (Blue Line) is just off the route at 2.3 miles, with weekday parking available. The starting point is inside the Capital Beltway.

LENGTH: 15.4 miles.

TERRAIN: Level. A few short, unpaved stretches on the trail in Holmes Run Park.

POINTS OF INTEREST: Alexandria National Cemetery at 0.8 miles. Cameron Run, Holmes Run and Four Mile Run. Cameron Run Regional Park at 3.8 miles has many facilities, including a wave pool and water slide; Dora Kelley Nature Park (wildlife sanctuary) at 6.5 miles. Northern Virginia Community College, Alexandria Campus at 8.2 miles.

FOOD: Food at start, 8.8 and 10.2 miles. Picnic areas in Cameron Run, Holmes Run and Four Mile Run Parks.

MAPS: *Recreational Facilities and Bike Trails Map* (City of Alexandria, Va.).

MILES   DIRECTIONS & COMMENTS

0.0   **Left** out of King Street Metro station on **DIAGONAL ROAD. Right** on **DAINGERFIELD ROAD** at first traffic light.

0.2   **Left** on **DUKE STREET**. *Caution: traffic.*

0.5   **Right** on **HENRY STREET** (US 1 South)**. Bear right immediately** to stay on **HENRY STREET**, while US 1 traffic bears left.

0.7   **Right** on **WILKES STREET**. Historic Alexandria cemeteries and Alexandria National Cemetery straight ahead.

0.8   **Left** on **PAYNE STREET.**

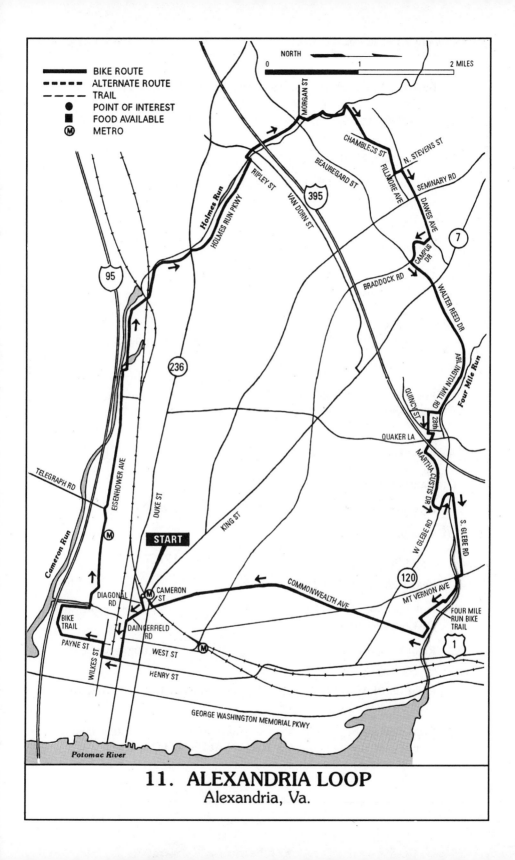

11. ALEXANDRIA LOOP
Alexandria, Va.

1.2 **Bear right** onto **TRAIL**, just after passing Alexandria Animal Shelter. Alexandria Sanitation Authority plant is on the right. Trail runs alongside the Capital Beltway, then turns right to follow Cameron Run.

1.7 Follow trail to left.

1.9 Trail joins **EISENHOWER AVENUE**. Trail is on left (south) side of Eisenhower Avenue.

2.3 Eisenhower Avenue Metro station.

2.5 Cross Telegraph Road on overpass. Hill.

3.8 **TRAIL** crosses to **right** (north) side of Eisenhower Avenue. Cameron Run Regional Park.

4.3 **Bear right** on **TRAIL** into Holmes Run Park.

5.1 "Bicentennial Tree" on right. Willow Oak tree more than 270 years old.

5.9 Trail sign for "urban trail" straight ahead or "scenic trail" to the left. Route follows **SCENIC TRAIL**. Portions of scenic trail route unpaved and prone to minor flooding. Urban trail route follows Van Dorn Street and Sanger Avenue and rejoins scenic trail at mile 6.9.

6.4 Cross Beauregard Street at Morgan Street. *Caution: traffic.* Just past intersection, **take immediate right** to stay on **TRAIL**. Dora Kelley Nature Park next 0.5 miles.

6.9 **Right** on **CHAMBLISS STREET**. Urban trail route rejoins here.

7.0 **Straight** on **TRAIL**.

7.3 Trail ends. **Straight on NORTH CHAMBLISS STREET**.

7.4 **Bear right** on **FILLMORE AVENUE**.

7.6 **Left** on **NORTH STEVENS STREET**, then after one block, **right** on **DAWES AVENUE**.

8.2 **Right** on **CAMPUS DRIVE** (Northern Virginia Community College, Alexandria Campus).

8.5 **Right** on **BRADDOCK ROAD**, then **left** on **BEAUREGARD STREET**. *Caution: traffic.*

8.8 Cross King Street (VA 7). Bike shop and food at intersection. Beauregard Street becomes **SOUTH WALTER REED DRIVE**.

9.5   **Right** on **SOUTH ARLINGTON MILL ROAD**. Take trail on north side of road.

10.2   **Right** on **SOUTH QUINCY STREET**. Shirlington Village on right. Bike shop and food.

10.4   **Left** on **28TH STREET SOUTH**. Stay on sidewalk on left side of 28th Street South to cross I-395 (Shirley Highway) on pedestrian overpass.

10.6   **Left** on **MARTHA CUSTIS DRIVE** at bottom of overpass.

11.1   **Left** on **WEST GLEBE ROAD**. *Caution: traffic.*

11.3   **Right** on **SOUTH GLEBE ROAD** then immediately turn onto **TRAIL**.

11.7   **Bear right** to continue on **TRAIL** just before Meade Drive.

12.0   Cross under Mount Vernon Avenue. (Sign says Arlington Ridge Road.) Follow trail to **left** back around to **MOUNT VERNON AVENUE.**

12.1   **Left** on **MOUNT VERNON AVENUE**. Cross overpass and make **immediate left** on **FOUR MILE RUN TRAIL.** Wildlife refuge on left.

13.0   **Right** on **COMMONWEALTH AVENUE** (unmarked, just past softball field).

15.3   **Right** on **CAMERON STREET.**

15.4   **Arrive** at **KING STREET METRO STATION.**

12. ANACOSTIA HEADWATERS LOOP

This ride forms a loop that will take you through the woods, fields and wetlands of the Anacostia Headwaters, before returning you on well-traveled roads to your starting point. About two-thirds of the ride uses the Anacostia Tributary Trail System, a series of seven different trails that connect at various intersections along the many tributaries of the Anacostia River. There are virtually no trail markers on the entire route, so keep track of where you are!

The remaining third of the ride uses major roadways. Although some of these are well-traveled vehicular roads, the proximity of the University of Maryland generally makes them good roads for bicycling. There are wide shoulders or sidewalks on most of the roads.

The route also passes Lake Artemesia, a man-made lake created by Metro; the College Park Airport and Museum, the world's oldest continually operating airport, where Wilbur Wright instructed Army officers in the first government airplane; and Adelphi Mill, built in 1796, reputed to be the oldest and largest mill in the Washington metropolitan area.

START/METRO START: Greenbelt Metro station (Green Line) at Exit 24 of the Capital Beltway, in Greenbelt, Md. Parking available. The starting point is just inside the Capital Beltway.

LENGTH: 21.6 miles.

TERRAIN: Level.

POINTS OF INTEREST: Lake Artemesia at 2.7 miles; College Park Airport and Museum at 3.6 miles; Adelphi Mill at 11.7 miles.

FOOD: This route passes through parks and woods, but there are numerous shopping centers and restaurants in the surrounding communities.

MAPS: Maryland National Capital Park and Planning Commission map of the Anacostia Tributary Trail System (301-952-3522). (*Note: this map's rendering of the roads around the University of Maryland is incomplete and should not be used as a guide.*)

MILES   DIRECTIONS & COMMENTS

0.0   On east side of Metro station, **follow GREENBELT METRO DRIVE** around parking area to T intersection with Cherrywood Lane.

0.5   **Right** on **CHERRYWOOD LANE** at T.

1.5   **Right** on **GREENBELT ROAD** (MD 193) at traffic light.

1.7   Cross **GREENBELT ROAD** at traffic light (Branchville Road/58th Avenue) and **follow the sidewalk** on the left side of Greenbelt Road for about 50 feet. **Left** on **57TH AVENUE** then immediately **begin INDIAN CREEK TRAIL** on right.

2.0   Cross Berwyn Road.

2.7   Cross bridge over Indian Creek then **immediate left** on **NORTHEAST BRANCH TRAIL.** (Trails to the right and straight ahead go around Lake Artemesia.)

3.6   College Park Airport and Museum on right.

3.9   Cross under Good Luck Road.

4.0   Fitness Circuit and Dennis Wolf Rest Stop. Ellen Linson Swimming Pool on right and Herbert Wells Ice Rink on left.

5.0   Cross under East-West Highway.

5.1   Cross Riverdale Road.

6.0   Cross Decatur Street.

Fording a stream on the Anacostia Headwaters Trail.

6.5   **Right** on **NORTHWEST BRANCH TRAIL** (unmarked) after passing under highway bridge. If you cross bridge over Northwest Branch, you have gone too far. **Bear left** at top of hill. Trail follows Armentrout Drive on sidewalk.

6.8   Cross Rhode Island Avenue (US 1). Melrose Neighborhood Playground on left.

7.5   Cross 38th Avenue.

8.0   **Bear right** after crossing bridge.

8.4   **Bear right** across bridge.

8.5   Cross Queens Chapel Road (MD 500).

8.8   West Hyattsville Metro station on right.

9.0   **Bear right** to continue on **NORTHWEST BRANCH TRAIL** at junction with Sligo Creek Trail.

9.2   **Straight** to remain on trail. Do not cross bridge to left.

9.6   Cross under Ager Road.

10.0   Cross under East-West Highway.

11.1   Cross University Boulevard. Adelphi Shopping Center with restaurants to left. Lane Manor Aquatic Facility and Recreation Center and University of Maryland to right.

11.3   Trail intersects with other trails. Go straight here and at subsequent trail intersections.

11.7   Cross under Riggs Road (MD 212). Adelphi Mill on right.

12.1   Trail crosses small stream. *Caution!*

12.5   Cross under New Hampshire Avenue (MD 650), then **left** at T. You are still on **NORTHWEST BRANCH TRAIL.**

13.3   Another small stream crossing. *Caution!*

13.7   At end of paved trail, walk 0.3 miles up steep hill on **right** to **OAKVIEW DRIVE.** Proceed straight on Oakview Drive.

14.6   Just before New Hampshire Avenue, **follow sidewalk to right** approximately 20 feet to **AVENEL ROAD.** Follow Avenel Road.

14.9   **Left** on **DILSTON ROAD.** Cross New Hampshire Avenue. Dilston Road becomes **ADELPHI ROAD.**

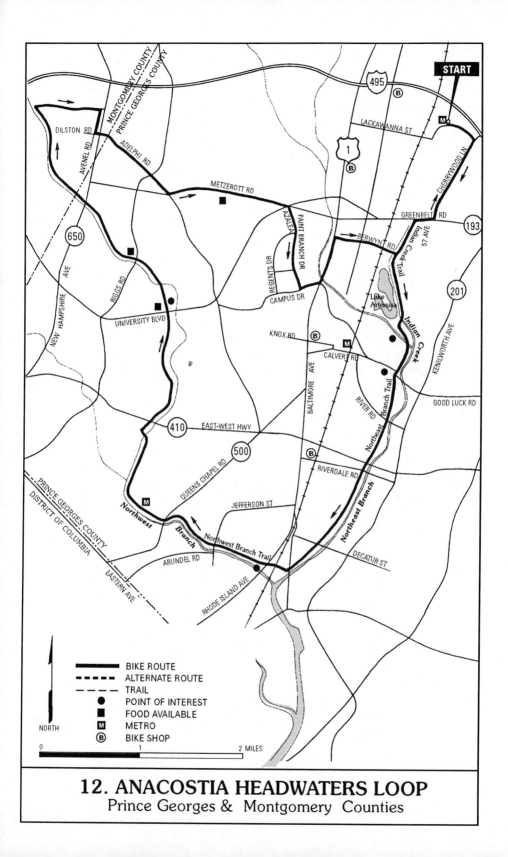

START

495

LACKAWANNA ST

1

DILSTON RD

AVENEL RD

ADELPHI RD

METZEROTT RD

GREENBELT RD

193

BERWYNT RD.

650

AZALEA

PAINT BRANCH DR

REGENTS DR

CAMPUS DR

57 AVE

Indian Creek Trail

Lake Artemisa

201

RIGGS RD

NEW HAMPSHIRE AVE

UNIVERSITY BLVD

KNOX RD

M

CALVERT RD

Indian Creek

KENILWORTH AVE

GOOD LUCK RD

RIVER RD

BALTIMORE AVE

410

EAST-WEST HWY

500

QUEENS CHAPEL RD

Northeast Branch Trail

M

PRINCE GEORGES COUNTY

DISTRICT OF COLUMBIA

EASTERN AVE

Northwest Branch

JEFFERSON ST

RIVERDALE RD

Northwest Branch Trail

Northeast Branch

ARUNDEL RD

RHODE ISLAND AVE

DECATUR ST

MONTGOMERY COUNTY
PRINCE GEORGES COUNTY

CHERRYWOOD LN

NORTH

——— BIKE ROUTE
- - - - ALTERNATE ROUTE
– – – TRAIL
● POINT OF INTEREST
■ FOOD AVAILABLE
Ⓜ METRO
Ⓑ BIKE SHOP

0   1   2 MILES

12. ANACOSTIA HEADWATERS LOOP
Prince Georges & Montgomery Counties

15.7   Cross Riggs Road (MD 210). 7-Eleven on corner. Grocery and fast food on right.

15.9   **Left** on **METZEROTT ROAD.** Pass National Archives and University of Maryland on right at 15.0 miles.

17.2   Cross University Boulevard and continue **straight** on **AZALEA LANE.** Becomes **PAINT BRANCH DRIVE** almost immediately.

18.1   **Left** on **CAMPUS DRIVE** at T.

18.2   **Left** on **BALTIMORE AVENUE** (US 1) at traffic light. Food. *Caution: traffic.*

18.8   **Right** on **BERWYN ROAD.**

19.3   Bridge over Metro tracks.

19.6   **Left** on **INDIAN CREEK TRAIL.**

20.0   At end of trail, proceed to Greenbelt Road and turn **right** (east) on **GREENBELT ROAD** sidewalk. At 58th Avenue traffic light, **cross road**, then continue east on sidewalk.

20.2   **Left** on **CHERRYWOOD LANE.**

21.1   **Left** on **GREENBELT METRO DRIVE.**

21.6   **Arrive** at **GREENBELT METRO STATION.**

Not Too Far Away

13. MONOCACY AQUEDUCT RIDE

From its start in western Montgomery County, Md., to the famous C&O Canal Monocacy Aqueduct, this loop features generally level terrain with plenty of lush greenery. Constructed in 1833 from white quartzite quarried near Sugarloaf Mountain, the aqueduct looms as the highlight of the tour.

START: Poolesville High School on West Willard Road in Poolesville, Md. From the Capital Beltway, take I-270 North and exit on MD 28 West (Rockville exit). Continue 12 miles and turn left on MD 107. Continue five miles to West Willard Road. Turn left and continue one block; the school is on left. Alternatively, from the Capital Beltway take River Road west to West Willard Road. Turn right. The school is approximately 3.5 miles on the right. Poolesville is 21 miles northwest of the Capital Beltway.

LENGTH: 27.7 miles.

TERRAIN: Level, with a steep hill on Big Woods Road.

POINTS OF INTEREST: Monocacy Aqueduct at 17.7 miles.

FOOD: Markets near start and at 9.5, 15,9 and 27.3 miles. Restaurants at 9.5, 11.9, 24.9 and 27.3 miles.

MAPS: Montgomery County, Md. road map; Maryland state highway map.

MILES   DIRECTIONS & COMMENTS

0.0   **Left** out of Poolesville High School, to go south on **WEST WILLARD ROAD.**

4.3   **Left** on **RIVER ROAD** at T.

4.7   **Left** on **HUGHES ROAD.** Polo club on left.

8.5   **Straight** on **WOOTTON AVENUE.**

9.5   **Right** on **ELGIN ROAD.** After one block it becomes **MD 109.** Food available in town at markets and restaurant.

9.8   **Stay to left** on **MD 109** (Beallsville Road) when Elgin Road branches to right.

11.9   Cross MD 28. Food at inn.

13.3   **Left** on **BIG WOODS ROAD.**

15.9   **Right** on **DICKERSON ROAD** (MD 28). Food at left, railroad overpass on right.

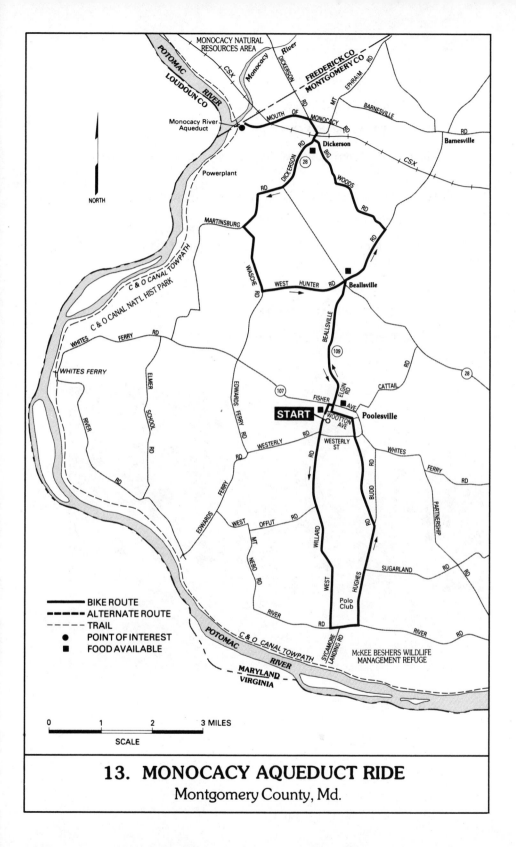

13. MONOCACY AQUEDUCT RIDE
Montgomery County, Md.

16.3   **Left** on **MOUTH OF MONOCACY ROAD**.

17.7   **Arrive** at **AQUEDUCT. Reverse direction.**

19.0   **Right** on **DICKERSON ROAD** (MD 28).

20.6   **Right** on **MARTINSBURG ROAD.** Becomes a narrow concrete road, after bearing left.

21.9   **Left** on **WASCHE ROAD.** *Caution: gravel at intersection.*

23.2   **Left** on **WEST HUNTER ROAD.**

24.9   **Right** on **MD 28,** then **immediate right** on **BEALLSVILLE ROAD** (MD 109). Food at intersection.

27.3   **Right** on **FISHER AVENUE.** Food available.

27.4   **Left** on **WEST WILLARD ROAD.**

27.7   **Arrive** at **POOLESVILLE HIGH SCHOOL.**

Watch for flying corn.

14. POOLESVILLE - LEESBURG LOOP

Rural roads and historic towns present a diverse experience on this tour. The charming towns of Poolesville, Leesburg and Waterford are interspersed with farmland scenes of days gone by. An abandoned railroad right-of-way and two crossings of the Potomac River — one by ferry and one by bridge — offer additional highlights. This popular tour also includes sweeping vistas of the distant Blue Ridge Mountains.

START: Poolesville High School on West Willard Road in Poolesville, Md. From the Capital Beltway, take I-270 North and exit on MD 28 West (Rockville exit). Continue 12 miles and turn left on MD 107. Continue five miles to West Willard Road. Turn left and continue one block; the school is on left. Alternatively, from the Capital Beltway take River Road west to West Willard Road. Turn right. The school is approximately 3.5 miles on the right. Poolesville is 21 miles northwest of the Capital Beltway.

LENGTH: 44.1 miles.

TERRAIN: Hilly. Good shoulder on MD 28. Heavy traffic with no paved shoulder on US 15 for 1.2 miles.

POINTS OF INTEREST: Whites Ferry (301-349-5200) at 6.3 miles, the only continually operating ferry on the Potomac River ($0.50 for bicycles, 7 days a week); Waterford at 18.3 miles, an 18th century town that maintains the look and feel of days gone by; and Point of Rocks, Md. on the Potomac River at 29.8 miles, with restored 19th century railroad station.

FOOD: Markets or restaurants available near start (Poolesville), mile 10.5 (Leesburg), mile 18.3 (Waterford), mile 24.2 (Taylorstown), mile 29.4 (Point of Rocks), mile 38.0 (Dickerson), and mile 41.4 (Beallsville).

MAPS: Montgomery and Frederick Counties, Md. and Loudoun County, Va. road maps.

MILES   DIRECTIONS & COMMENTS

0.0   **Right** out of Poolesville High School to go north on **WEST WILLARD ROAD. Left** on **FISHERS AVENUE** (MD 107), which becomes **WHITES FERRY ROAD.**

6.3   Cross Potomac River on Whites Ferry. Go **south** on **VA 655.**

7.6   **Left** on **US 15**. *Caution: trucks and heavy traffic on road with no paved shoulder.*

8.8   **Straight** on **BUS US 15.**

10.5   **Right** on **WEST CORNWALL STREET**, just after North Street in Leesburg. Food available in Leesburg.

10.9   **Left** on **AYR STREET**. Continue **straight** on **DRY MILL ROAD**, cross W&OD Trail. Pass Loudoun County High School.

13.1   **Bear right** to stay on **DRY MILL ROAD**.

15.2   **Right** on **VA 9** (Charles Town Pike) crossing over VA 7.

16.3   **Right** on **VA 662**, just before Texaco station.

18.3   **Straight** on **VA 665** (High Street) in Waterford. This road later becomes **LOYALTY ROAD.** Food available at Waterford Grocery (closed Sunday).

24.2   **Left** on **TAYLORSTOWN ROAD** in Taylorstown. General Store open every day (closed Sunday morning).

26.3   **Right** on **VA 672** (Lovettsville Road).

29.0   **Left** on **US 15**. Cross Potomac River into Maryland.

29.4   **Right** on **MD 28** (Tuscarora Road). Enter Point of Rocks. Restored train station on right. Food available at several markets.

34.2   **Right** to stay on **MD 28** (Dickerson Road) where MD 85 goes straight.

38.0   Enter Dickerson. Food at general store.

41.4   **Right** on **MD 109** in Beallsville. Restaurant and ice cream stand (closed Mondays).

43.9   **Right** on **MD 107** in Poolesville.

44.1   **Left** on **WEST WILLARD ROAD. Left** into **POOLESVILLE HIGH SCHOOL.**

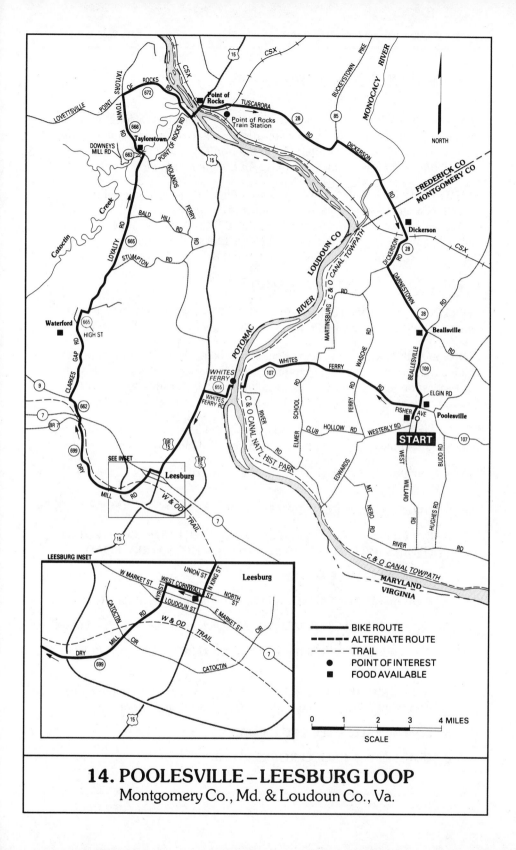

NORTH

Point of Rocks

Point of Rocks
Train Station

TAYLORS
POINT OF ROCKS RD
672
LOVETTSVILLE
668
Taylorstown
663
DOWNEYS
MILL RD
15

CSX

TUSCARORA

28
85

MONOCACY RIVER
BUCKEYSTOWN PIKE

DICKERSON RD

FREDERICK CO
MONTGOMERY CO

NOLANDS
FERRY RD
BALD HILL RD
STUMPTON RD
LOYALTY RD
665

Catoctin Creek

Waterford
665
HIGH ST

CLARKES GAP RD

9
7
BR 7
662
699
DRY

SEE INSET

Leesburg

MILL RD
W & OD TRAIL
15
7

BR
15
BP
15

Dickerson
28
DICKERSON RD
DARNESTOWN RD
CSX

28
Beallsville
109
ELGIN RD
FISHER AVE
Poolesville
107

LOUDOUN CO

MARTINSBURG C & O CANAL TOWPATH

POTOMAC RIVER

WHITES
FERRY
655
WHITES FERRY RD
107
WHITES
FERRY RD

C & O CANAL NATL HIST PARK

RIVER RD
ELMER SCHOOL RD
CLUB HOLLOW RD
WESTERLY RD
EDWARDS RD
MT NEBO RD
WEST WILLARD RD
HUGHES RD
BUDD RD
107

WASCHE RD
FERRY RD

START

C & O CANAL TOWPATH

MARYLAND
VIRGINIA

LEESBURG INSET

UNION ST
W MARKET ST
WEST CORNWALL ST
KING ST
NORTH ST
Leesburg
CATOCTIN MILL RD
AYR ST
LOUDOUN ST
E MARKET ST
CIR
W & OD TRAIL
CIR
DRY
699
CATOCTIN
7
15

—— BIKE ROUTE
– – – ALTERNATE ROUTE
- - - TRAIL
● POINT OF INTEREST
■ FOOD AVAILABLE

0   1   2   3   4 MILES
SCALE

14. POOLESVILLE – LEESBURG LOOP
Montgomery Co., Md. & Loudoun Co., Va.

15. BACK OF SUGARLOAF

The scenic Sugarloaf Mountain is a "must-cycle" for the Washington area bicycle tourist! Circling the mountain, this tour features mostly quiet roads with views of the Catoctin Mountains to the north. We include a shortcut to leave more time for mountain climbing. An excellent fall colors ride!

START: Poolesville High School on West Willard Road in Poolesville, Md. From the Capital Beltway, take I-270 North and exit on MD 28 West (Rockville exit). Continue 12 miles and turn left on MD 107. Continue five miles to West Willard Road. Turn left and continue one block; the school is on left. Poolesville is 21 miles northwest of the Capital Beltway.

LENGTH: 50.5 miles. **ALTERNATE ROUTE:** 21.3 miles.

TERRAIN: Well-maintained roads, rolling hills. Three steep hills at 25.1, 33.0 and 34.2 miles. Local cyclists refer to Flint Hill (mile 25.1) as "The Wall."

POINTS OF INTEREST: Dickerson Regional Park at 5.0 miles; Point of Rocks at 11.2 miles, with 19th century railroad station; Lilypons Water Gardens at 23.3 miles, one of the world's largest goldfish and water lily breeding areas; Urbana Lake at 29.1 miles; and Sugarloaf Mountain Park at 38.0 miles.

FOOD: Markets at start, 7.4, 15.1, 15.7, 26.1 and 35.4 miles. Restaurants at start and 35.4 miles. Only the Dickerson market (7.4 miles) on alternate route.

MAPS: Montgomery and Frederick Counties, Md. road maps.

MILES   DIRECTIONS & COMMENTS

0.0   **Right** out of school to go north on **WEST WILLARD ROAD. Left** on **FISHERS AVENUE** (MD 107). Becomes **WHITES FERRY ROAD.**

2.3   **Right** on **WASCHE ROAD.**

5.0   **Right** on **MARTINSBURG ROAD.** Dickerson Regional Park on left.

6.3   **Left** on **DICKERSON ROAD** (MD 28). Dickerson Market at 7.4 miles.

7.5   After underpass, **bear left** to remain on **MD 28.** ALTERNATE ROUTE (see end of cues).

11.1   **Left** on **MD 28** at intersection with MD 85. *Caution: heavy traffic.* Pass Point of Rocks train station on left. Good snack spot.

15.8   **Right** on **BALLENGER CREEK ROAD.**

19.6   **Sharp right** on **CALICO ROCKS ROAD.**

A barn, back of Sugarloaf.

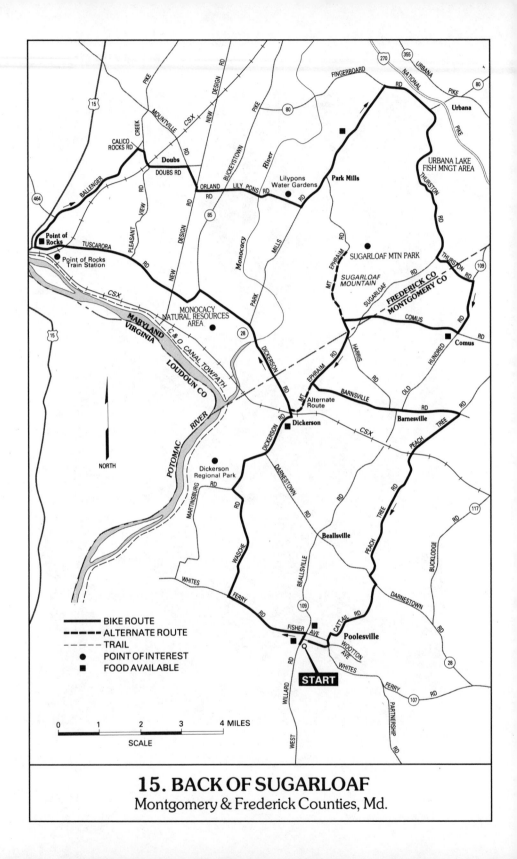

15. BACK OF SUGARLOAF
Montgomery & Frederick Counties, Md.

19.7 **Right** on **DOUBS ROAD**.

20.1 **Left** to stay on **DOUBS ROAD,** just after crossing railroad tracks.

21.1 **Right** on **MOUNTVILLE ROAD**.

21.6 **Right** on **NEW DESIGN ROAD**.

21.7 **Left** on **ORLAND ROAD**.

22.4 **Straight** on **LILY PONS ROAD**.

23.2 Lilypons Water Gardens.

24.3 **Left** on **PARK MILLS ROAD** at T. Steep hill at mile 25.1.

27.8 **Right** on **FINGERBOARD ROAD**.

29.1 **Right** on **THURSTON ROAD**. Urbana Lake on left.

33.0 **Bear left** to remain on **THURSTON ROAD**. Begin mile-long climb.

34.2 **Right** on **OLD HUNDRED ROAD** (MD 109) at T. Steep hill.

35.4 **Right** on **COMUS ROAD** in Comus. Grocery and Comus Inn.

37.9 **Arrive** at **SUGARLOAF MOUNTAIN PARK. Left** on **MOUNT EPHRAIM ROAD** to continue ride. Right on Mount Ephraim Road to climb mountain.

39.8 **Left** on **BARNESVILLE ROAD**.

43.2 **Right** on **PEACH TREE ROAD**.

44.3 **Quick left and right** to remain on **PEACH TREE ROAD**.

47.5 **Left** on **MD 28** (Darnestown Road).

47.7 **Right** on **CATTAIL ROAD**.

49.6 **Left** at stop sign to remain on **CATTAIL ROAD** (unmarked).

49.8 **Left** on **MD 107** (Fisher Avenue; Whites Ferry Road) in Poolesville.

49.9 **Right** on **WOOTTON AVENUE**.

50.5 **Left** into **POOLESVILLE HIGH SCHOOL**.

ALTERNATE ROUTE

At 7.6 miles, turn **right** on **MOUNT EPHRAIM ROAD.** Ride 2.7 miles to Sugarloaf Mountain. After climb, **reverse direction.** Pick up cues at 37.9 miles.

16. SENECA - POOLESVILLE LOOP

Enjoy bucolic country scenes and views of Sugarloaf Mountain on this route as you loop between Seneca and Poolesville. Orchards and seasonal fruit stands provide a "taste" of Seneca that should not be missed! For a brief history of Seneca sandstone, see the Seneca Mini-Tour (Tour 17).

START: Riley's Lock (Lock 24), abutting the C&O Canal on Riley's Lock Road in Seneca, Md. From the Capital Beltway, take River Road (MD 190) west 11 miles and turn left on Riley's Lock Road. Follow road to canal parking lot. Seneca is 12 miles northwest of the Capital Beltway.

LENGTH: 33.9 miles.

TERRAIN: Hilly, with a short gravel stretch.

POINTS OF INTEREST: C&O Canal and Seneca Aqueduct at start; Seneca Creek State Park at 9.8 miles. Fruit stands and views of Sugarloaf Mountain.

FOOD: Markets at 0.7 (closed Sundays), 9.8 and 23.7 miles.

MAPS: *Lower Montgomery County Bicycle Route Map;* Montgomery County, Md. road map.

MILES   DIRECTIONS & COMMENTS

0.0   **Right** out of parking lot to go north on **RILEY'S LOCK ROAD.**

0.7   **Left** on **RIVER ROAD.** Poole's General Store on right.

1.0   **Right** on **MONTEVIDEO ROAD.**

2.0   Cross narrow bridge.

3.3   **Right** on **SUGARLAND ROAD.** *Narrow pavement for 0.5 miles.*

4.8   Cross Whites Ferry Road (MD 107).

4.9   **Left** on **DARNESTOWN ROAD** (MD 28) at T.

5.0   **Right** on **WHITE GROUND ROAD** (MD 121).

6.6   Cross narrow bridge.

8.6   Cross narrow bridge.

9.5   **Right** on **CLOPPER ROAD.**

9.6   **Left** on **CLARKSBURG ROAD.**

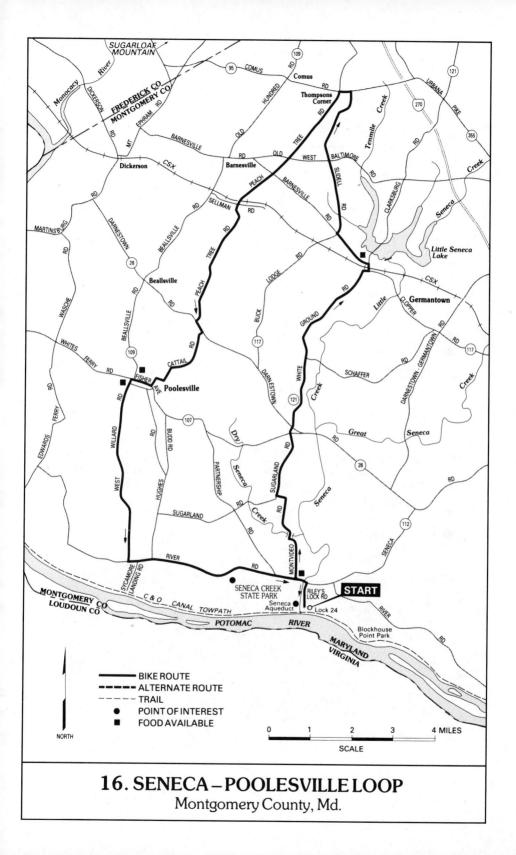

16. SENECA – POOLESVILLE LOOP
Montgomery County, Md.

9.7   **Left** on **BARNESVILLE ROAD** (MD 117). Go through underpass at railroad and **bear left.** Little Seneca Lake to right. Boyd's Store.

10.8   **Right** on **SLIDELL ROAD.**

14.5   **Left** on **COMUS ROAD** (MD 95).

14.7   **Left** on **PEACH TREE ROAD.** Sugarloaf Mountain to right.

18.3   Cross narrow bridge. **Bear left** to stay on **PEACH TREE ROAD** at Sellman Road.

21.5   **Left** on **DARNESTOWN ROAD** (MD 28) at T. Fruit stand on left.

21.7   **Right** on **CATTAIL ROAD.**

23.5   **Left** at school yard corner to stay on **CATTAIL ROAD.**

23.7   **Right** on **FISHER AVENUE** (MD 107). Food in Poolesville.

24.3   **Left** on **WEST WILLARD ROAD.**

28.8   **Left** on **RIVER ROAD** at T.

33.2   **Right** on **RILEY'S LOCK ROAD.**

33.9   **Arrive** at **RILEY'S LOCK.**

Pastoral scene in Montgomery County.

17. SENECA MINI-TOUR

A path of historic structures, mills, homes and farms of the industrial age marks this tour through Montgomery County, Md. Try this tour in autumn for spectacular colors.

The ride loops through the once-bustling quarry town of Seneca. The sandstone quarried from Seneca was used to construct the Smithsonian "Castle" on the Washington Mall, as well as most of the District of Columbia's other post-Civil War buildings. Once cut, the stone was hauled to town by barge via the C&O Canal.

Seneca's economy declined in the 1920s, as architectural preferences shifted away from sandstone. The C&O Canal faced a similar decline: unable to compete with the railroad, it folded in 1924. The local grist mill also succumbed to the industrial age, and it too closed in 1931.

START: Violet's Lock, abutting the C&O Canal on Violet's Lock Road in Montgomery County, Md. From the Capital Beltway, take River Road (MD 190) west 11 miles and turn left on Violet's Lock Road. (Road is marked with a yellow sign with an arrow. Turnoff comes up very quickly after the sign.) After turning, continue 0.6 miles to Potomac River. Parking on left. Violet's Lock is 12 miles northwest of the Capital Beltway.

LENGTH: 10.7 miles.

TERRAIN: Rolling hills, with dirt roads and hard-packed dirt on the C&O Canal.

POINTS OF INTEREST: Violet's Lock at start (named after Ab Violette, the last lock tender), a lift lock that could raise or lower canal boats eight feet; the remains of a 2,500-foot rock dam, built in 1928 at the head of the Seneca rapids in the Potomac River near start; Seneca Aqueduct (1929) at 0.6 miles, the first of 11 aqueducts between Georgetown and Cumberland, Md., carrying canal boats over Seneca Creek; site of Tschiffely Mill (1780) at 0.9 miles and the narrow-gauge railroad that took mill products to grain boats; Rocklands (1870), an Italianate showplace of the agrarian community; Sandstone School House (1863) at 8.1 miles, built of Seneca sandstone; and Montevideo (1825) at 8.5 miles, built for J.P.C. Peters, owner of the quarry and great-grandson of Martha Custis Washington. Rouser's Ford, where Confederate General J.E.B. Stuart crossed the Potomac during the Gettysburg campaign, at 8.9 miles.

FOOD: Market at 1.9 miles (closed Sundays).

MAPS AND INFORMATION: Montgomery County, Md. road map. The Montgomery County Parks and Planning Commission (301-495-4600) offers a complete guide to this tour.

MILES   DIRECTIONS & COMMENTS

0.0   From Violet's Lock parking lot, go **right** (west, upstream) on the **C&O CANAL TOWPATH.** Note remains of 1928 rock dam at head of Seneca rapids. Cross Seneca Creek on **AQUEDUCT.**

1.0   **Right** turn after wood bridge on **TSCHIFFELY MILL ROAD** (unmarked). Pool next to the road is the turning basin, where 90-foot canal boats turned around. Remains of Tschiffely Mill (red sandstone structure) are on left.

1.9   Cross River Road (MD 190), then **bear left** on **OLD RIVER ROAD.** Poole's General Store on right.

2.2   **Right** on **MONTEVIDEO ROAD.**

3.5   Cross Dry Seneca Creek.

5.0   **Left** on **SUGARLAND ROAD.**

5.7   Cross Dry Seneca Creek again.

6.1   **Left** on **PARTNERSHIP ROAD.** *Caution: traffic.*

8.1   **Left** on **RIVER ROAD** (MD 190). *Caution: traffic.* Sandstone School House on right.

8.5   Montevideo house on left. Smaller buildings are Overseer's House and the slaves' quarters.

9.8   **Right** to stay on **RIVER ROAD.**

10.0   **Right** on **VIOLET'S LOCK ROAD.**

10.7   **Arrive** at **VIOLET'S LOCK.**

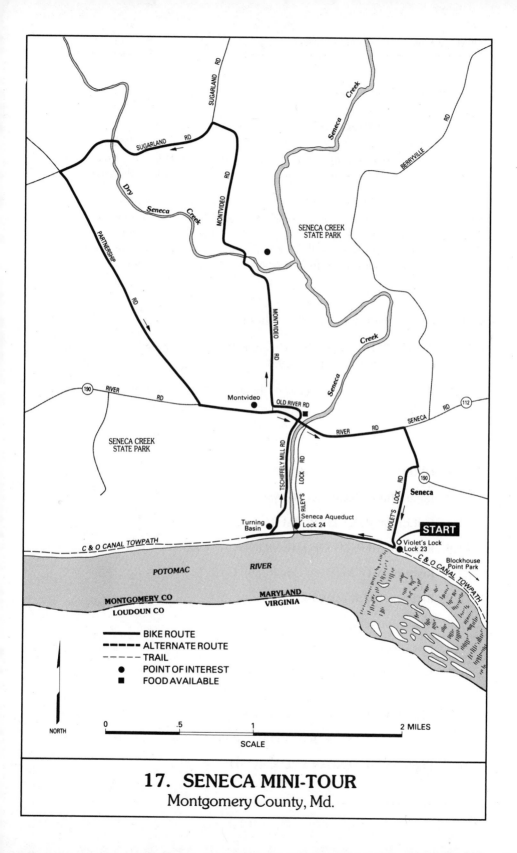

17. SENECA MINI-TOUR
Montgomery County, Md.

18. LILYPONS LOOP

This moderately hilly ride passes through farmlands and several small towns in Montgomery and Frederick Counties, Md. A tasty break in Middletown for homemade ice cream should not be missed! Later you will visit Lilypons Water Gardens, an enjoyable respite for bird watchers and aquatic plant lovers.

START: Monocacy Elementary School on Barnesville Road in Montgomery County, Md. From the Capital Beltway, take I-270 North 22 miles and exit on MD 109 South (Old Hundred Road) toward Barnesville. Continue 5.3 miles and turn right at T on Barnesville Road. Continue one mile; school is on the right. The starting point is 28 miles northwest of the Capital Beltway.

LENGTH: 59.2 miles.

TERRAIN: Hilly, with some level stretches mid-ride.

POINTS OF INTEREST: Main's Ice Cream Parlor at 27.4 miles; and Lilypons Water Gardens (301-874-5133) at 49.3 miles.

FOOD: Markets at 9.2, 13.3 (closed Sunday), 27.4, 42.7 and 48.1 miles. Sandwich shop at mile 27.4.

MAPS: Montgomery and Frederick Counties, Md. road maps.

MILES   DIRECTIONS & COMMENTS

0.0	**Right** on **BARNESVILLE ROAD**.
1.3	**Left** on **MOUNT EPHRAIM ROAD**.
1.9	**Right** on **MOUTH OF THE MONOCACY ROAD**.
2.2	**Right** on **MD 28** (Dickerson Road). Cross Monocacy River.
4.0	**Right** on **PARK MILLS ROAD**.
9.2	Market on left.
9.4	**Left** on **FLINT HILL ROAD**.
10.5	**Left** on **MD 80** (Fingerboard Road) at stop sign. Cross Monocacy River.
12.1	**Right** on **MD 85** (Buckeystown Pike).
13.3	**Left** on **MANOR WOOD ROAD**. Market (closed Sunday).
16.1	**Right** on **BALLENGER CREEK ROAD**.

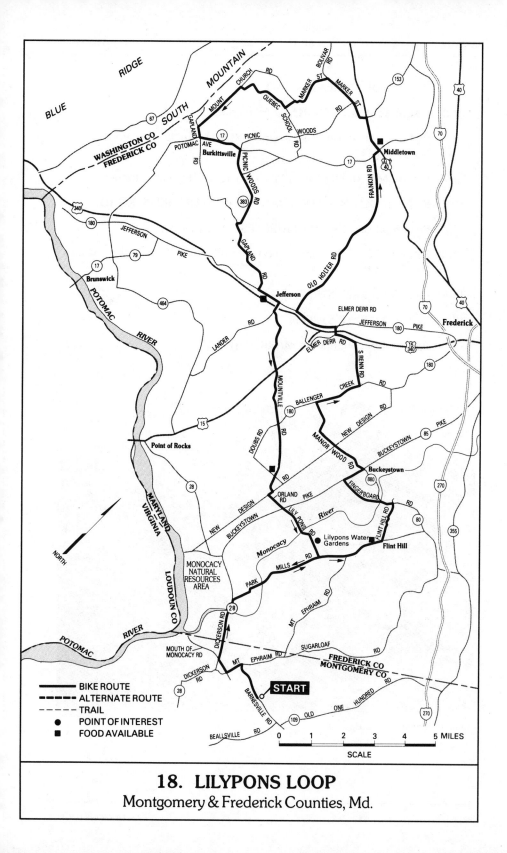

BLUE RIDGE

SOUTH MOUNTAIN

67

WASHINGTON CO.
FREDERICK CO.

MOUNT CHURCH RD

QUEBEC SCHOOL RD

MARKER ST

BOLIVAR RD

MARKER ST

153

40

70

GARLAND AVE

POTOMAC RD

17

Burkittsville

PICNIC WOODS

PICNIC WOODS RD

WOODS RD

17

Middletown

FRANKLIN RD

40

340

180

JEFFERSON PIKE

79

17

Brunswick

464

383

GARLAND RD

Jefferson

OLD HOLTER RD

ELMER DERR RD

ELMER DERR RD

JEFFERSON PIKE

180

Frederick

70

40

POTOMAC RIVER

LANDER RD

S RENN RD

CREEK

RD

15
340

180

MOUNTVILLE RD

BALLENGER

NEW DESIGN RD

85 PIKE

BUCKEYSTOWN

15

Point of Rocks

DOUBS RD

MANOR WOOD RD

Buckeystown

880

270

28

MARYLAND
VIRGINIA

NEW DESIGN

BUCKEYSTOWN

ORLAND RD

PIKE

LILY PONS RD

Monocacy River

FINGERBOARD RD

FLINT HILL RD

Flint Hill

80

355

LOUDOUN CO.

MONOCACY
NATURAL
RESOURCES
AREA

PARK

MILLS RD

Monocacy

Lilypons Water
Gardens

NORTH

POTOMAC RIVER

DICKERSON RD

28

MOUTH OF
MONOCACY RD

MT EPHRAIM RD

MT EPHRAIM RD

SUGARLOAF RD

FREDERICK CO.
MONTGOMERY CO.

RD

DICKERSON RD

28

BARNESVILLE RD

START

109 OLD ONE HUNDRED

270

BEALLSVILLE RD

——— BIKE ROUTE
----- ALTERNATE ROUTE
- - - TRAIL
● POINT OF INTEREST
■ FOOD AVAILABLE

0   1   2   3   4   5 MILES

SCALE

18. LILYPONS LOOP
Montgomery & Frederick Counties, Md.

17.6   **Left** on **SOUTH RENN ROAD**.

19.0   **Left** on **ELMER DERR ROAD** (unmarked) at T.

19.6   **Right** to remain on **ELMER DERR ROAD**. Single lane tunnel under US 340/US 15.

19.7   **Left** on **MD 180** (Jefferson Pike) at T (unmarked) after tunnel.

21.2   **Right** on **OLD HOLTER ROAD**. Becomes **FRANKLIN ROAD**.

27.3   **Bear right** on **SOUTH CHURCH STREET** (unmarked) at T.

27.4   **Left** on **ALT US 40** (Main Street) in Middletown. Sandwiches. Main's Ice Cream Parlor.

28.5   **Left** on **MARKER STREET**.

30.3   **Left** on **MARKER STREET**.

31.8   **Bear left** to continue on **MARKER STREET**.

A mill in Frederick County.

32.1 **Right** on **QUEBEC SCHOOL ROAD** at T. Becomes **MARKER STREET** again.

33.8 **Left** on **MOUNT CHURCH ROAD**.

35.6 **Left** on **GAPLAND ROAD** at T.

36.1 **Left** on **MD 17** in Burkittsville at stop sign.

37.4 **Right** on **PICNIC WOODS ROAD**.

39.8 **Left** on **GAPLAND ROAD**.

42.2 **Left** on **MD 180** (Jefferson Pike).

42.7 Market on right.

43.1 **Right** on **LANDER ROAD**.

43.3 **Left** on **MOUNTVILLE ROAD** just after overpass.

45.4 Cross US 15 at bottom of steep hill. *Caution: traffic.*

48.1 Store with food in Adamstown.

49.3 **Right and left dogleg** on **ORLAND ROAD**. Becomes **LILY PONS ROAD** after Buckeystown Pike. Lilypons Water Gardens on left.

51.8 **Right** on **PARK MILLS ROAD** at T.

55.0 **Left** on **MD 28** (Dickerson Road, unmarked) at T.

56.8 **Left** on **MOUTH OF THE MONOCACY ROAD**.

57.3 **Left** on **MOUNT EPHRAIM ROAD**.

57.9 **Right** on **BARNESVILLE ROAD**.

59.2 **Left** into **MONOCACY ELEMENTARY SCHOOL**.

19. WASHINGTON TO HARPERS FERRY

From its start in downtown Washington, D.C., this scenic tour takes you through prime Montgomery County biking territory (including Seneca, Beallsville and Point of Rocks) and delivers you to the HI-Harpers Ferry Lodge in Knoxville, Md., just across the Potomac River from Harpers Ferry.

Harpers Ferry is a restored 19th century town at the confluence of the Potomac and Shenandoah Rivers, where Maryland, Virginia and West Virginia meet. Site of one of the nation's first gun factories, the town and its arsenal were seized by the abolitionist John Brown in 1859, in an event that foreshadowed the Civil War. The town changed hands repeatedly during the war. Destruction caused by the war and repeated flooding in the years following it were responsible for the town's decline.

The Harpers Ferry Lodge is on the Appalachian Trail, a hiking trail that extends from Maine to Georgia. The hostel also serves as a terminus for tours to the Antietam Battlefield (Tour 61) and HI-Bear's Den Lodge (Tour 63), as well as a waypoint on the C&O Canal Towpath (Tour 7).

The tour offers sweeping views of the Potomac River and rolling farmland. Allow time for the long, steep hills on MD 464, just west of Point of Rocks. An alternate route swings through Brunswick, adding a popular restaurant and some small-town scenery.

START: Washington Circle at Pennsylvania Avenue NW and 23rd Street NW in Washington, D.C. The starting point is within the Capital Beltway. Glen Echo Park, on MacArthur Boulevard at mile 6.8, offers an alternative start. **METRO START:** From the Foggy Bottom Metro station (Blue and Orange Lines), go north one block on 23rd Street NW to Pennsylvania Avenue NW.

LENGTH: 62.0 miles.

TERRAIN: Hilly.

POINTS OF INTEREST: Montrose Park at 0.8 miles; Dumbarton Oaks at 0.8 miles, site of the drafting of the United Nations Charter (1944); Glover Archibald Park at 1.7 miles; Dalecarlia Reservoir at 2.8 miles; Bonfield's Texaco station (1927) at 4.5 miles; Glen Echo Park at 6.8 miles; Cabin John Bridge at 9.0 miles; Monocacy Aqueduct (1833) at 37.5 miles; C&O Canal and Point of Rocks at 43.5 miles, with restored 19th century railroad station; Harpers Ferry National Historical Park, with visitor center, near end.

FOOD: Markets near start and at 8.2, 13.3, 24.1, 37.0 and 45.2 miles. Restaurants near start, at 13.3 19.0 and 55.9 miles, and at end (Cindy Dee's has good pies), and on alternate route at 54.0 miles.

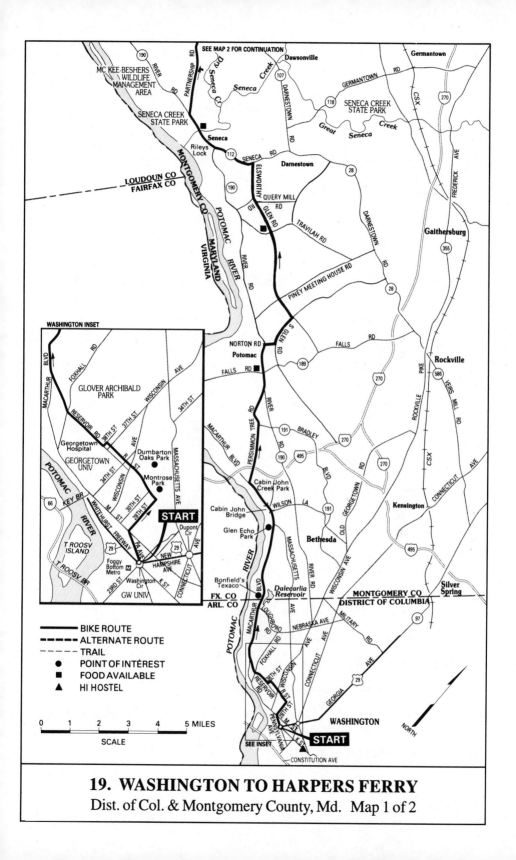

19. WASHINGTON TO HARPERS FERRY
Dist. of Col. & Montgomery County, Md.   Map 1 of 2

LODGING: Near Harpers Ferry, HI-Harpers Ferry Lodge, 19123 Sandy Hook Road, Knoxville, Md. (301-834-7652); and Hilltop House (800-338-8319), on Ridge Street, 10 blocks from C&O Canal Towpath.

MAPS: *ADC's Washington Area Bike Map;* Montgomery, Frederick and Washington Counties, Md. road maps.

MILES   DIRECTIONS & COMMENTS

0.0   Go **west** on **PENNSYLVANIA AVENUE NW** toward Georgetown.

0.3   **Right** on **28TH STREET NW,** just before Pennsylvania Avenue NW merges with M Street NW.

0.8   **Left** on **R STREET NW** at T. Pass Montrose Park and Dumbarton Oaks on right.

1.3   Cross Wisconsin Avenue NW.

1.7   **Left** on **38TH STREET NW** at T, then **first right** on **RESERVOIR ROAD NW** at T. Georgetown Hospital on left. Pass through Glover Archibald Park.

2.3   **Bear right** to stay on **RESERVOIR ROAD NW.** Cross Foxhall Road NW.

2.8   **Bear right** on **MACARTHUR BOULEVARD NW.** Pass Dalecarlia Reservoir and enter Montgomery County. [Note: the Capital Crescent Trail right-of-way passes underneath at mile 5.5 (see Tour 3). To connect with the trail, take paved trail on right at intersection of MacArthur Boulevard, Madaket Road and Sangamore Road.]

6.8   Glen Echo Park.

8.2   Bethesda Food Co-op. Pass through Cabin John Park, over one-lane Cabin John Bridge, the world's largest stone arch when built (220 feet).

9.4   **Right** on **PERSIMMON TREE ROAD.**

10.0   **Straight** to stay on **PERSIMMON TREE ROAD.**

11.4   Cross Bradley Boulevard.

13.0   **Left** on **RIVER ROAD** (MD 190). *Caution: traffic.*

13.3   Cross Falls Road (MD 189) in Potomac. Restaurants, fast food and general stores.

14.0   **Right** on **NORTON ROAD.**

14.6   **Left** on **SOUTH GLEN ROAD.** Stables along road.

15.8   **Left** on **GLEN ROAD**, cross bridge, then **left** again to stay on **GLEN ROAD.**

19.0   Cross Travilah Road (food on left).

19.9   **Left** on **QUERY MILL ROAD.**

20.5   **Right** on **ESWORTHY ROAD.**

21.8   **Left** on **SENECA ROAD** (MD 112).

23.4   **Straight** on **RIVER ROAD.**

24.1   Cross Great Seneca Creek. Riley's Lock one mile to left on C&O Canal. Poole's General Store on right.

24.8   **Right** on **PARTNERSHIP ROAD**. [End of Map 1 instructions.]

28.7   **Bear left** on **MD 107.**

31.2   **Right** on **BEALLSVILLE ROAD** (MD 109) in Poolesville.

33.7   **Left** on **MD 28** (Darnestown Road) in Beallsville.

37.0   Enter Dickerson. MD 28 becomes **DICKERSON ROAD.** Store. Pass under railroad tracks. Mount Ephraim Road to right leads to Sugarloaf Mountain. At 37.4 miles, Mouth of Monocacy Road to left leads to Monocacy Aqueduct. Stay on **DICKERSON ROAD** (MD 28).

40.8   **Left** to stay on **MD 28** (Tuscarora Road) at fork. MD 85 (Buckeystown Pike) goes right. *Caution: MD 28 seems to go down to right.*

45.2   Enter Point of Rocks. Food, train station, C&O Canal Towpath.

45.6   **Right** on **BALLENGER CREEK ROAD.** *Caution: fast traffic.*

46.6   **Left** on **MD 464.** Very hilly.

46.7   Cross US 15.

53.8   **Right** on **SOUDER ROAD** (MD 464) at traffic light. (Sign may say Cummings Drive.) ALTERNATE ROUTE stays straight (see end of cues).

54.8   **Straight** on **MD 17.**

55.9   **Left** on **MD 180** (Jefferson Pike). McDonald's at intersection.

57.6   Enter Knoxville. **Bear right** to remain on **MD 180.**

59.9   **Bear left** to merge onto **US 340.** *Caution: heavy traffic.*

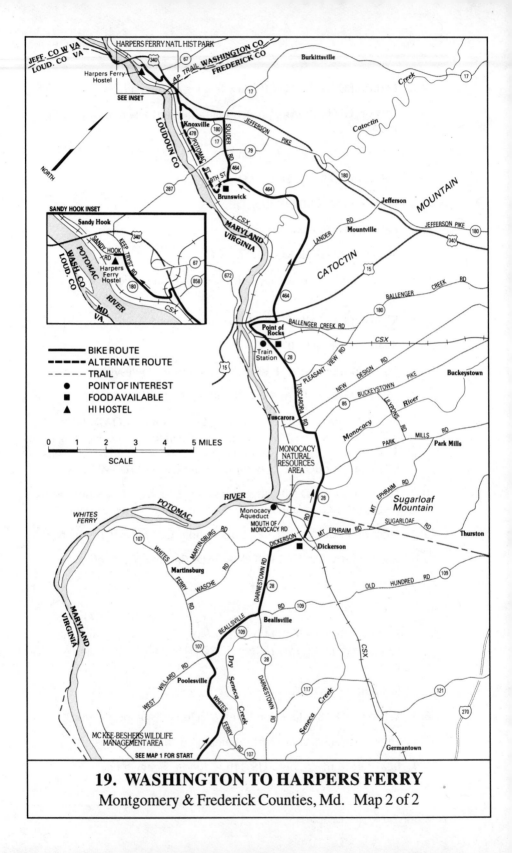

19. WASHINGTON TO HARPERS FERRY
Montgomery & Frederick Counties, Md. Map 2 of 2

61.6   **Left** on **KEEP TRYST ROAD** up hill.

61.8   **Right** on **SANDY HOOK ROAD/HARPERS FERRY ROAD.**

62.0   **Left** into **HI-HARPERS FERRY LODGE.**

ALTERNATE ROUTE

At 53.8 miles, go **straight** on **SOUDER ROAD** (MD 464) at traffic light. This route passes through Brunswick; its quaintness may compensate for the added traffic. This alternative adds less than one mile to the main route.

53.8   **Straight** on **9TH STREET** into Brunswick.

54.0   Berlin Cafe. Good food here.

55.0   **Left** on **MD 478** at blinking light. Follow as it bends sharply back to right and descends to **POTOMAC STREET.**

56.2   Pass under bridge over Potomac River. Stay on **MD 478.**

58.3   **Left** on **MD 180** in Knoxville. Pick up main route at 57.6 miles.

The train station in Dickerson.

20. THREE COVERED BRIDGES

As you bicycle through the scenic valleys of Frederick County with the Catoctin Mountains rising in the distance, you will experience the three historic covered bridges that distinguish this tour. One, at Loy's Station Park, provides a scenic picnic spot along a cool stream and an old mill race. Visible along the northern section of the route, the imposing shrine of St. Mary's College (built in 1839) nestled in the mountains further highlights the trip.

START: Holiday Inn at the intersection of US 15 and US 40 in Frederick, Md. From the Capital Beltway, take I-270 North and bear left at fork on US 15 North (to Frederick). Continue two miles to US 40 West; motel is visible before exit. Frederick is 33 miles northwest of the Capital Beltway.

LENGTH: 44.7 miles. **ALTERNATE ROUTE:** 25.0 miles.

TERRAIN: Gentle hills. Traffic is increasing around Frederick because of development. Use caution, especially on Rosemont Avenue and Oppossumtown Pike.

POINTS OF INTEREST: Covered bridges at 10.1, 15.6 and 21.5 miles. MD 806 passes a wildlife park and historic Catoctin Furnace, and also passes near Cunningham Falls State Park.

FOOD: Numerous restaurants and markets available in Frederick and Thurmont (27.1 miles). Fruit stand (in season) at 8.8 miles.

LODGING: In Frederick, Holiday Inn (301-662-5141) at start. In the Frederick area, bed-and-breakfasts include Spring Bank Inn (301-694-0440), Turning Point Inn (301-831-8232), Tyler-Spite House (301-831-4455) and Rosebud Inn (301-845-2221). In Thurmont, Thurmont's Cozy Motel (301-271-4301), at 27.1 miles, welcomes bicyclists. Camping is available at Cunningham Falls State Park, on US 15, near Catoctin Furnace.

MAPS AND INFORMATION: *A Frederick Cycling Guide,* available for $5.70 postpaid from Frederick County Tourism Council, 19 East Church Street, Frederick, MD 21701-5401 (301-663-8687); Frederick County, Md. road map.

MILES   DIRECTIONS & COMMENTS

0.0   **Right** out of motel parking lot to go north on **BAUGHMANS LANE.**

0.6   **Right** on **SHOOKSTOWN ROAD.**

0.8   **Right** on **ROSEMONT AVENUE.**

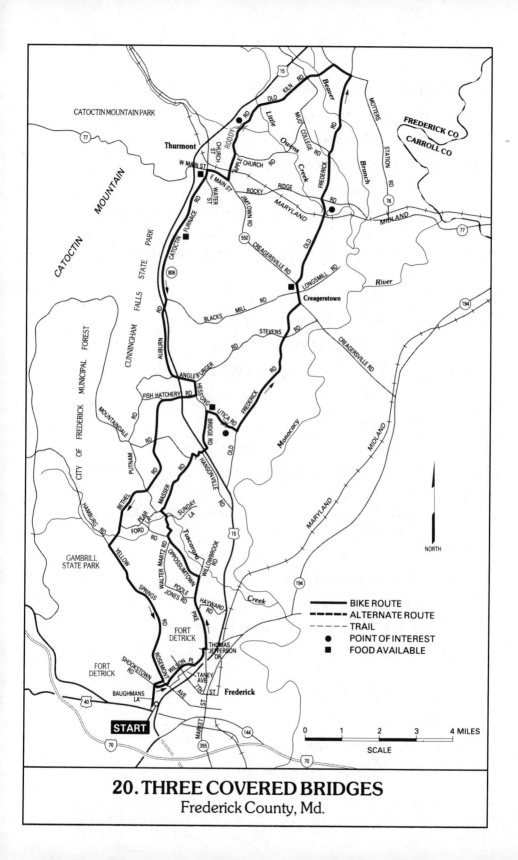

20. THREE COVERED BRIDGES
Frederick County, Md.

0.9   **Immediate left** on **WILSON PLACE.**

1.9   **Left** on **TANEY AVENUE.**

2.4   **Right** on **THOMAS JEFFERSON DRIVE.**

2.5   **Left** on **OPPOSSUMTOWN PIKE.**

4.5   **Bear left** to remain on **OPPOSSUMTOWN PIKE.**

5.9   **Bear right** and continue on main road **(OPPOSSUMTOWN PIKE)** at Ford Road.

6.5   **Bear left** and continue on main road **(OPPOSSUMTOWN PIKE)** at Sunday Lane.

6.7   **Right** on **MASSER ROAD.**

8.4   **Right** on **MOUNTAINDALE ROAD.**

8.8   **Left** on **HANSONVILLE ROAD** (unmarked).

9.0   Cross US 15 to **left** on **HESSONG BRIDGE ROAD.**

10.1   **Right** on **UTICA ROAD** over covered bridge.

11.0   **Left** on **OLD FREDERICK ROAD.**

15.0   **Bear left** on **CREAGERSVILLE ROAD** at stop sign. Store on right.

15.3   **Right** on **OLD FREDERICK ROAD.** Covered bridge at Loy's Station Park.

21.3   **Left** at fourth paved road after covered bridge on **MOTTERS STATION ROAD** (unmarked); red barn on right.

21.9   **Left** on **OLD KILN ROAD** (unmarked).

24.4   **Left** on **RODDY ROAD** at T.

26.0   **Straight** on **APPLE CHURCH ROAD.**

26.4   **Right** on **EAST MAIN STREET** (MD 77; unmarked).

27.1   **Left** on **WATER STREET** (MD 806). Restaurants.

27.2   **Right** on **FREDERICK ROAD** to remain on **MD 806**. This becomes **CATOCTIN FURNACE ROAD.**

31.1   **Straight** to **AUBURN ROAD** crossing US 15.

33.1   **Left** on **ANGLEBURGER ROAD** crossing US 15.

33.6   **Right** on **HESSONG BRIDGE ROAD.**

34.0   **Right** on **FISH HATCHERY ROAD**. *Caution at US 15.*

34.9   **Left** on **BETHEL ROAD**.

39.7   **Left** on **YELLOW SPRINGS ROAD**. This becomes **ROSEMONT AVENUE**.

43.9   **Right** on **BAUGHMANS LANE**.

44.7   **Left** into motel **PARKING LOT**.

ALTERNATE ROUTE

For a shorter route (approximately 25 miles) that still crosses all three covered bridges, begin on **UTICA ROAD** (mile 10.1), follow all directions to mile 34.0, then return to Utica via **HESSONG BRIDGE ROAD**.

The Roddy Road bridge.

21. GAITHERSBURG GETAWAY

Pedal through new subdivisions and old farm country on this diverse route, which also takes you through the scenic towns of Damascus and Laytonsville.

START: Behind the Roy Rogers/Hardee's in Montgomery Village Shopping Mall at the corner of Montgomery Village Avenue and Club House Road in Gaithersburg, Md. From the Capital Beltway, take I-270 North for 11 miles and exit at Montgomery Village Avenue. Continue east for approximately two miles to shopping mall. Start from corner of service road behind Roy Rogers/Hardee's and Club House Road. Gaithersburg is 12 miles north of the Capital Beltway. **METRO START:** The ride starts approximately five miles from the Shady Grove Metro station (Red Line). From the station, exit on Frederick Avenue (MD 355) and turn right. Bear right on North Summit Avenue. Turn left on Centerway Road. Turn right at Montgomery Village Avenue. Club House Road is one block away.

LENGTH: 35.3 miles.

TERRAIN: Hilly at first, then rolling hills.

POINTS OF INTEREST: Town of Laytonsville at 8.5 miles; Rachel Carson Regional Park at 9.0 miles; and town of Damascus at 21.9 miles.

FOOD: Markets at 8.5, 21.9 and 33.3 miles. Restaurants at start and 33.3 miles.

MAPS: Montgomery County, Md. road map.

MILES   DIRECTIONS & COMMENTS

0.0   **Left** to go west on **CLUB HOUSE ROAD** (away from Montgomery Village Avenue).

0.2   **Right** on **WATKINS MILL ROAD** at T. Hills for next three miles.

1.8   **Right** on **BLUNT ROAD.**

3.4   **Right** on **BRINK ROAD** (MD 420) at stop sign.

3.7   **Bear left** to stay on **BRINK ROAD** at stop sign.

4.7   **Right** on **GOSHEN ROAD** at T.

5.4   **Left** on **WARFIELD ROAD** at stop sign.

8.5   **Left** on **LAYTONSVILLE ROAD** at T. At right is shopping center with pizza shop, convenience store and antique shops.

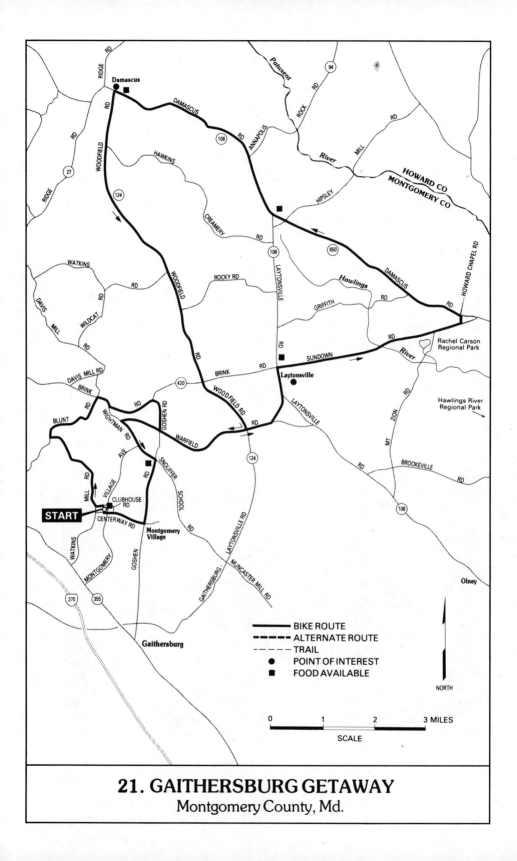

BIKE ROUTE
ALTERNATE ROUTE
TRAIL
POINT OF INTEREST
FOOD AVAILABLE

0   1   2   3 MILES

SCALE

NORTH

21. GAITHERSBURG GETAWAY
Montgomery County, Md.

9.0   **Right** on **SUNDOWN ROAD** at traffic light. Notable old homes. Pass Rachel Carson Regional Park on right, just past Mount Zion Road.

12.6   **Left** on **HOWARD CHAPEL ROAD.**

12.8   **Left** on **DAMASCUS ROAD** at stop sign.

17.5   **Straight** on **MD 108** (Damascus Road). Seasonal produce stand.

21.9   **Left** on **WOODFIELD ROAD** (MD 124) at traffic light in Damascus. *Caution: heavy traffic.* Supermarket just ahead.

29.4   **Right** on **WARFIELD ROAD.**

32.2   **Sharp left** on **WIGHTMAN ROAD.**

33.3   **Right** on **GOSHEN ROAD.** Supermarket and restaurants on right.

34.6   **Right** on **CENTERWAY ROAD.**

35.3   **Arrive** at **MONTGOMERY VILLAGE.**

When cows lie down, the chance of rain is high.

22. TRIADELPHIA RESERVOIR

This scenic jaunt around the Triadelphia Reservoir in Patuxent River State Park provides a short but strenuous workout. The route crosses Brighton Dam and passes through hilly countryside with occasional thick forests and glimpses of the reservoir. There are no towns along the route.

START: Corner of Georgia Avenue (MD 97) and New Hampshire Avenue (MD 650) in Montgomery County, Md. From the Capital Beltway, take Georgia Avenue north 17 miles to its intersection with New Hampshire Avenue. Parking at start and at Brighton Dam. The starting point is 17 miles north of the Capital Beltway.

LENGTH: 18.1 miles.

TERRAIN: Hilly, especially first half.

POINTS OF INTEREST: Triadelphia Reservoir; Patuxent River State Park (301-924-2127); Brighton Dam (301-774-9124) at 4.1 miles. Near the dam is a 5-acre azalea garden, an experimental tree plantation, short hiking trails and a visitor center. Picnic grounds at various stops along the reservoir at the end of Triadelphia Mill Road.

FOOD: Convenience store, with short order grill, at start, open daily. No other food on route.

MAPS: *ADC's Washington Area Bike Map;* Montgomery and Howard Counties, Md. road maps.

MILES   DIRECTIONS & COMMENTS

0.0   Go **southeast** on **NEW HAMPSHIRE AVENUE** (MD 650).

3.0   **Left** on **BRIGHTON DAM ROAD.**

4.1   Cross Brighton Dam. Picnic area, toilet facilities, soda machines, information.

5.7   **Left** on **HIGHLAND ROAD.**

7.0   **Left** on **TRIADELPHIA MILL ROAD.**

8.8   **Right** on **GREEN BRIDGE ROAD** then immediate left to stay on **TRIADELPHIA MILL ROAD.**

10.3   Picnic ground and reservoir on left.

12.5   **Left** on **ROXBURY ROAD** at bottom of steep hill.

14.1   **Left** on **DORSEY MILL ROAD** at T.

14.7   **Left** on **MD 97** (Roxbury Mills Road, then Georgia Avenue) at T. *Caution: swiftly moving traffic, no shoulder in some stretches.*

17.0   Cross Patuxent River into Montgomery County.

18.1   **Arrive** at **MD 650** intersection (Damascus and New Hampshire Avenues).

Howard County farmhouse.

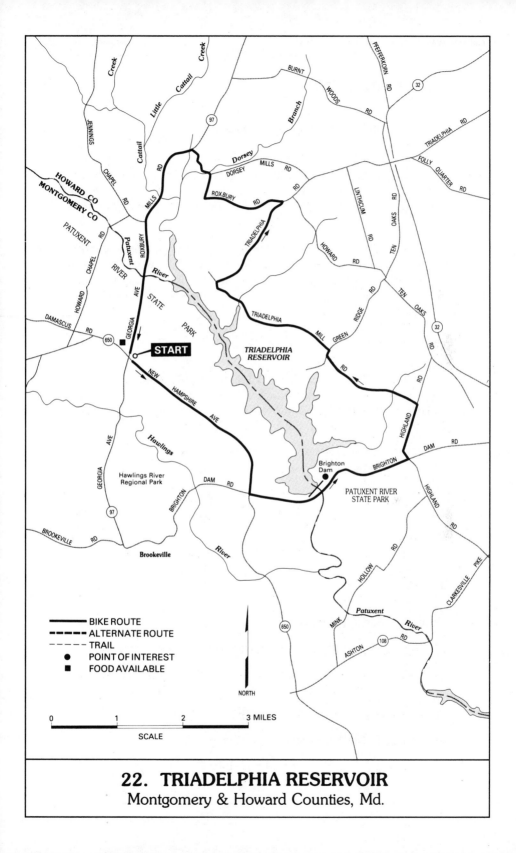

22. TRIADELPHIA RESERVOIR
Montgomery & Howard Counties, Md.

23. ELLICOTT CITY LOOP

The historic town of Ellicott City, on the south bank of the Patapsco River, marks the midpoint of this loop. The city was established in 1774 with the construction of George Ellicott's grist and flour mill. The town flourished with the laying of the Cumberland Road and the arrival of the B&O Railroad in 1830. The old granite buildings wedged into the rocky hillside attest to the area's history. Today, Ellicott City hosts America's oldest remaining railroad station (1831), now the home of the B&O Railroad Museum.

START: Baltimore County Library (Randallstown Branch) on Liberty Road in Baltimore County, Md. From the Baltimore Beltway, take Liberty Road (exit 18) west. Continue two miles; library is on right after intersection with Old Court Road. The starting point is 34 miles north of the Capital Beltway.

LENGTH: 23.0 miles.

TERRAIN: Hilly.

POINTS OF INTEREST: In Ellicott City at 12.5 miles: B&O Railroad Museum, open daily (except Monday) spring through fall and on weekends during winter (410-461-1944 for directions and information); Tongue Row; 1840 houses converted into shops; Town Hall; Patapsco Female Institute (1835) on Church Road overlooking the city; antique shops; and Patapsco River State Park.

FOOD: Markets at start and 12.1 miles. Restaurants at start, 6.1, 12.1 and 14.5 miles.

LODGING: At Patapsco River State Park (410-461-5005), public campgrounds.

MAPS AND INFORMATION: *Baltimore Area Bike Map;* Baltimore and Howard Counties, Md. road maps. Howard County Chamber of Commerce (410-730-4111).

MILES   DIRECTIONS & COMMENTS

  0.0   Go **right** (southwest) on **OLD COURT ROAD.**

  6.1   **Straight** on **WOODSTOCK ROAD** (MD 125), crossing Patapsco River. Restaurant on left.

  7.2   **Left** on **MD 99** (Old Frederick Road) at T.

10.1   **Right** on **ST. JOHNS LANE.**

12.1   Cross US 40. Grocery store and restaurant.

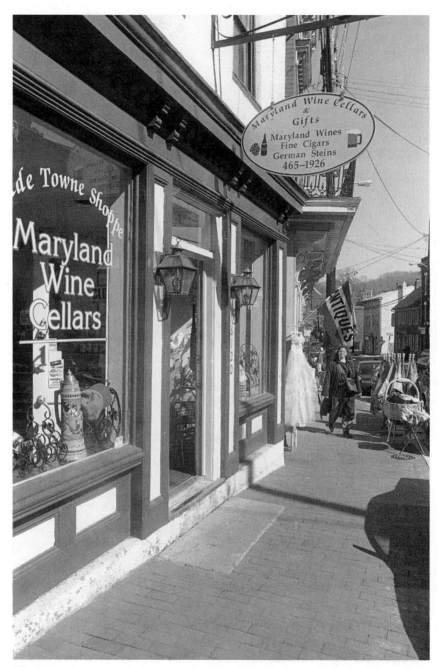

Ellicott City.

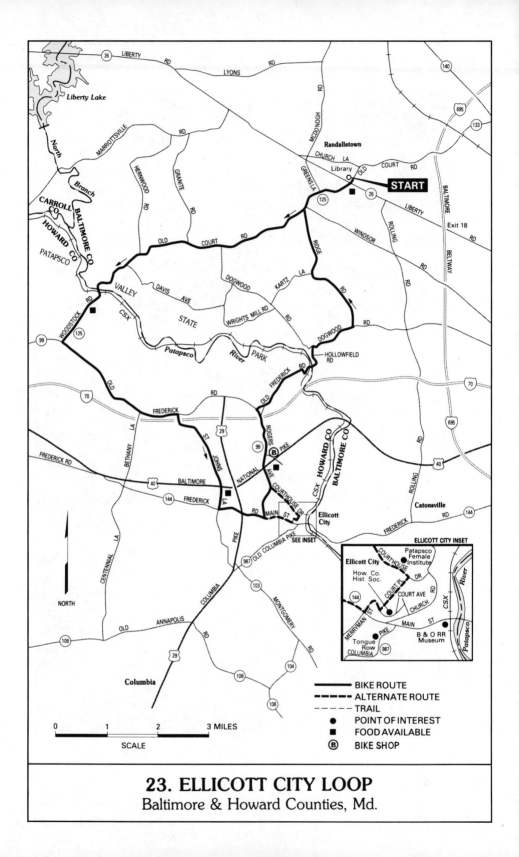

23. ELLICOTT CITY LOOP
Baltimore & Howard Counties, Md.

12.5   **Left** on **FREDERICK ROAD** (MD 144) and enter Ellicott City.

13.5   **Left** on **ROGERS AVENUE.**

(To see more of Ellicott City, do not turn on Rogers Avenue. Continue on Frederick Road for one mile. To leave Ellicott City and return to the route, from Main Street heading toward the river, turn left on Merryman Street (street sign on right). Turn left on unmarked street at Howard County Historical Society. Turn right on Court Place. Turn left on Courthouse Drive. Merge right on Rogers Avenue to continue route.)

14.5   Cross US 40. Restaurant.

15.4   **Left** to stay on **ROGERS AVENUE** (MD 99) at T.

15.8   **Right** on **OLD FREDERICK ROAD,** just past I-70.

17.4   **Straight** on **HOLLOWFIELD ROAD,** crossing Patapsco River.

17.9   **Right** on **DOGWOOD ROAD** at T.

19.0   **Left** on **RIDGE ROAD.**

21.8   **Right** on **OLD COURT ROAD** (MD 125).

23.0   **Left** into **LIBRARY.**

24. HOWARD'S HILLS

After the steep hills of the first leg, this tour settles down to rolling countryside. The miles of corn fields, punctuated by an occasional pumpkin patch and horse ranch, charm you as you leave behind the bustle of the metropolitan area. If you begin the ride early in the day, you will find few cars on the first five miles of the route along New Hampshire Avenue (except on Sundays when churchgoers attend services in the area).

START: Safeway at the corner of New Hampshire Avenue (MD 650) and Briggs Chaney Road, in Cloverly, Md. From the Capital Beltway, take New Hampshire Avenue north for 6.5 miles. Safeway is on the right, past Briggs Chaney Road. Cloverly is six miles north of the Capital Beltway.

LENGTH: 43.6 miles. **ALTERNATE ROUTE:** 31.4 miles.

TERRAIN: Hilly.

POINTS OF INTEREST: Brighton Dam at 8.2 miles. Vegetable stands on New Hampshire Avenue and open countryside along the route.

FOOD: Markets at start, 3.5, 13.2, 19.4 and 25.3 miles. Pub at 11.5 miles.

MAPS: *Lower Montgomery County Bicycle Route Map;* Howard and Montgomery Counties, Md. road maps.

MILES   DIRECTIONS & COMMENTS

0.0   **Right** from parking lot to go north on **NEW HAMPSHIRE AVENUE** (MD 650).

3.5   Cross MD 108. Grocery store at right.

4.8   **Right** on **HAVILAND MILL ROAD.**

7.2   **Right** on **BRIGHTON DAM ROAD** at T. (Brighton Dam is one mile to the left from this intersection.)

8.3   **Left** on **HIGHLAND ROAD.**

10.0   **Bear left** on **TEN OAKS ROAD** at stop sign.

11.5   **Right** to stay on **TEN OAKS ROAD.** Pub on right.

13.2   **Left** on **TRIADELPHIA ROAD.** General store on right. ALTERNATE ROUTE begins here (see end of cues).

13.6   **Right** on **IVORY ROAD.**

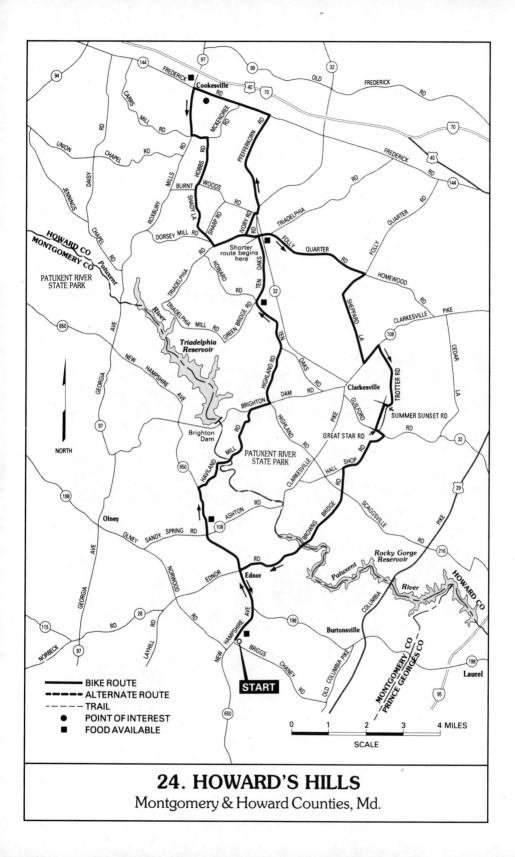

24. HOWARD'S HILLS
Montgomery & Howard Counties, Md.

14.2   **Right** on **BURNT WOODS ROAD,** then **immediate left** on **MD 32.** *Caution: traffic.*

14.4   **Left** on **PFEFFERKORN ROAD.**

17.1   **Left** on **MD 144** (Frederick Road) at T.

19.4   **Left** on **MD 97** (Roxbury Mills Road). General store on right. Site of Civil War skirmish on left.

20.7   **Left** on **McKENDREE ROAD.**

21.1   **Right** on **HOBBS ROAD.**

22.4   **Right** on **BURNT WOODS ROAD** at stop sign.

22.6   **Bear left** on **SHADY LANE.** Do not take Burnt Woods Road, which continues to the right.

Corn galore.

24.0   Shady Lane becomes **SHARP ROAD.** Do not turn left on Sharp Road!

24.2   **Bear left** at Dorsey Mill to stay on **SHARP ROAD.**

24.4   **Left** on **TRIADELPHIA ROAD.**

25.3   Cross Ten Oaks Road at stop sign. General store on right.

26.0   **Bear right** on **FOLLY QUARTER ROAD.**

29.0   **Right** on **SHEPPARD LANE,** where Folly Quarter Road goes left.

31.7   **Left** on **MD 108** (Clarksville Pike) at T.

32.2   **Right** on **TROTTER ROAD.**

34.4   **Right** on **SUMMER SUNSET ROAD.**

34.5   **Left** on **GREAT STAR ROAD**, crossing over MD 32.

35.1   **Left** on **OLD MD 32** (Guilford Road) at T.

35.5   **Right** on **HALL SHOP ROAD.**

37.0   **Bear left** on **BROWNS BRIDGE ROAD.**

37.6   Cross MD 216. Stables to right. Browns Bridge Road becomes **EDNOR ROAD,** crossing Patuxent River.

41.5   **Left** on **NEW HAMPSHIRE AVENUE** (MD 650) at traffic light.

43.6   **Left** into **SAFEWAY.**

ALTERNATE ROUTE

At 13.2 miles, turn **right** instead of left on **TRIADELPHIA ROAD,** then pick up cues at 26.0 miles.

25. WASHINGTON TO BALTIMORE

With the vibrant city of Baltimore as its destination, this tour provides a circuitous but relatively low-traffic route from downtown Washington, D.C. Baltimore boasts a nationally acclaimed aquarium, a beautifully renovated harbor, the nation's largest railroad museum, the birthplace of Babe Ruth and an interesting historic district.

Starting from Washington's Union Station, the trip is also ideal for out-of-town tourists who want to experience both cities. The tour ends at HI-Baltimore, conveniently located a few blocks from the Baltimore Inner Harbor and the Camden Yards baseball stadium. A few hilly stretches lie along the way, but most bicyclists should be able to complete the ride in one day.

START: West side of Union Station at Massachusetts Avenue NE and 1st Street NE in Washington, D.C. The starting point is within the Capital Beltway. **ALTERNATE START:** Greenbelt Metro station (Green Line) at Exit 24 of the Capital Beltway in Greenbelt, Md. **METRO STARTS:** Union Station Metro station (Red Line) at start; Rhode Island Avenue Metro station (Red Line) at 1.3 miles; Greenbelt Metro station (Green Line) is at alternate start.

LENGTH: 44.0 miles. From **ALTERNATE START:** 32.6 miles.

TERRAIN: Relatively level, with some hilly stretches. Demands some skills with traffic. [Note: the proposed Metropolitan Branch Trail runs from Union Station to Takoma Park/Silver Spring with a connecting trail to Prince Georges County and, when built, may substitute for the on-street route up to mile 5.5.]

POINTS OF INTEREST: National Shrine of the Immaculate Conception (202-526-8300) at 2.5 miles; Northwest Branch and Northeast Branch parks, starting at 5.5 miles; College Park Airport with museum at 9.4 miles, the nation's oldest continuously operating general aviation facility; National Agricultural Research Station at 14.1 miles; old Richmond-to-Philadelphia stage coach route at 18.8 miles; Elkridge Furnace Inn, built in 1744 and beautifully restored as a restaurant, at 34.7 miles; Carroll Park at 40.2 miles, home of a signer of the Declaration of Independence. In Baltimore at end: Oriole Park at Camden Yards; Harborplace (410-332-4191) with U.S.S. Constellation (410-539-1797), built in 1797; National Aquarium (410-576-3800); B&O Railroad Museum (410-752-2490); Lexington Market; Babe Ruth birthplace and museum; Pratt Library; and scenic neighborhoods.

FOOD: Frequent along the route.

LODGING: In Baltimore, HI-Baltimore, 17 West Mulberry Street (410-576-8880). Inns include: Admiral Fell, 888 South Broadway (410-522-7377); Celie's Waterfront Bed and Breakfast, 1714 Thames Street (410-522-2323);

Shirley Madison Inn, 205 West Madison Street (410-728-6550); Society Hill Hotel, 58 West Biddle Street (410-244-7227); Governor's House, 1125 North Calvert Street; and Hopkins Inn, 3404 St. Paul Street (410-235-8600).

MAPS: *ADC's Washington Area Bike Map; Baltimore Area Bike Map.*

MILES   DIRECTIONS & COMMENTS

0.0   **Right** on **1ST STREET NE** (downhill on sidewalk). **Follow BIKEROUTE U.** Pass Trailways/Greyhound Station. For ALTERNATE START from Greenbelt Metro station, see end of cues.

0.8   **Jog right** at end of road at **FLORIDA AVENUE NE** to **ECKINGTON PLACE NE.**

1.0   **Right** on **R STREET NE** at end of road.

1.1   **Left** on **3RD STREET NE.**

1.3   **Right** on **T STREET NE,** then **left** on **4TH STREET NE.** Cross Rhode Island Avenue NE (US 1). Rhode Island Avenue Metro station on right. Proposed Metropolitan Branch Trail lies west of railroad tracks.

2.5   **Right** on **MICHIGAN AVENUE NE** at National Shrine of the Immaculate Conception. *Caution: traffic.*

2.7   Cross over Metro tracks.

3.7   Cross South Dakota Avenue NE (use trail on right).

3.9   **Bear right** on **VARNUM STREET NE** at traffic light (use roadway).

4.2   **Left** on **22ND STREET NE** at end of road. Cross Eastern Avenue and enter Maryland. **Straight** on **ARUNDEL ROAD** (Arundel Road is a marked Bike Route).

4.9   **Right** on **34TH STREET** at traffic light, then **left** on **WINDOM STREET.**

5.3   **Left** on **38TH STREET.**

5.5   **Right** on **TRAIL** after crossing Northwest Branch.

6.3   Cross Rhode Island Avenue (US 1) at Melrose Neighborhood Playground. Trail parallels Charles Armentrout Way.

6.5   **Right** to follow unmarked **TRAIL** downhill 75 feet before T intersection, then **immediate left** on **NORTHEAST BRANCH TRAIL.** Cross under ALT US 1.

6.9   Cross Decatur Street.

7.7   Cross Riverdale Road.

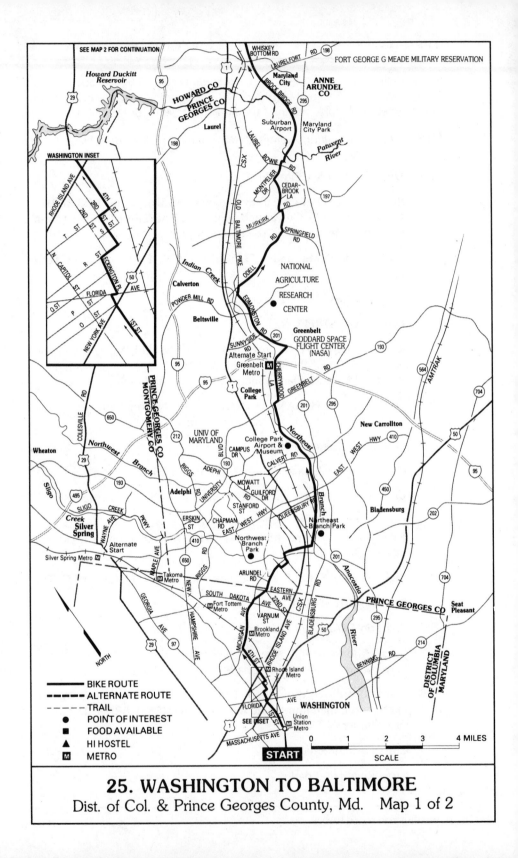

25. WASHINGTON TO BALTIMORE
Dist. of Col. & Prince Georges County, Md.   Map 1 of 2

7.8   Cross under East-West Highway.

8.7   Cross under Good Luck Road.

9.0   College Park Airport with museum on left.

9.8   **Right** to cross bridge, then **immediate left** on **INDIAN CREEK TRAIL**.

10.9   Trail ends. **Right** on **GREENBELT ROAD SIDEWALK.**

11.0   **Left** on **CHERRYWOOD LANE** (use roadway). ALTERNATE START joins Cherrywood Lane at 11.8 miles; see end of cues. Cross over Capital Beltway at 12.0 miles.

12.6   **Left** on **EDMONSTON ROAD** (MD 201) at end of road.

13.5   Pass Sunnyside Avenue.

14.1   National Agriculture Research Station.

14.7   **Right** on **OLD BALTIMORE ROAD.** *Caution: steep uphill.*

15.0   **Right** on **ODELL ROAD.** *Caution: narrow, poor pavement.* Site of Van Horn Tavern marker.

16.2   **Bear right** to stay on **ODELL ROAD** at Ellington Road by electrical substation. Pass through wooded portion of Research Station. Cross Springfield Road.

17.4   **Sharp left** on **MUIRKIRK ROAD**, then **right** on **CEDARBROOK LANE.** Pass recreation center with swimming pool.

18.3   **Right** on **MONTPELIER DRIVE.**

18.7   Cross Laurel Bowie Road (MD 197) at traffic light.

18.8   **Left** on **BROCK BRIDGE ROAD** (this is the old stagecoach route between Richmond and Philadelphia).

19.0   Cross Brock Bridge (county line). *Caution: may be standing water after heavy rains.*

19.3   **Jog right** onto **TRAIL** in Maryland City Park.

19.7   Airport.

20.6   **Straight** at end of trail to rejoin roadway (**BROCK BRIDGE ROAD**). Pass store. [End of Map 1 instructions.]

21.4   Cross Laurel Fort Road (MD 198) at traffic light. Stores. Pass Laurel Raceway Stables. Cross Whiskey Bottom Road at 22.0 miles and Little Patuxent River at 23.2 miles.

23.9   **Right** on **DORSEY RUN ROAD.** Cross over MD 32.

24.8   **Right** on **GUILFORD ROAD.**

25.2   **Left** on **BROCK BRIDGE ROAD.** Pass Maryland Surplus Property store. Cross Dorsey Run at 26.1 miles. Pass prison at 26.5 miles.

27.3   **Right** on **JESSUP ROAD** (MD 175).

27.5   **Left** on **RACE ROAD** (before MD 295). Hilly.

27.8   **Bear right** to stay on **RACE ROAD.**

30.1   **Bear right** to stay on **RACE ROAD** at Faulkner Road.

30.3   **Left** on **DORSEY ROAD** (MD 176) at T.

30.6   **Right** on **COCA COLA DRIVE**, crossing highway.

31.1   **Right** on **PARK CIRCLE DRIVE.**

31.3   **Left** on **RACE ROAD.**

32.6   **Left** on **HANOVER ROAD,** then **right** on **RACE ROAD.**

34.7   **Right** on **FURNACE ROAD.** Elkridge Furnace Inn. Cross Deep Run.

34.8   **Left** on **FURNACE ROAD.** Uphill. Cross Stony Run, then cross under railroad tracks and I-195.

35.2   **Left** on **FURNACE ROAD.** Becomes **RIVER ROAD.**

35.5   **Bear left** to stay on **RIVER ROAD.**

36.4   **Left** on **WEST NURSERY ROAD.**

37.0   **Left** on **HAMMONDS FERRY ROAD** at traffic light. Stores. Cross under I-695 (Baltimore Beltway) at 37.4 miles. Cross Patapsco River. Cross under I-895 (Tunnel Thruway) at 37.7 miles.

38.0   **Right** on **HOLLINS FERRY ROAD** at traffic light.

39.0   Cross Lansdowne Road.

39.5   Enter Baltimore. Railroad tracks.

40.9   More railroad tracks, these at a bad angle. *Use caution!*

41.0   **Right** on **WASHINGTON BOULEVARD.** Cross under I-95, then cross river and railroad tracks.

41.5   Pass Carroll Park on left.

42.2   **Right** on **CROSS STREET** at traffic light at bend.

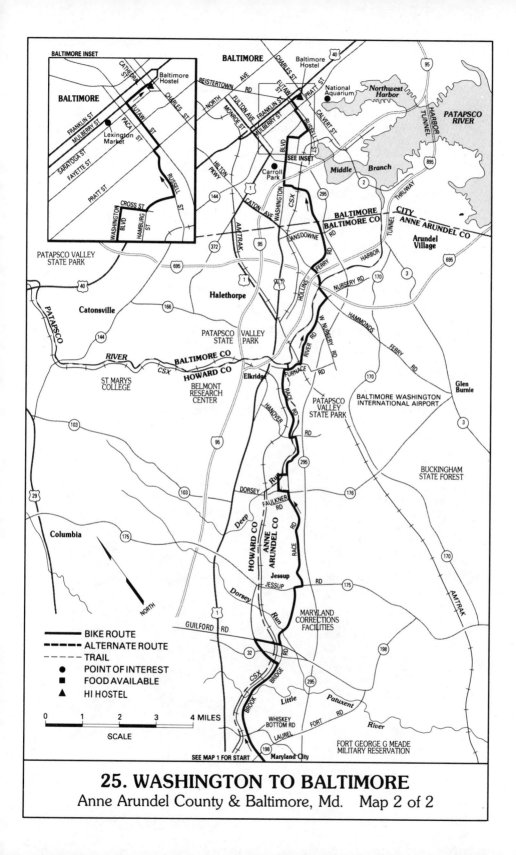

25. WASHINGTON TO BALTIMORE
Anne Arundel County & Baltimore, Md.   Map 2 of 2

42.4   **Left** on **HAMBURG STREET** at traffic light.

42.7   **Left** on **RUSSELL STREET**. Turns into **PACA STREET**. *Caution: traffic; avoid ramps to King Drive and I-95.*

43.1   **Right** on **PRATT STREET** for one block, then **left** on **EUTAW STREET**. [Note: B&O Railroad Museum is 0.5 miles to left on Pratt Street.]

43.7   **Right** on **MULBERRY STREET**.

44.0   **Arrive** at **BALTIMORE HOSTEL,** 17 West Mulberry Street, on right.

ALTERNATE START

0.0   From Greenbelt Metro station, **follow GREENBELT METRO DRIVE** around parking area to T intersection with Cherrywood Lane.

0.5   **Left** on **CHERRYWOOD LANE.** Continue cues at mile 12.6.

Baltimore's Inner Harbor, with the U.S.S. Constellation.

26. CAPITAL TO CAPITAL (AND BACK!)

This ride takes you on a round trip from the nation's capital (or at least its Metro system) to Annapolis, the capital of Maryland. Traffic is increasing at both the D.C. and Annapolis ends of the route, but Annapolis is a wonderful destination, a charming and historic city on the western shore of the Chesapeake, with a wide choice of eating establishments. Out and back makes a nice day trip for the experienced cyclist.

START/METRO START: New Carrollton Metro station (Orange Line), off US 50, just inside the Capital Beltway, in Prince Georges County, Md.

LENGTH: 57.7 miles.

TERRAIN: Rolling hills.

POINTS OF INTEREST: U.S. Naval Academy (off route at 27.6 miles); Maryland State House, the oldest U.S. state capitol in continuous legislative use (1772), with exhibits of Annapolis colonial life, at 28.3 miles; Annapolis Waterfront at 28.7 miles.

FOOD: Annapolis, at the mid-point of the ride, has great seafood and a wide variety of places to eat. There are also convenience stores or markets along the route at 9.1, 19.6, 37.8 and 48.4 miles.

LODGING: In Annapolis, inns include Charles Inn (410-268-1451), Prince Georges Inn (410-263-6418), Green Street Inn (410-263-6631) and Historic Inns at Annapolis (410-263-2641). For more information on lodging, contact the Annapolis and Anne Arundel County Visitor Bureau (410-268-TOUR).

MAPS AND INFORMATION: County maps for Prince Georges and Anne Arundel Counties, Md.; *ADC's Washington, D.C. 50-mile Radius Map*. City of Annapolis Office of Tourism (410-263-7940); Annapolis Visitor's Center (410-268-8687).

MILES   DIRECTIONS & COMMENTS

0.0   From New Carrollton Metro station, go **south** on **GARDEN CITY DRIVE**, which becomes **ARDWICK-ARDMORE ROAD** after crossing under US 50 overpass at 0.2 miles. *Caution: truck traffic.*

1.2   Cross Martin Luther King Highway.

1.4   Cross Capital Beltway (I-495).

3.4   **Right** on **LOTTSFORD VISTA ROAD** at T.

4.3   **Left** on **LOTTSFORD ROAD** at T.

5.0   Cross Enterprise Road (MD 193). Proceed **straight** on **WOODMORE ROAD.** *Caution: Speeding traffic and little to no shoulder room on some portions of this road.*

7.5   **Left** on **CHURCH ROAD** at T.

7.6   **Right** on **MOUNT OAK ROAD.**

9.1   **Right** on **MITCHELVILLE ROAD.** 7-Eleven near corner.

10.6   Cross US 301. **Straight** on **QUEEN ANNE BRIDGE ROAD**.

12.8   **Left** on **CENTRAL AVENUE** (MD 214). Busy road, but good shoulder.

13.3   Cross bridge over Patuxent River into Anne Arundel County.

16.0   Cross Davidsonville Road.

17.1   **Left** on **RIVA ROAD** at traffic light. Gas station on right at intersection.

19.6   Riva Food Market on right after fire station.

20.0   Cross South River Bridge.

22.4   Cross MD 665. Shopping center on right.

23.2   **Left** on **DEFENSE HIGHWAY** (MD 450). Go under US 50.

23.3   **Right** on **JENNIFER STREET** at traffic light.

24.4   **Left** on **ADMIRAL DRIVE** at T.

25.1   **Right** on **BESTGATE ROAD** at T.

25.9   **Left** on **NORTH BESTGATE ROAD** at traffic light.

26.3   **Right** on **RIDGELY AVENUE.**

26.6   Cross US 50.

26.9   Cross bridge.

27.4   **Left** on **TAYLOR AVENUE.**

27.5   **Right** on **ANNAPOLIS STREET.**

27.6   **Right** on **KING GEORGE STREET** near Naval Academy sign.

27.9   Cross bridge.

28.3   Cross Maryland Avenue. Maryland State House to right.

28.6   **Right** on **RANDALL STREET.**

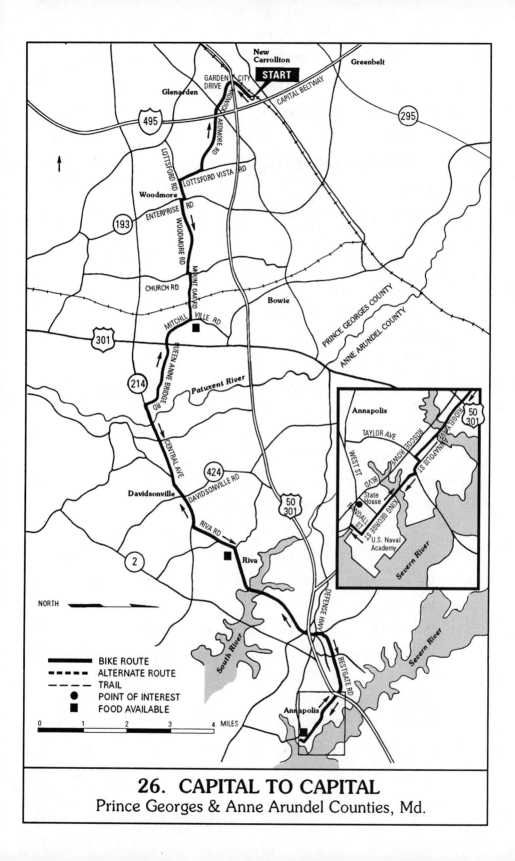

26. CAPITAL TO CAPITAL
Prince Georges & Anne Arundel Counties, Md.

28.7   Arrive at **ANNAPOLIS WATERFRONT. Reverse direction** for return.

28.8   **Left** on **KING GEORGE STREET.**

29.4   Cross bridge.

29.7   **Left** on **ANNAPOLIS STREET** at T.

29.9   **Left** on **TAYLOR AVENUE.**

30.0   **Right** on **RIDGELY AVENUE.**

30.6   Cross bridge.

30.9   Cross US 50.

31.3   **Left** on **NORTH BESTGATE ROAD.**

31.7   **Right** on **BESTGATE ROAD** at traffic light.

32.5   **Left** on **ADMIRAL DRIVE** at traffic light.

33.2   **Right** on **JENNIFER STREET.**

34.3   **Left** on **DEFENSE HIGHWAY** (MD 450) at traffic light. Go under US 50.

34.4   **Right** on **RIVA ROAD** immediately after bridge.

37.8   Riva Food Market on left before fire station.

38.8   **Bear left** at Y intersection to remain on **RIVA ROAD.**

40.4   **Right** on **CENTRAL AVENUE.** Gas station at intersection.

41.5   Cross Davidsonville Road.

44.2   Cross bridge over Patuxent River into Prince Georges County.

44.8   **Right** on **QUEEN ANNE BRIDGE ROAD.**

46.8   **Bear left** at Y.

47.0   Cross US 301. Road becomes **MITCHELVILLE ROAD.**

48.4   **Left** on **MOUNT OAK ROAD** at stop sign. 7-Eleven on right near corner.

50.0   **Left** on **CHURCH ROAD.**

50.1   **Right** on **WOODMORE ROAD.** *Caution: Fast traffic, no shoulder.*

52.6   Cross Enterprise Road (MD 193) at traffic light. Road becomes **LOTTSFORD ROAD.**

53.2 **Right** on **LOTTSFORD VISTA ROAD.**

54.1 **Left** on **ARDWICK-ARDMORE ROAD.**

55.8 **Bear left** at Y to stay on **ARDWICK-ARDMORE ROAD**.

56.1 Cross over Capital Beltway (I-495).

56.3 Cross Martin Luther King Highway.

57.1 **Right** on **PENNSY ROAD** at traffic light. Cross over US 50.

57.6 **Left** on **CORPORATION DRIVE** at traffic light.

57.7 **Arrive** at **NEW CARROLLTON METRO STATION.**

Annapolis.

27. BALTIMORE AND ANNAPOLIS TRAIL / BWI TRAIL

The Baltimore and Annapolis (B&A) Trail travels through refreshing stands of tulip poplar and expansive open space, offering you a relaxing bicycle trip within one mile of half of Anne Arundel County, Md.'s population. This 112-acre linear park is the county's most popular and lies near quiet residential neighborhoods, schools, offices and a variety of shops.

The B&A Trail runs between Glen Burnie and historic Annapolis, first settled in 1649. Parking, restrooms, food and information are easy to find along the entire length of the trail. The trail is patrolled by park rangers and maintained with safety in mind.

At its northern terminus, the B&A Trail links with the new BWI Trail, the first section of which opened in 1994. This trail can take you an additional 4.4 miles to the Linthicum station of Baltimore's light rail system (bikes are welcome on board!). A two-mile spur to the west, through Sawmill Creek Park and Friendship Park, takes you to the BWI Aircraft Observation Area, at the end of BWI's main north-south runway. Eventually this spur may link the B&A Trail to Patapsco State Park to the north and west, as part of a statewide bikeway system.

START: Park and Ride lot on MD 450 in Annapolis, Md. From the Capital Beltway, take US 50 East (toward Annapolis) and exit on MD 450 South (toward Naval Academy; second exit after Severn River Bridge). Stay in right lane; parking lot is immediately on the right. Annapolis is 33 miles east of the Capital Beltway.

LENGTH: 19.7 miles.

TERRAIN: Level, smooth asphalt surface.

POINTS OF INTEREST: United States Naval Academy and Museum (410-263-6933) near start; Maryland State House (410-974-3400) also near start, the oldest U.S. State house in continuous legislative use (1772), with exhibits of Annapolis colonial life. Many historic sites and museums in Annapolis, including Banneker-Douglass Museum, 84 Franklin Street (410-974-2893) and Museum of African-American Art and Culture. Severna Park at approximately 6.0 miles. Along the B&A Trail, markers note historically significant points. Ranger station (an 1889 train station) at mile 7.0 has further information. BWI Aircraft Observation Area at 15.3 miles. Historic Benson-Hammond House at 18.6 miles.

FOOD: Market at 9.0 miles. Restaurants at 1.0, 7.0, 9.0, 9.5, 10.0, 12.0 and 13.0 miles. Other options frequent along the route.

LODGING: No lodging next to trail, but many places available along Ritchie Highway and in Annapolis. In Annapolis, inns include Charles Inn (410-268-1451), Prince Georges Inn (410-263-6418), Chamis Bed and Breakfast (410-263-6631) and Historic Inns at Annapolis (410-263-2641). For more information on lodging, contact the Annapolis and Anne Arundel County Visitor Bureau (410-268-TOUR).

MAPS AND INFORMATION: B&A Trail map available from B&A Trail Headquarters, P.O. Box 1007, Severna Park, MD 21146-8007 (410-222-6244). City of Annapolis Office of Tourism (410-263-7940); Annapolis Visitor's Center (410-268-8687).

MILES   DIRECTIONS & COMMENTS

0.0   **U-turn** out of parking lot to go north on **BOULTER ROAD.**

0.3   Start of **B&A TRAIL.**

1.0   Cross Arnold Road. Arnold Station Shopping Center on right with food and water.

3.0   Pass the Power House, once a power generation station for the railroad, now the B&A Trail's maintenance building. Restrooms and water available.

3.5   Park and Ride at Jones Station Road. Anne Arundel Historical Society. For bike shop, take Jones Station Road east, crossing MD 2. Shop is on right, shortly after crossing intersection.

4.9   Severna Park Railroad Club.

5.0   Cross McKinsey Road. Water fountain on left. Bike shop on north side of McKinsey Road to the right.

7.0   Cross Earleigh Heights Road. Ranger station on left (open every day but Mondays). Restrooms, phone, water, parking and first aid available. Food (open Monday through Saturday 8 a.m. - 8 p.m., Sunday 8 a.m. - 5 p.m.).

9.0   Rest stop on left. Lucky's Market (open 7:30 a.m. - 10:30 p.m. every day) is behind rest stop, across the street (on Elvaton Road). The tin walls of Lucky's Market are unusual, typical of an urban Baltimore style at the turn of the century. At one time there was a dance floor upstairs.

9.5   Jumpers Mall Junction on right. Food, restrooms in mall area.

10.5   Cross MD 100 on pedestrian bridge. Marley Station Mall on right. Food, restrooms and other amenities available.

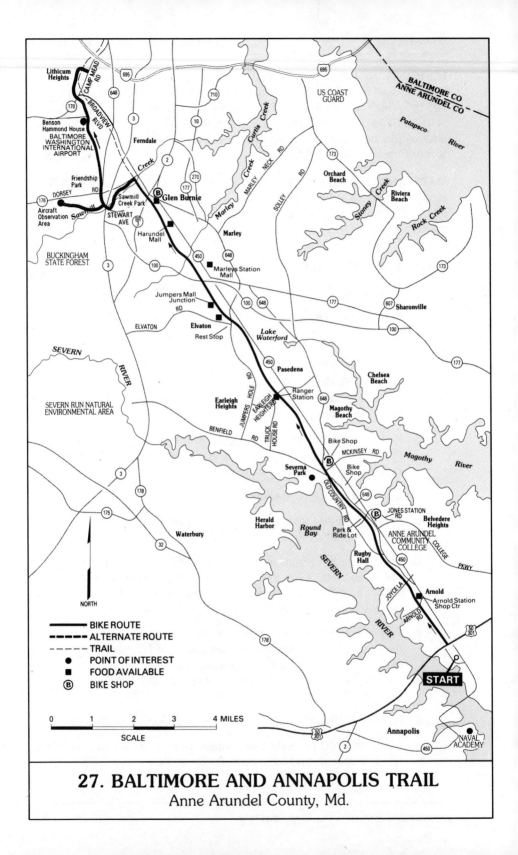

27. BALTIMORE AND ANNAPOLIS TRAIL
Anne Arundel County, Md.

12.0   Harundale Mall with restrooms and food on right. Harundale Mall was the first enclosed, air-conditioned shopping mall east of the Mississippi River.

12.7   Cross BUS MD 3.

13.0   Enter Glen Burnie. Parking garage deck with restrooms, bike shop and restaurants on right.

13.3   B&A Trail ends at Dorsey Road (MD 176). **Left** to begin **BWI TRAIL.**

14.1   Cross Sawmill Creek and continue on trail.

14.3   Cross I-97, then take **sharp left** at Y on **TRAIL** to Friendship Park and BWI Aircraft Observation Area.

15.3   Arrive at BWI Aircraft Observation Area. Portable toilets. **Reverse direction.**

16.3   **Left** on **TRAIL** at T.

16.5   Cross Dorsey Road (MD 176).

18.6   Benson-Hammond House, a historic plantation house, on left.

18.7   Cross Aviation Boulevard.

19.0   Cross BWI Light Rail line.

19.1   Cross Camp Meade Road.

19.2   **Right** to stay on **TRAIL** at North County High School. Cross Andover Road.

19.4   Cross Hammonds Ferry Road.

19.7   **Arrive** at **LINTHICUM LIGHT RAIL STATION.**

28. ANNE ARUNDEL ADVENTURE

Developed by the Annapolis Bike Club, this loop and other roads in the area can provide a variety of rides over traffic-free county roads. The ride passes working farms, country homes and grazing horses. A midpoint stop in Galesville provides a glimpse of life on the Chesapeake.

This area is so popular with local cyclists that on Saturday mornings you may see more bicycles than cars.

START: Park and Ride lot on MD 424, just south of US 50 in Anne Arundel County, Md. From the Capital Beltway, follow US 50 east (toward Annapolis) for 10 miles. Take Exit 16, MD 424. Bear left on the exit ramp for MD 424 North to Crofton. At the traffic light, cross MD 424 and enter the Park and Ride lot. The starting point is 10 miles east of the Capital Beltway.

LENGTH: 36.7 miles.

TERRAIN: Mostly level, with a few easy hills. Wide shoulders on main roads. Other roads are lightly traveled.

POINTS OF INTEREST: The area's colonial heritage is still evident in place names and occasional historic markers. Galesville was originally settled by Quakers, and several markers refer to visits by William Penn.

FOOD: Country stores, convenience marts and restaurants in Galesville at mile 15.4. There are no facilities at the start, but stores, restaurants, gas stations and restrooms are available approximately three miles north on MD 424.

LODGING: Variety of accommodations available in Annapolis, approximately eight miles east off US 50. For more information, call 410-263-7940.

MAPS: Anne Arundel County, Md. road map.

MILES   DIRECTIONS & COMMENTS

0.0   **Right** out of Park and Ride lot to go northwest on **MD 424**. *Caution: Keep to right, but beware of traffic that may be taking the US 50 on-ramp.*

0.4   **Right** on **ROSSBACK ROAD.**

1.7   **Follow** road to the **right**. Becomes **RUTLAND ROAD.**

2.3   US 50 underpass.

2.6   **Left** on **ST. GEORGE BARBER ROAD.**

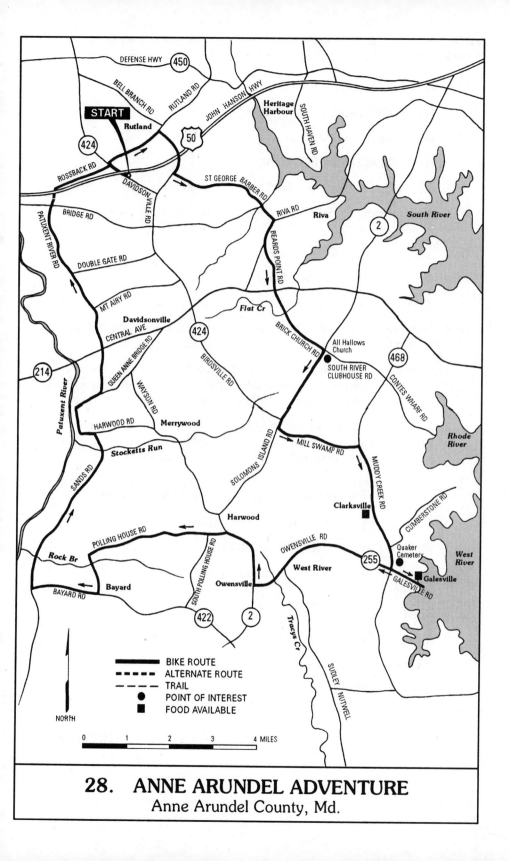

28. ANNE ARUNDEL ADVENTURE
Anne Arundel County, Md.

4.2   Begin winding descent.

4.9   **Left** on **GOVERNOR'S BRIDGE ROAD.**

5.2   **Right** on **RIVA ROAD** at T.

5.7   **Left** on **BEARD'S POINT ROAD.**

6.7   Cross MD 214. Becomes **BRICK CHURCH ROAD.**

8.3   **Right** on **MD 2** (Solomon's Island Road). All Hollows Episcopal Church on the right was founded in 1692.

10.0 **Left** on **MILL SWAMP ROAD.**

11.9 **Right** on **MUDDY CREEK ROAD** (MD 468).

13.4 Zang's Produce Stand on the left.

14.4 **Left** on **GALESVILLE ROAD** (MD 255). Dixon's service station has restrooms and cold drinks.

15.4 West River Market on the left (open 7 a.m. - 8 p.m.) is a favorite stop of local cyclists for cranberry muffins. Picnic tables. Historic marker on the right mentions visits by William Penn and George Washington.

15.5 **Arrive** at **GALESVILLE WATERFRONT**. Restaurants include Steamboat Landing, Pirate's Cove and Topside Inn. Portable toilet in season. **Reverse direction.**

16.6 Historic marker and colonial era Quaker cemetery on right. Cross Muddy Creek Road (MD 468). Becomes **OWENSVILLE ROAD.**

18.3 Historic marker on left commemorates visit by William Penn in 1682.

19.1 **Right** on **OWENSVILLE-SUDLEY ROAD.**

19.7 Restrooms available at South County Recreation Center on left, if it is open.

20.4 **Right** on **MD 2** (Solomon's Island Road).

20.7 **Left** on **POLLING HOUSE ROAD.**

24.4 **Right** on **BAYARD ROAD** at T.

25.7 **Right** on **SANDS ROAD** at T.

28.8 Cross Stockett's Run.

29.2 **Left** at T on **HARWOOD ROAD. Becomes PATUXENT RIVER ROAD SOUTH**.

30.0 Sharp right turn. *Beware of gravel. Also watch for flooding after rain.*

30.7 **Left** to remain on **PATUXENT RIVER ROAD** at intersection with Queen Anne's Bridge Road.

31.5 Cross MD 214.

35.0 US 50 underpass. Follow road to **right.** Becomes **ROSSBACK ROAD.**

36.3 **Right** on **MD 424.** Stay to the right until you cross over US 50, then move to the left.

36.7 **Left** into **PARK AND RIDE LOT.**

Polling House Road, near Owensville.

29. GEESE GALORE

This relaxing and refreshing loop visits Merkle Wildlife Sanctuary, a 2,000-acre preserve of marshes, farm fields and woods on the Patuxent River, and uncovers the once-prosperous city of Nottingham, a late colonial era town, in Prince Georges County, Md.

The wildlife sanctuary is named for Edgar Merkle, a Washington area printer and publisher, who, beginning in 1932, purchased mated pairs of Canada geese from Arkansas and Missouri and reintroduced them to the western shore of the Chesapeake Bay at his farm, which forms the nucleus of the sanctuary. Today, as many as 10,000 Canada geese migrate to the area each fall. Two hundred other species of birds may also be seen at the sanctuary.

The ride then leads to Nottingham. The British camped here during the War of 1812 after landing at Benedict (14 miles downriver). They burned the city before marching on to Washington. No trace of Nottingham remains today. Nottingham Road, the straight main roadway into the former town, was popular as a race track and was frequented by George Washington.

START: Mattaponi Elementary School in Rosaryville, Md., about 10 miles southeast of the Capital Beltway. From the Beltway, take exit 11, Pennsylvania Avenue (MD 4) south for three miles. Exit at Woodyard Road (MD 223). After 2.5 miles, bear left on Rosaryville Road and follow for three miles to intersection with US 301. At the intersection, cross US 301 and follow Old Indian Head Highway south. After 0.3 miles, road bears left, becoming Duley Station Road. Mattaponi Elementary School is 0.4 miles on right, across from Holy Rosary Parish.

LENGTH: 18.2 miles.

TERRAIN: Rolling hills. Good roads with light traffic.

POINTS OF INTEREST: St. Thomas Parish Church at 3.1 miles, completed in 1745. Merkle Wildlife Sanctuary at 6.9 miles has trails, a visitor center, and lots of geese (in season). *Note:* On Saturdays, from 10 a.m. - 3 p.m., and other times by advance reservation (301-888-1410), bicyclists can access a 4-mile, self-guided tour that connects Merkle Wildlife Sanctuary and the Jug Bay Natural Area. The tour, known as the Chesapeake Bay Critical Area Driving Tour, includes educational displays, a 1,000-foot bridge across Mattaponi Creek, and a 40-foot tall observation tower that affords a spectacular panoramic view of the Patuxent River.

FOOD: Markets at 2.9 and 13.1 miles.

MAPS: Prince Georges County, Md. road map.

MILES DIRECTIONS & COMMENTS

0.0 **Right** out of school parking lot to the stop sign and intersection.

0.1 **Left** on **DULEY STATION ROAD.**

0.4 **Right** to remain on **DULEY STATION ROAD**.

0.5 Cross railroad tracks.

2.7 **Right** on **CROOM ROAD** at T.

2.9 More's Country Store. Open daily 6:30 a.m. to 8 p.m., except Sundays (open 8 a.m. to noon). Makes sandwiches.

3.0 **Left** on **ST. THOMAS CHURCH ROAD** (brown sign for Merkle Wildlife Sanctuary). Turns into **FENNO ROAD.**

3.1 St. Thomas Parish Church, completed in 1745, on left.

6.0 **Left** into **MERKLE WILDLIFE SANCTUARY.** Sanctuary open 8 a.m. to 5 p.m. daily. [See Points of Interest above, for information on access to self-guided tour.]

6.9 Visitors Center, open 10 a.m. - 4 p.m. Tuesday through Sunday. **Return** to Fenno Road.

8.0 **Left** on **FENNO ROAD.** Rough surface.

8.9 **Left** on **NOTTINGHAM ROAD** at T (stop sign).

10.0 Nottingham Historical Marker.

10.1 Arrive at Patuxent River.

10.3 **Reverse direction. Right** on **NOTTINGHAM ROAD** at Y intersection with Candy Hill Road.

11.3 **Bear left** to continue on **NOTTINGHAM ROAD** at Fenno Road.

13.1 **Right** on **CROOM ROAD** at T (stop sign). Buffalo Bill's Market, open 6 a.m. - 8 p.m. Monday - Saturday, 7 a.m. - 4:30 p.m. Sunday. *Caution: traffic. Use shoulder.*

14.1 **Left** on **MOLLY BERRY ROAD.**

14.7 **Right** on **VAN BRADY ROAD.**

15.4 Bear right at intersection of Van Brady Road and Windsor Manor Road.

17.4 **Bear right** at intersection of Van Brady Road and Van Brady Road (this is not a typo!).

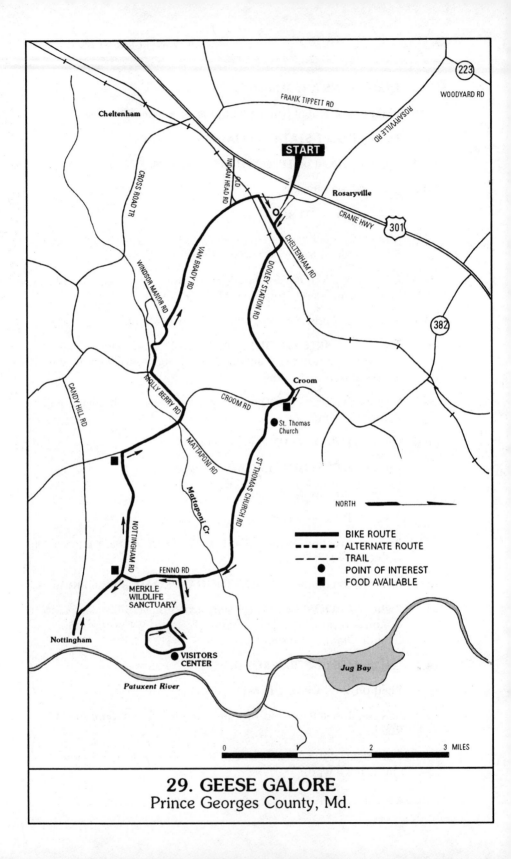

29. GEESE GALORE
Prince Georges County, Md.

17.6   **Right** on **OLD INDIAN HEAD ROAD** at T (stop sign).

17.7   Cross railroad tracks.

17.8   **Right** on **CHELTENHAM ROAD** at Y intersection.

18.2   **Left** on **DULEY STATION ROAD** (stop sign). **Arrive** at **MATTAPONI ELEMENTARY SCHOOL.**

St. Thomas Church.

30. PORTSIDE PACER

Enjoy historic Charles County, Md. on this tour through the towns of Port Tobacco and La Plata.

Port Tobacco was once an important river port and the designated Charles County seat. By 1895, however, the Port Tobacco River filled with so much silt that ships could no longer reach the town. Trade collapsed and Charles County moved its seat to La Plata. Today, both Port Tobacco and La Plata boast historic churches and courthouses, with a museum in Port Tobacco that recounts its local history.

The tour runs primarily on pleasant, tree-lined roads with broad shoulders and little traffic. Along the way, road markers tell the histories of Dr. Gustavus Brown (a surgeon and friend of George Washington), and the flight of John Wilkes Booth after the assassination of President Abraham Lincoln.

Stop at the National Colonial Farm for a rewarding side trip. Just north of the ride's starting point, the farm, with its staff dressed in period costume and its assortment of colonial crops, takes you back to life during colonial times.

START: Bryans Road Shopping Center at the intersection of MD 210 and MD 227, in Charles County, Md. From the Capital Beltway, exit on MD 210 (exit 3A, Indian Head Highway), east of Woodrow Wilson Bridge. Continue south into Charles County, to junction of MD 210 and MD 227 (Marshall Hall Road). The starting point is 16 miles south of the Capital Beltway.

LENGTH: 31.8 miles.

TERRAIN: Easy hills.

POINTS OF INTEREST: Port Tobacco at 10.0 miles, with museum, historic courthouse (301-475-2467), marina and restaurant on Port Tobacco River; St. Ignatius Church at Chapel Point with a famous river view at 13.5 miles, the oldest continuously active Catholic parish in America; Chapel Point State Park at 13.5 miles; La Plata at 21.1 miles, with colonial-era Episcopal Church, courthouse with undulating brick wall and farmers market; and Myrtle Grove Wildlife Refuge at 25.6 miles, an 800-acre scenic reserve. Also many tobacco farms along the route.

FOOD: Markets at start, 15.8, 21.0 and 22.0 miles. Restaurant at start. Barbecue stands at 9.7 and 19.1 miles.

MAPS: Charles County, Md. road map. *Southern Maryland Bicycle Map* from the St. Mary's Chamber of Commerce, 301-884-5555.

MILES   DIRECTIONS & COMMENTS

0.0   Cross MD 210 at stop sign to go **southeast** on **MD 227.** Restaurant.

1.4   **Left** to stay on **MD 227** (Pomfret Road).

4.6   **Right** on **MARSHALL CORNER ROAD.**

6.7   **Straight** on **ROSE HILL ROAD.** Historical marker. Cross MD 225.

9.4   **Left** on **MD 6** (Doncaster Road).

9.7   **Right** on **CHAPEL POINT ROAD.** Barbecue stand, store.

10.0   Port Tobacco Courthouse Historical Site and Museum on right. Water from pump in front yard.

13.5   St. Ignatius Church with scenic river view. **Left** to stay on **CHAPEL POINT ROAD.** Water available from spigot in front of church. Chapel Point State Park on left.

13.8   Historical marker, St. Ignatius Church.

15.8   **Straight** on **BEL ALTON-NEWTOWN ROAD,** crossing US 301. Convenience store.

16.1   **Left** on **FAIRGROUNDS ROAD.** Pass historical marker.

18.6   **Right** on **US 301** (shoulder).

19.1   **Right** on **ST. MARYS AVENUE.** Ribs on corner.

21.0   **Right** on **CHARLES STREET** in La Plata. Historical courthouse and Episcopal church. Farmers market and supermarket one block away.

21.0   **Quick left** on **WASHINGTON AVENUE.**

21.8   **Left** on **HAWTHORNE DRIVE.**

22.0   **Straight** on **MD 225** (La Plata Road), crossing US 301. Fast food, convenience store.

25.2   **Right** on **MARSHALL CORNER ROAD.**

25.3   **Left** on **BUMPY OAK ROAD.** Pass Myrtle Grove Wildlife Refuge on left, Maryland Airport on right. Refuge entrance is on MD 225, 2.2 miles west of Bumpy Oak Road.

29.9   **Right** on **LIVINGSTON ROAD** (MD 224) at stop sign.

30.4   **Merge left** on **MD 227.**

31.8   **Arrive** at **BRYANS ROAD SHOPPING CENTER.**

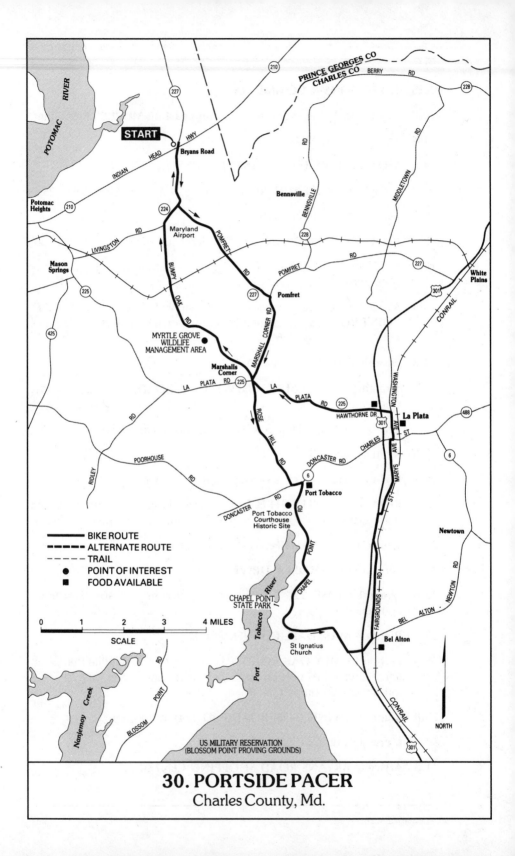

30. PORTSIDE PACER
Charles County, Md.

31. CHESAPEAKE TO PATUXENT

This ride, over quiet country roads, passes through several old Bayside resort towns. It offers views of Chesapeake Bay and the Patuxent River, wetlands, wildlife and historic homes.

Chesapeake Beach, complete with amusement park, was a major weekend destination for Washingtonians in the early 1900s. The resort's heyday, when it was served by the Chesapeake Beach Railway Company, is detailed in a collection of historical photos and artifacts in the railway's only remaining station, in Chesapeake Beach.

This tour also passes historic Lower Marlboro, one of the oldest towns in Maryland, where several 18th century homes still stand.

Thanks to Tom Roberts of Patuxent Area Cycling Enthusiasts (PACE), who developed this ride and allowed us to use it.

START: Northern High School parking lot in Chaneyville, Md. From the Capital Beltway, take Exit 11 (MD 4) 21 miles east and south to Chaneyville. At the traffic light in Chaneyville, take a right on Chaneyville Road. School parking lot is 0.9 miles west of MD 4 on the left. Chaneyville is 21 miles southeast of the Capital Beltway.

LENGTH: 41.0 miles.

TERRAIN: Nice mix of level terrain and rolling hills, lightly traveled roads.

POINTS OF INTEREST: Resort towns of North Beach and Chesapeake Beach at 11.5 and 13.7 miles; public pier and beach in North Beach; Chesapeake Beach Railway Museum, free, open daily, 1 p.m. - 4 p.m.; Chesapeake Beach Water Park, open 11 a.m. - 7 p.m. from Memorial Day to the first day of school, admission $12; Lower Marlboro historic area, near 38.0 miles.

FOOD: You won't starve on this route. There are markets and lots of restaurants in North Beach (11.5 miles), Chesapeake Beach (13.7 miles) and Huntingtown (31.0 miles). Besides crabs and seafood, you can find Caribbean, Southwest and Cajun (all in one restaurant! — Lagoon's Island Grille in Chesapeake Beach). There's great hickory smoked beef, chicken and ribs at John's Open Pit Barbecue in Huntingtown. And there's a wide variety of ambiance: volleyball and horseshoes, in addition to crabs and crabcakes at Chaney's in Chesapeake Beach; outside deck with bay view at Lagoon's Island in Chesapeake Beach; bingo and live entertainment at the Rod n' Reel, also in Chesapeake Beach; and country family cooking recommended by the locals at the Survey Inn Restaurant a mile off route on Solomon's Island Road South in Huntingtown.

LODGING: Angels in the Attic Bed and Breakfast, North Beach (410-855-2607); Back Woods Bed and Breakfast in Huntingtown, with stream, fish pond, hot tub and pool (410-535-4627); Serenity Acres Bed and Breakfast in Huntingtown, a Victorian residence with five acres (410-535-3744).

MAPS AND INFORMATION: Calvert County Map (available for $2.50 at the Calvert County Tourist Information Center on the right on MD 4, just before the turn on Chaneyville Road). *Southern Maryland Bicycle Map* from the St. Mary's Chamber of Commerce, 301-884-5555.

MILES   DIRECTIONS & COMMENTS

0.0   Turn **right** on **CHANEYVILLE ROAD** from school parking lot.

0.9   Cross MD 4 on service road.

1.0   Follow service road to **left.**

1.1   **Right** on **FOWLER'S ROAD** at end of service road.

2.5   At end of Fowler's Road, cross Mount Harmony Road and **bear right** on **GROVER'S TURN ROAD.**

3.5   **Straight** on **OLD SOLOMON'S ROAD** (MD 778N) at stop sign.

4.4   Cross MD 260.

6.0   **Right** on **FRIENDSHIP ROAD** (MD 261 East).

9.0   Enter Rose Haven. Friendship Road becomes **LAKE SHORE ROAD.**

10.0   Lake Shore Road becomes **WALNUT AVENUE** (MD 261 South).

11.5   Enter North Beach.

11.9   **Right** on **MD 261** when Walnut Avenue becomes one-way the wrong way. Then **first left** on **CHESAPEAKE AVENUE** (MD 261). Continue on MD 261 (becomes **BAYSIDE ROAD**).

13.7   **Right** on **OLD BAYSIDE ROAD** at Beach Elementary School. Becomes **DALRYMPLE ROAD.**

21.0   **Left** on **HARDESTY ROAD.**

23.7   **Bear left** on **PONDS WOOD ROAD.**

25.0   **Right** on **MD 261.**

25.7   **Right** on **PLUM POINT ROAD.**

28.3   **Right** on **COX ROAD.**

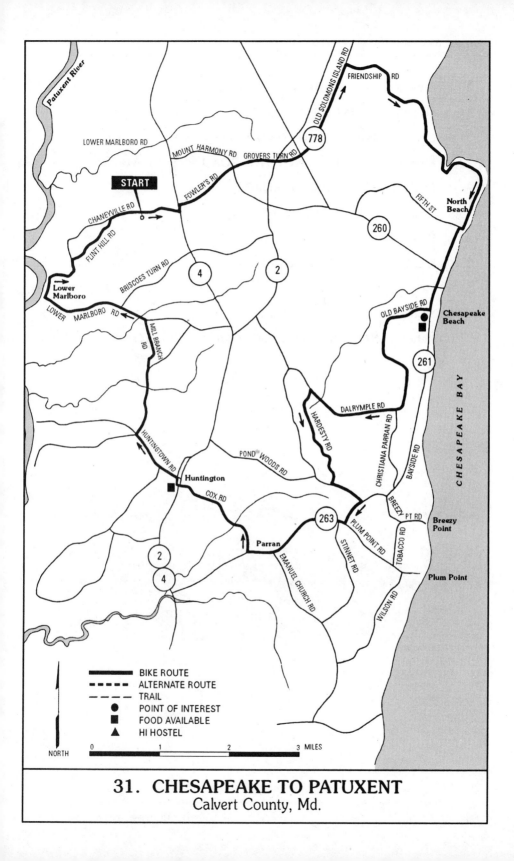

31. CHESAPEAKE TO PATUXENT
Calvert County, Md.

30.9   Cross MD 4 to **OLD TOWN ROAD.**

31.2   **Left** on **HUNTINGTOWN ROAD.**

31.6   Continue **straight** on **HUNTINGTOWN ROAD**.

32.6   **Right** to stay on **HUNTINGTOWN ROAD** at microwave antenna.

34.1   **Straight** on **MILL BRANCH ROAD.**

35.5   **Left** on **LOWER MARLBORO ROAD.**

37.8   Pass airfield.

38.0   **Right** on **CHANEYVILLE ROAD.**

38.5   Patuxent River on left.

39.0   **Straight** on **FLINT HILL ROAD.**

41.0   **Return** to **NORTHERN HIGH SCHOOL PARKING LOT.**

Wetlands along the Bay.

32. PRINCE WILLIAM PARK

Featuring the roads and trails of Prince William Forest Park, this ride will give the outdoor enthusiast ample opportunity to view white-tailed deer, wild turkey and beaver.

Prince William Forest Park is located on land formerly farmed by Scottish settlers. After years of soil depletion and extensive erosion, the land was reclaimed by the Civilian Conservation Corps in the 1930s. The National Park Service now operates a park and nature center, where rangers and volunteers explain the delicate ecological balance.

Surprisingly close to Washington, the park contains 17,000 acres of forestland, with picnic grounds, fishing, hiking trails, and the chance for cyclists to pedal without traffic.

START: Headquarters of Prince William Park on Fuller Road in Prince William County, Va. From the Capital Beltway, take I-95 South approximately 20 miles and exit on VA 619 West (Fuller Road). Turn right and continue 0.5 miles to park entrance; bear right to the park headquarters. The starting point is 21 miles southwest of the Capital Beltway.

LENGTH: 13.5 miles.

TERRAIN: Rolling hills and well-maintained roads. No shoulders.

POINTS OF INTEREST: Prince William Park (703-221-7181) with hiking trails and wildlife; and Turkey Run Environmental Center at 9.7 miles.

FOOD: None in the park. Choices in historic Dumfries, just east of the park.

LODGING: Regular and primitive campsites available (a written permit is required for the latter).

MAPS AND INFORMATION: *Prince William Forest Park* guide, available at Park Headquarters.

MILES   DIRECTIONS & COMMENTS

0.0   Leave Park Headquarters on **PARK ROAD, bearing right** past entrance road.

2.2   **Bear right** on **SCENIC DRIVE.**

9.3   **Left** to **TURKEY RUN ENVIRONMENTAL CENTER.**

9.7   Environmental Center to your left. **Reverse direction.** Continue past Scenic Drive loop.

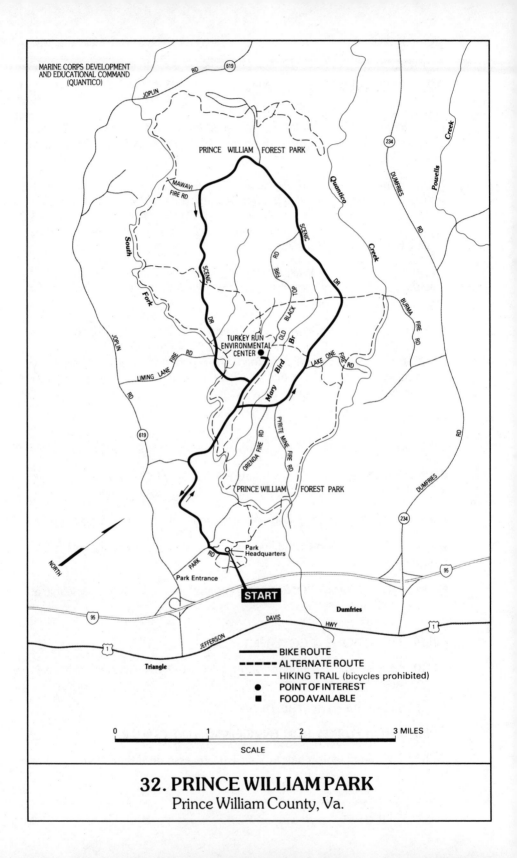

MARINE CORPS DEVELOPMENT
AND EDUCATIONAL COMMAND
(QUANTICO)

PRINCE WILLIAM FOREST PARK

MAWAVI FIRE RD

South Fork

SCENIC DR

TURKEY RUN ENVIRONMENTAL CENTER

LIMING LANE FIRE RD

JOPLIN RD

619

ORENDA FIRE RD

PYRITE MINE FIRE RD

PRINCE WILLIAM   FOREST PARK

FIRE RD

OLD BLACK TOP

Mary Bird Br

SCENIC DR

LAKE ONE FIRE RD

BURMA FIRE RD

Quantico   Creek

234

DUMFRIES RD

Powells   Creek

DUMFRIES RD

234

95

Park Headquarters

PARK RD

Park Entrance

START

Dumfries

DAVIS   HWY

JEFFERSON

Triangle

95

1

1

NORTH

JOPLIN   RD

619

—————— BIKE ROUTE
■■■■■■ ALTERNATE ROUTE
---------- HIKING TRAIL (bicycles prohibited)
● POINT OF INTEREST
■ FOOD AVAILABLE

0   1   2   3 MILES
SCALE

32. PRINCE WILLIAM PARK
Prince William County, Va.

13.0   Straight past park entrance.

13.5   **Arrive** at **PARK HEADQUARTERS.**

A beaver lodge in Prince William Forest Park.

33. HILL HATERS HALF HUNDRED KILOMETERS

Boasting easy hills, aromatic evergreen forests, scenic views of the distant Blue Ridge Mountains and low-traffic roads, this tour offers an ideal route for novice cyclists. Parks and country stores along the way provide rest stops for eating, dawdling or napping. For even lighter traffic, try the alternate route.

START: Nokesville Community Park in Nokesville, Va. From the Capital Beltway, take I-66 West for 11 miles and exit on VA 28 South. Continue south for 14 miles and turn left on VA 652 (Fitzwater Drive). Continue one mile; at end of road, turn right and go 0.2 miles south on Aden Road to Nokesville Community Park. Nokesville is 26 miles southwest of the Capital Beltway.

LENGTH: 31.5 miles. **ALTERNATE ROUTE:** 19.6 miles.

TERRAIN: Easy rolling hills, well maintained surfaces. This route had relatively light traffic in 1997, but the area is developing rapidly, and traffic may become much heavier in the near future.

POINTS OF INTEREST: Quantico Marine Base with National Cemetery and Marine Corps Museum at 5.8 miles; George Hellwig Memorial Park at 12.8 miles; Brentsville Recreational Area at 17.7 miles, with fitness par course, creek and rope swings; Brentsville Historic Area also at 17.7 miles, with historic marker, jail and courthouse (c.1822) and county parks information center; and Bristow Manor at 20.2 miles, a beautifully preserved old mansion. Dairy farms, hardwood and evergreen forests along the route.

FOOD: Markets (open Sundays) at 5.8, 12.3, 17.7 and 25.4 miles.

MAPS: Prince William County, Va. road map.

MILES   DIRECTIONS & COMMENTS

0.0   Go **north** on **ADEN ROAD** (VA 646).

1.0   **Right** on **COLVIN LANE** (VA 671).

2.9   **Right** on **VALLEY VIEW DRIVE** (VA 611). Pass cemetery on right.

3.9   **Right** on **PARKGATE DRIVE** (VA 653).

4.1   **First left** on **FLEETWOOD DRIVE** (VA 611).

5.8   **Left** on **ADEN ROAD** (VA 646). General store at Aden Crossroads. Traffic. Pass Quantico Marine Base with cemetery and museum on right. ALTERNATE ROUTE begins here (see end of cues).

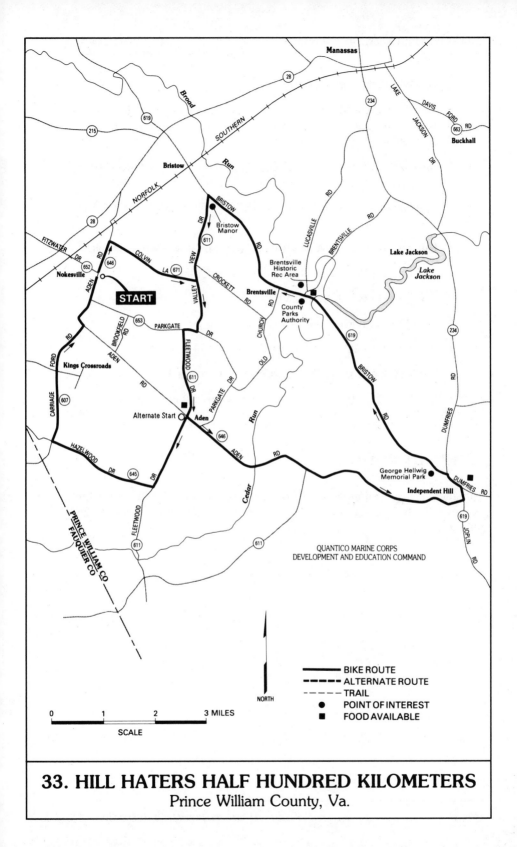

33. HILL HATERS HALF HUNDRED KILOMETERS
Prince William County, Va.

12.0 **Left** on **JOPLIN ROAD** (VA 619).

12.3 **Left** on **DUMFRIES ROAD** (VA 234) in Independent Hill. *Caution: busy intersection and heavy traffic. Narrow shoulder.* General store, park office, old courthouse.

12.7 **Bear left** on **BRISTOW ROAD** (VA 619). George Hellwig Memorial Park (with toilets) on left. Shaded road through forest.

17.7 Brentsville Recreational Area on right. General store and Brentsville Historic Area.

20.2 **Left** on **VALLEY VIEW DRIVE** (VA 611). Bristow Manor on left.

22.8 **Right** on **PARKGATE ROAD** (VA 653) at Golf Club sign.

23.2 **Left** on **FLEETWOOD DRIVE** (VA 611).

25.4 Aden Road intersection. General store.

26.9 **Right** on **HAZELWOOD DRIVE** (VA 645).

28.3 **Right** on **CARRIAGE FORD ROAD** (VA 607) at T.

30.8 **Left** on **ADEN ROAD** (VA 646) at T. Victory Baptist Church on left.

31.5 **Right** into **NOKESVILLE COMMUNITY PARK.**

ALTERNATE ROUTE

This alternate route eliminates the more-trafficked first loop of the tour. Simply skip over the first few cues and begin at 5.8 miles, following all cues to 25.4 miles.

34. VINEYARD VISIT

Cycle through Virginia's rich wine region and view picture-postcard plantations in horse and hunt country. Enjoy a picnic lunch at Meredyth Vineyards and return to the historic town of Middleburg to see its beautiful homes and craft shops. Later, ride through The Plains, another quaint town of shops and antique stores. Except for a half-mile stretch on U.S. 50, most of the roads have very little traffic.

Middleburg was acquired by Rawleigh Chinn in 1731 from the so-called Northern Neck Proprietary, a wilderness area. George Washington, Chinn's cousin, surveyed the area in 1787 and incorporated 50 acres as Middleburg. In 1863 Leven Powell purchased the town, divided it into lots and named all the streets after his Federalist friends. Middleburg soon became renowned for its bountiful hunting opportunities.

Meredyth Vineyards has grown hybrid grapes since 1970. Sip in moderation though — one of the route's big hills awaits you upon your return to Middleburg!

START: Middleburg Elementary School on VA 626 in Middleburg, Va. From the Capital Beltway, take I-66 West for 33 miles to The Plains/Middleburg exit. Turn right on VA 55 in The Plains and then take an immediate left on VA 626. Continue 8.4 miles to Middleburg. Turn right on US 50 then left on VA 626 by the Red Fox Tavern. Continue for 0.2 miles; school is on right. Middleburg is 42 miles west of the Capital Beltway.

LENGTH: 36.8 miles.

TERRAIN: Rolling hills, except for three sizable climbs. Almost two miles of dirt road traveling to and from the vineyard.

POINTS OF INTEREST: Middleburg shops, buildings and Red Fox Tavern near start; The Plains at 22.8 miles; Meredyth Vineyards (540-687-6277) at 28.7 miles, which produces wine under its own label (open 10 a.m. to 4 p.m. daily, with free tours); and Piedmont Vineyards (a side trip) on VA 626, 1.7 miles past right turn on VA 679 (at 26.6 miles). Horse farms along the route.

FOOD: Markets near start and at 9.2 miles (open until noon on Sundays). Restaurants near start, 22.8 and 36.3 miles.

LODGING: In Middleburg, Red Fox Inn and Tavern (540-687-6301). Near Middleburg, Welbourne Inn (540-687-3201), a 1775 farm listed on the National Register of Historic Places, on VA 743 one mile west of VA 611.

MAPS: Loudoun and Fauquier Counties, Va. road maps.

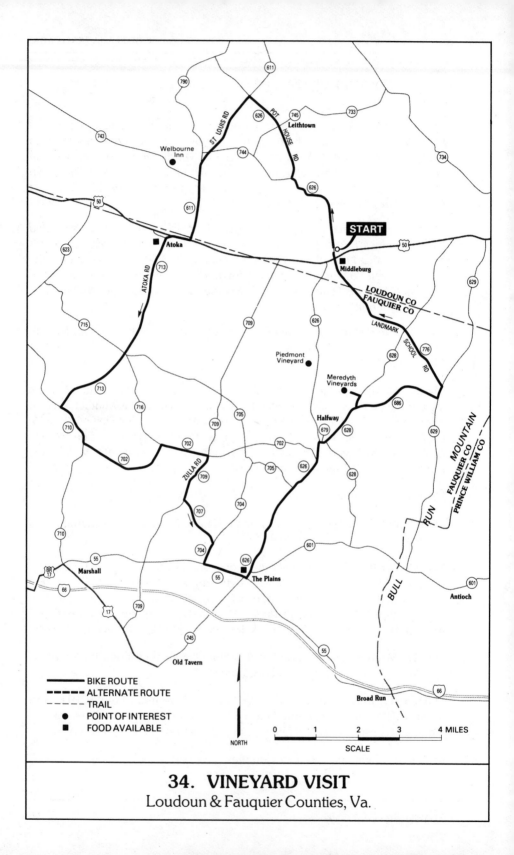

34. VINEYARD VISIT
Loudoun & Fauquier Counties, Va.

MILES   DIRECTIONS & COMMENTS

0.0   **Right** out of school parking lot to go north on **VA 626** (Pot House Road).

4.9   **Left** on **VA 611** (St. Louis Road) at stop sign.

8.7   **Right** on **US 50** at T. *Caution: heavy traffic.*

9.2   **First left** on **VA 713.**

9.4   **Bear left** to stay on **VA 713** (Atoka Road). General store (open until noon on Sundays).

14.4   **Left** on **VA 710** at T.

15.5   **Left** on **VA 702.**

19.1   **Right** on **ZULLA ROAD** (VA 709).

20.3   **Left** on **VA 707.**

21.6   **Bear right** on **VA 704.**

22.2   **Left** on **VA 55** at T.

23.2   Enter The Plains. Railway Stop store and Steubemart's General Store. Last food before vineyard.

23.3   **Left** on **VA 626.** Some traffic.

27.0   **Right** on **VA 679** which immediately becomes **VA 628.** [To reach Piedmont Vineyards, continue instead on VA 626 for 1.7 miles.]

28.2   **Left** to stay on **VA 628** at Meredyth Vineyards sign. Dirt road.

28.5   **Left** into **STIRLING FARM.**

29.1   **Arrive** at **MEREDYTH VINEYARDS**. Picnicking and tours. **Reverse direction.**

29.7   **Right** on **VA 628** at farm gate.

30.1   **Left** on **VA 686** at stop sign.

32.3   **Bear left** on **VA 629.**

32.5   **Left** on **VA 776.**

36.7   **Straight** on **VA 626,** crossing US 50 at blinking light. Red Fox Tavern.

36.8   **Right** into **MIDDLEBURG ELEMENTARY SCHOOL.**

35. PEDALING THE PIEDMONT

The Virginia Piedmont offers you rolling meadows, rural countryside and an occasional steep hill — a visual treat and physical challenge to the well-trained cyclist. Farmhouses from the 18th and 19th centuries dot the landscape, along with open fields and Blue Ridge Mountain vistas.

START: Marshall Commuter Lot in Marshall, Va. From the Capital Beltway, take I-66 West for 36 miles and exit on US 17 (toward Marshall/Warrenton). Continue north for 0.7 miles on BUS US 17 into Marshall. Turn left on Main Street (VA 55) at the stop sign. Turn right after 0.1 miles on Frost Street. Continue straight to the dead end and commuter lot. Marshall is 37 miles west of the Capital Beltway.

LENGTH: 55.2 miles.

TERRAIN: Rolling hills to moderately hilly.

POINTS OF INTEREST: Naked Mountain Vineyard at 33.7 miles, and Sky Meadows State Park at 40.2 miles. Views of Blue Ridge Mountains and farmhouses along the route. Peach orchards near Markham.

FOOD: Markets in Marshall near start, 19.9 and 44.4 miles.

MAPS: Fauquier County, Va. road map.

MILES   DIRECTIONS & COMMENTS

0.0   **Straight** out of parking lot on **FROST STREET.**

0.1   **Left** on **MAIN STREET.**

0.2   **Right** on **VA 710.**

1.2   **Right** on **VA 691** (Carters Run) after crossing I-66.

9.6   **Left** to stay on **VA 691.**

12.1   **Right** to stay on **VA 691** (Old Waterloo Road).

14.2   **Right** on unmarked **VA 688** (Leeds Manor Road) in Waterloo.

19.9   Pass through Orlean. Markets on left, before intersection with VA 732, and on right after intersection.

26.2   Pass through Hume.

31.8   **Left** to follow **VA 688.**

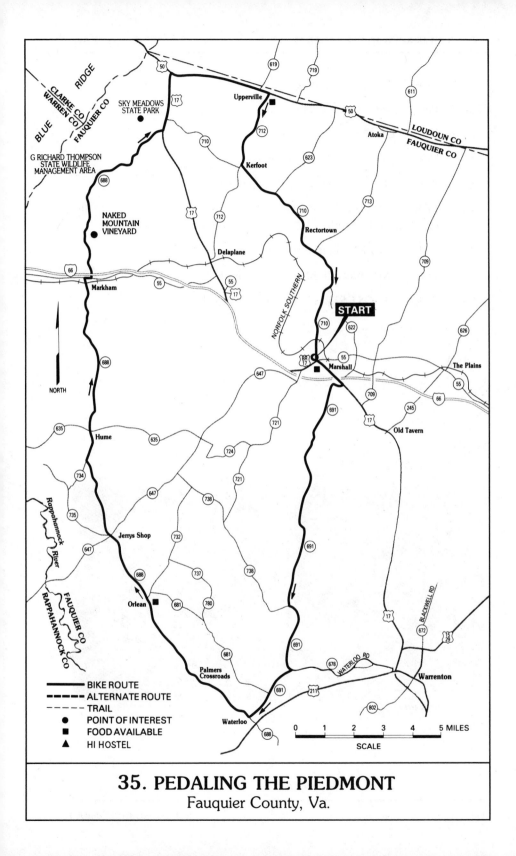

35. PEDALING THE PIEDMONT
Fauquier County, Va.

31.9   Cross VA 55 and continue under I-66.

33.7   Pass Naked Mountain Vineyard.

38.7   **Left** on **US 17** (Winchester Road). *Caution: heavy traffic.*

40.2   Sky Meadows State Park on left.

40.6   **Right** on **US 50** (John S. Mosby Highway).

44.1   **Right** on **VA 712** (Delaplane Grade Road). Town of Upperville. General store at mile 44.4. Water at firehouse on right.

46.7   **Left** on **VA 710** (Rectortown Road).

55.1   Town of Marshall. **Right** on **MAIN STREET.**

55.2   **Right** on **FROST STREET.** Parking lot straight ahead.

Meredyth Vineyards.

36. VIRGINIA HUNT COUNTRY

A quiet respite from the bustle of urban life, this pleasant ride through Virginia Hunt Country offers you smooth cycling on country roads. Views of the Blue Ridge Mountains serve as a backdrop to the many elegant country estates, expansive farmland and grazing horses.

START: Middleburg Elementary School on VA 626 in Middleburg, Va. From the Capital Beltway, take I-66 West for 33 miles to The Plains/Old Tavern exit (Exit 31 North). Turn right on VA 55 in The Plains and then take an immediate left on VA 626. Continue 8.4 miles to Middleburg. Turn right on US 50 then left on VA 626 by the Red Fox Tavern. Continue for 0.2 miles; school is on right. Middleburg is 42 miles west of the Capital Beltway.

LENGTH: 44.8 miles.

TERRAIN: Rolling hills to moderately hilly.

POINTS OF INTEREST: Middleburg at start and The Plains at 31.8 miles. Views of the Blue Ridge Mountains and country estates and horse farms along the route.

FOOD: Markets near start and at 10.0, 11.5 (closed Saturday afternoon and Sunday), 19.3 and 31.8 miles. Restaurants near start and at 31.8 miles.

LODGING: In Middleburg, Red Fox Inn and Tavern (540-687-6301). Near Middleburg, Welbourne Inn (540-687-3201), on VA 743 one mile west of VA 611, a 1775 farm listed on the National Register of Historic Places.

MAPS: Fauquier County, Va. road map.

MILES   DIRECTIONS & COMMENTS

   0.0   **Left** out of parking lot on **VA 626** (Madison Street).

   0.1   **Right** on **US 50** (Washington Street). *Caution: traffic.*

   1.4   **Left** on **VA 709** (Zula Road).

   6.5   **Right** on **VA 702** (Frogtown Road). Sign may be obscured.

 10.0   **Right** on **VA 710** at T. General store.

 11.5   General Store in Rectortown, closed Sunday and after 1 p.m. Saturday.

 13.7   **Right** on **VA 623** (Rokeby Road).

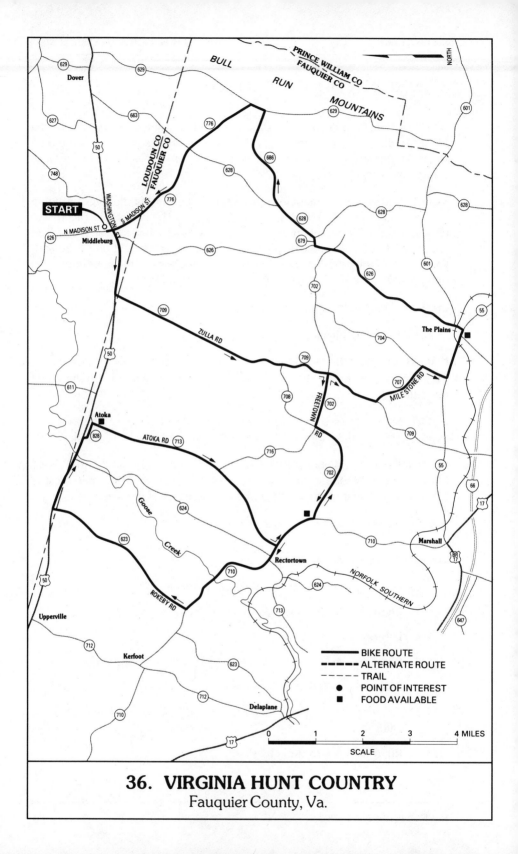

BIKE ROUTE
ALTERNATE ROUTE
TRAIL
● **POINT OF INTEREST**
■ **FOOD AVAILABLE**

0 1 2 3 4 MILES
SCALE

36. VIRGINIA HUNT COUNTRY
Fauquier County, Va.

17.3   **Right** on **US 50.** *Caution: high speed traffic.*

18.9   **Right** on **VA 828** (Rector's Lane).

19.3   **Right** on **VA 713** (Atoka Road). General store.

24.3   **Left** on **VA 710** at T.

25.3   **Left** on **VA 702** (Frogtown Road).

28.8   **Right** on **VA 709.**

30.0   **Left** on **VA 707** (Milestone Road).

31.3   **Bear right** on **VA 704.**

31.8   **Left** on **VA 55.** *Caution: traffic.* Enter The Plains. Restaurants and markets.

32.8   **Left** on **VA 626.**

36.7   **Right** on **VA 679.** Becomes **VA 628/686.**

36.9   **Bear left** on **VA 628.** Becomes **VA 686.**

40.2   **Bear left** on **VA 629.**

40.4   **Left** on **VA 776.** Becomes **SOUTH MADISON STREET** in Middleburg.

44.7   **Straight** on **SOUTH MADISON STREET** (VA 626). Cross US 50.

44.8   **Right** into **MIDDLEBURG ELEMENTARY SCHOOL.**

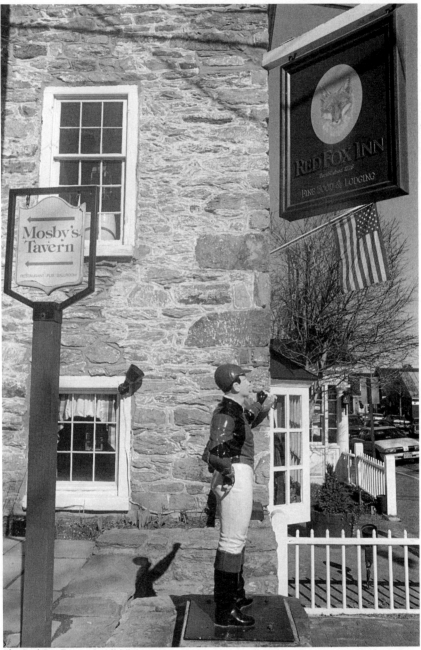

The Red Fox Tavern in Middleburg.

37. THE RESPLENDENT RAPPAHANNOCK

Traversing the foothills of the Blue Ridge Mountains, this challenging ride boasts spectacular views of the Upper Rappahannock River Valley, an important watershed for the Virginia Piedmont. The route passes through several small villages with quaint stone houses and hunt country estates surrounded by elegant stone fences. You will cross the Rappahannock River and its tributaries several times, offering cool relief in summer and views of colorful foliage in autumn. Oasis Vineyard is located six miles west of Hume on VA 635.

START: Marshall Commuter Lot in Marshall, Va. From the Capital Beltway, take I-66 West for 36 miles and exit at Exit 28 on US 17 (toward Marshall/Warrenton). Turn right at end of ramp on BUS US 17. Continue north for 0.7 miles on BUS US 17 into Marshall. Turn left at the stop sign on West Main Street (VA 55/US 17). Turn right after 0.1 miles on Frost Street. Continue straight to the dead end and commuter lot. Marshall is 37 miles west of the Capital Beltway.

LENGTH: 55.7 miles.

TERRAIN: Hilly.

POINTS OF INTEREST: Oasis Vineyard at 15.7 miles; and Rappahannock River at 16.5 miles. Views of the Blue Ridge Mountains along the route.

FOOD: Markets in Marshall and at 25.1 and 35.6 miles. Restaurant (Four and Twenty Blackbirds) in Flint Hill at 25.1 miles has Sunday brunch from 10 a.m. to 2 p.m. Several restaurants in Marshall.

MAPS: Fauquier and Rappahannock Counties, Va. road maps.

MILES   DIRECTIONS & COMMENTS

0.0   From Marshall Commuter Lot, go back out **FROST STREET.**

0.1   **Right** on **US 17/VA 55** (West Main Street). *Caution: traffic.*

0.7   **Left** on **VA 647.**

1.0   **Right** to stay on **VA 647.** Turn is just past I-66 bridge.

5.5   **Right** on **VA 635.**

9.7   Hume. *Caution: big hills and narrow curves follow.* Marriott Ranch on left.

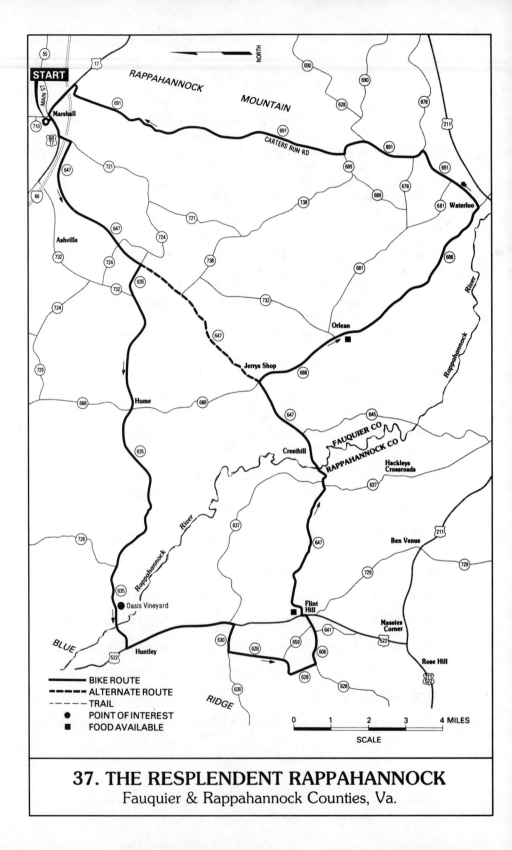

37. THE RESPLENDENT RAPPAHANNOCK
Fauquier & Rappahannock Counties, Va.

15.7　Oasis Vineyard (open 10 a.m. - 5 p.m. daily).

16.5　Cross the Rappahannock River.

17.1　**Left** on **US 522** (Zachary Taylor Highway). Arrive at the Blue Ridge! *Caution: fast traffic and no shoulder.*

20.2　**Right** on **VA 630.**

21.0　**Bear left** on **VA 628.**

23.0　**Bear left** to stay on **VA 628.**

23.7　**Left** on **VA 606.** Bed and Breakfast if you're too tired to go on.

25.1　**Left** on **US 522.** Flint Hill.

25.4　**Right** on **VA 647.** Food stores (open 8 a.m. - 7 p.m.). More hills follow.

33.1　**Right** on **VA 688.** [Note: for an alternate short-cut back to Marshall, do not turn here, and instead go straight on VA 647.]

35.6　Two food stores (one open 7 a.m. - 10 p.m.) in Orlean.

41.2　**Left** on **VA 691** in Waterloo. Climb!

43.4　**Left** to stay on **VA 691,** approaching Rappahannock Mountain.

45.2　**Bear left** to stay on **VA 691.**

45.9　**Right** at bottom of hill to stay on **VA 691** (Carter's Run Road).

54.3　**Left** on **US 17.** *Caution: traffic.* Arrive in Marshall.

55.4　**Left** on **US 17/VA 55** (West Main Street).

55.6　**Right** on **FROST STREET.**

55.7　**Arrive** at **MARSHALL COMMUTER LOT**.

38. WARRENTON WANDERLUST

The three Virginia counties of Fauquier, Rappahannock and Culpeper set the scene for this tour. Passing through serene, wooded countryside over lightly traveled roads, you also will experience a taste of history. Farms and small villages throughout the valley remain virtually unchanged since Civil War days. Views to the west afford excellent panoramas of the Blue Ridge Mountains.

The tour takes you through Brandy Station, location of the largest cavalry engagement in U.S. history. In June 1863, Union cavalry under Alfred Pleasonton clashed with J.E.B. Stuart's Confederate raiders. More than 21,000 mounted troops battled to a standoff.

START: Fauquier County High School on VA 678 in Warrenton, Va. From the Capital Beltway, take I-66 West for 22 miles and exit on US 29 South at Gainesville. Continue on US 29/211 for 12 miles and bear right on BUS US 29/15 (toward Warrenton/Winchester). Continue for 0.8 miles and turn right on US 211. Take first right on Rappahannock Street, then immediately left on VA 678. Continue for 0.5 miles; the high school is on the right. Warrenton is 36 miles west of the Capital Beltway.

LENGTH: 78.3 miles.

TERRAIN: Rolling hills to moderately hilly.

POINTS OF INTEREST: Rappahannock River at 16.7 miles; Brandy Station at 50.2 miles; and Victorian homes in Warrenton at 77.2 miles.

FOOD: Markets at 11.4, 21.5, 25.4, 57.5 and 77.2 miles.

MAPS: Fauquier, Rappahannock and Culpeper Counties, Va. road maps.

MILES   DIRECTIONS & COMMENTS

  0.0   Leave Fauquier County High School by turning **right** on **VA 678**. *Caution: traffic.*

  3.7   **Left** on **VA 691.**

  5.8   **Right** on **VA 688** in Waterloo.

 11.4   General stores in Orlean.

 13.8   **Left** on **VA 647.**

 16.7   Cross Rappahannock River into Rappahannock County.

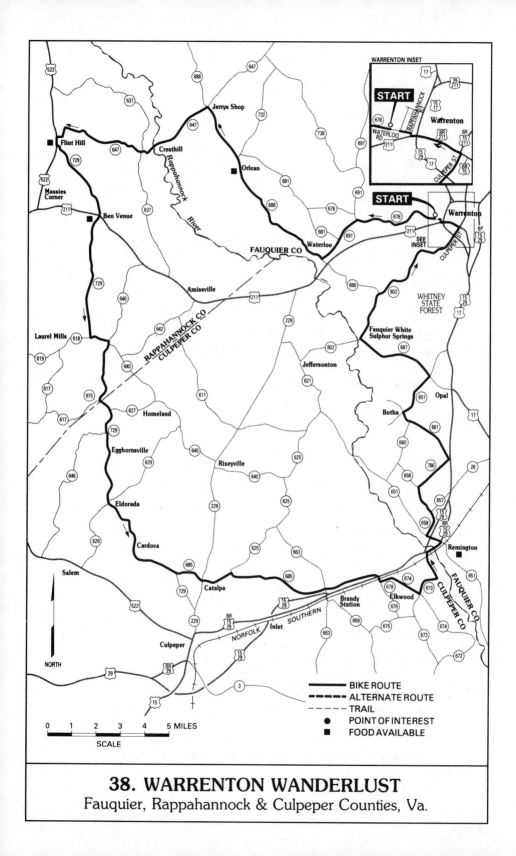

38. WARRENTON WANDERLUST
Fauquier, Rappahannock & Culpeper Counties, Va.

21.5   **Left** on **US 522.** General store in Flint Hill.

21.9   **Left** on **VA 729.**

25.4   Cross US 211. General store.

30.9   **Left** to stay on **VA 729.**

31.9   **Bear right** to stay on **VA 729.** [Note: VA 640 comes in from the left twice!]

34.6   **Left** to stay on **VA 729.** Enter Culpeper County.

35.1   **Bear right** to stay **VA 729.**

43.5   **Bear left** on **VA 685.**

44.7   Cross VA 229. Catalpa. Continue on VA 685.

46.0   **Right** to stay on **VA 685.**

50.2   Cross VA 663 at Brandy Station (left across US 29).

52.3   Cross US 29. **Left** on **VA 678.**

52.7   **Straight** on **VA 674.** Elkwood.

54.4   **Left** on **VA 673.**

56.8   **Right** on **BUS US 29.** Cross Rappahannock River.

57.5   **Left** on **VA 651.** General store in Remington.

58.0   Cross US 29.

58.1   **Right** on **VA 658.**

60.4   **Right** on **VA 786.**

62.1   **Left** on **VA 661.**

65.1   **Right** on **VA 651.**

67.0   **Left** on **VA 687.**

70.4   **Right** on **VA 802.** Fauquier White Sulphur Springs.

76.8   Cross US 29, on **CULPEPER STREET.**

77.2   **Left** on **BUS VA 15.** Downtown Warrenton. General stores.

78.0   Cross US 29. **Right** on **VA 678.**

78.3   **Right** into **FAUQUIER COUNTY HIGH SCHOOL.**

39. FRONT ROYAL HILLS

Offering beautiful views of the Blue Ridge Mountains, this challenging route travels round-trip from Marshall to Front Royal, Va. You will pass the Oasis Vineyard and the hilltop home of Chief Justice John Marshall.

The strenuous three-mile climb over Chester Gap is more than rewarded by a four-mile descent into Front Royal! During the long descent keep your eyes open for giraffes, wildebeest and other exotic animals at the Smithsonian Conservation and Research Center. The flea market in Front Royal, at the intersection of VA 522 and VA 55, offers another diversion.

Front Royal has two notable Civil War museums located next door to each other. The Belle Boyd Cottage at 101 Chester Street (540-636-1446), a former tavern, now houses a museum dedicated to the career of the "Siren of the South." When Union officers turned Boyd's house into a military headquarters during the Shenandoah campaigns of 1862, she spied on the officers and passed the information to Confederate leaders. Next door at 95 Chester Street is the Warren Rifles Confederate Museum (540-636-6982), operated by the United Daughters of the Confederacy.

START: Marshall Commuter Lot in Marshall, Va. From the Capital Beltway, take I-66 West for 36 miles and exit on US 17 (toward Marshall/Warrenton). Continue north for 0.7 miles on BUS US 17 into Marshall. Turn left on Main Street (VA 55) at the stop sign. Turn right after 0.1 miles on Frost Street. Continue straight to the dead end and commuter lot. Marshall is 37 miles west of the Capital Beltway.

LENGTH: 56.5 miles.

TERRAIN: Rolling hills, with one long hill on US 522.

POINTS OF INTEREST: Home of Chief Justice Marshall at 9.2 miles; Oasis Vineyard at 18.8 miles, on VA 635 just west of Hume; Smithsonian Conservation and Research Center at 30.2 miles; and Front Royal, with Civil War museums on Chester Street and flea market on Commerce Street, at 32.2 miles. At Front Royal, entrance to Shenandoah National Park and Skyline Drive.

FOOD: Markets at start, 27.6 (often closed), 32.2 and 40.9 miles. Restaurants and diners on Main Street in Marshall and restaurants in Front Royal at 32.5 miles.

MAPS: Fauquier and Warren Counties, Va. road maps.

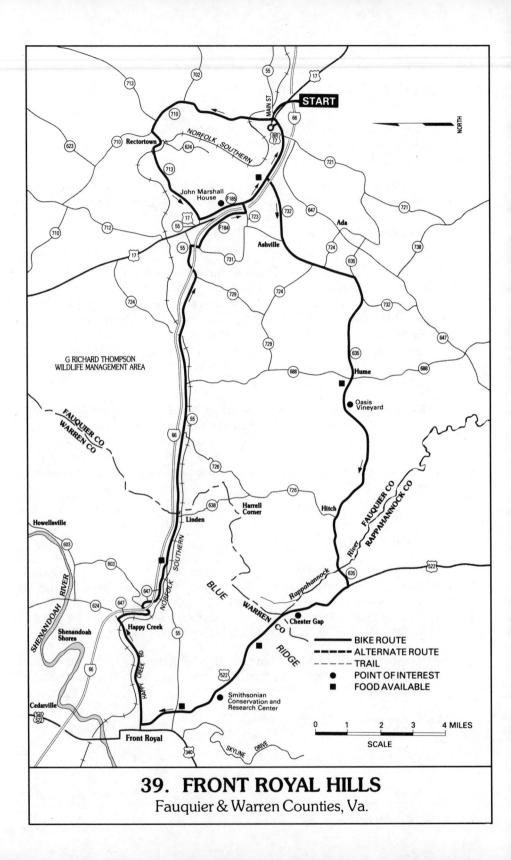

39. FRONT ROYAL HILLS
Fauquier & Warren Counties, Va.

MILES   DIRECTIONS & COMMENTS

0.0   **Straight** out of parking lot on **FROST STREET.**

0.1   **Left** on **MAIN STREET.**

0.2   **Left** on **VA 710.**

4.6   **Left** on **VA 713** in Rectortown.

5.0   **Straight** at fork to stay on **VA 713.**

5.5   Cross railroad tracks.

8.2   **Left** on **VA F-185.** DO NOT proceed one block to intersection of VA 55/17 and VA 713.

9.2   Chief Justice Marshall home.

10.8   **Right** on **VA 732.**

15.5   **Right** on **VA 635.**

18.8   **Straight** to stay on **VA 635** in Hume, crossing VA 688.

26.4   **Right** on **US 522** at T. *Caution: heavy traffic.* Begin 3-mile climb over Chester Gap.

27.6   Store (irregular hours).

30.2   Smithsonian Conservation and Research Center.

32.2   Fast food and convenience stores at intersection of VA 55 and US 522, where US 522 becomes **COMMERCE AVENUE** in Front Royal. Restaurants in Front Royal.

34.1   **Right** on **HAPPY CREEK ROAD** at traffic light. Becomes **VA 624.**

37.7   **Right** on **VA 647** (Dismal Hollow Road).

40.9   **Left** on **VA 55.** High's Dairy Store at intersection.

50.9   **Right** on **VA 731** at T. (VA 55 continues left.)

51.0   **Left** on **VA F-184,** immediately after crossing under I-66.

53.0   **Left** on **VA 723.**

53.1   **Right** on **VA F-185.** Becomes **MAIN STREET** in Marshall.

56.5   **Left** on **FROST STREET.** Straight ahead into **MARSHALL COMMUTER LOT.**

Virginia pastures.

40. LEESBURG-WATERFORD-HAMILTON TREK

Sporting a number of long steep hills with panoramic views of the neighboring countryside, this scenic loop takes you primarily on gravel and dirt roads. The towns of Waterford and Hamilton provide small-town diversions, with plenty of historic landmarks along the way.

START: Loudoun County High School on Dry Mill Road (VA 699) in Leesburg, Va. From the Capital Beltway, take VA 7 West for 28 miles to Leesburg. At the Leesburg city limits, continue straight to remain on BUS VA 7, and turn left on Catoctin Circle. At the third traffic light, turn left on Dry Mill Road (VA 699) and continue 200 yards; school parking lot is on right. Leesburg is 31 miles northwest of the Capital Beltway.

LENGTH: 32.1 miles.

TERRAIN: Rolling hills. *Mountain bike recommended*, as most of the roads are unpaved.

POINTS OF INTEREST: Leesburg at start; Waterford at 6.9 miles; W&OD Trail at 18.6 miles; and Hamilton at 19.6 miles. Historic landmarks and hillside views along the route.

FOOD: Markets and restaurants in Leesburg near start; market and restaurant at 19.6 miles, in Hamilton.

MAPS: Loudoun County, Va. road map.

MILES   DIRECTIONS & COMMENTS

0.0   **Left** on **DRY MILL ROAD** (VA 699) [paved]. Cross W&OD Trail.

0.7   **Right** on **CORNWALL STREET** [paved].

0.9   **Left** on **LIBERTY STREET** [paved].

1.0   **Bear left** on **NORTH STREET** [paved].

1.1   **Bear right** on **OLD WATERFORD ROAD** (VA 698) [paved and unpaved].

6.9   **Right** on **VA 665** (Taylorstown Road) [paved]. Waterford.

8.4   **Left** on **VA 662** (Old Mill Road) [unpaved].

11.0   **Right** on **VA 698** (Old Wheatland Road) [unpaved].

14.0   **Left** on **VA 9** (Charles Town Pike) [paved].

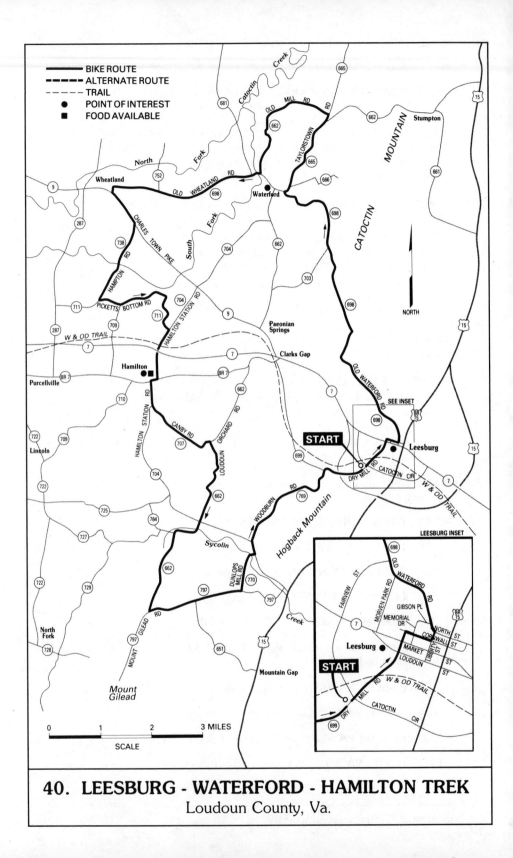

40. LEESBURG - WATERFORD - HAMILTON TREK
Loudoun County, Va.

14.7   **Right** on **VA 738** (Hampton Road) [unpaved].

16.4   **Left** on **VA 711** (Picketts Bottom Road) [unpaved].

16.9   **Bear left** to remain on **VA 711.**

18.6   **Right** on **VA 704** (Hamilton Station Road) [paved]. Cross W&OD Trail.

19.0   Cross VA 7 Bypass.

19.6   **Right** on **BUS VA 7** [paved]. Hamilton. General Store. Restaurant with outside dining.

19.7   **Left** on **VA 704** (Hamilton Station Road) [paved].

20.2   **Left** on **VA 707** (Canby Road) [unpaved].

21.7   **Right** on **VA 662** (Loudoun Orchard Road) [unpaved].

23.3   **Straight** to remain on **VA 662** [unpaved].

24.4   Cross VA 704 (Hamilton Station Road).

25.0   **Left** to remain on **VA 662** [unpaved and paved].

26.7   **Left** on **VA 797** (Mount Gilead Road) [unpaved].

28.5   **Left** on **VA 770** (Dunlops Mill Road) [unpaved].

29.3   **Left** on **VA 704** (Hamilton Station Road) [paved].

29.6   **Right** on **VA 769** (Woodburn Road) [unpaved and paved].

31.6   **Right** on **VA 699** (Dry Mill Road) [paved].

32.1   **Left** into **PARKING LOT.**

41. MOUNT GILEAD TO HAMILTON TREK

Featuring vistas of vineyards, mountains and horse farms, plus a few spectacular downhill runs, this very scenic ride takes you through the Mount Gilead area of Loudoun County, Va. The loop also passes through the communities of Hamilton and Goose Creek. This route is getting somewhat less rural as more development comes to Loudoun County, but still qualifies as quiet, secluded and scenic.

You can also start in Hamilton, which is near the Purcellville terminus of the W&OD Trail.

START: Junction of VA 621 and VA 771 in Loudoun County, Va. From the Capital Beltway, take the Dulles Toll Road. After 12 miles, exit right on Dulles Greenway (toll). Exit at VA 7 West. Exit left on VA BUS 7 (South King Street). Turn left on VA 621 (Evergreen Mills Road). Go 5.4 miles and turn right on VA 771 (The Woods Road). Park on the shoulder of VA 771. The starting point is 27 miles west of the Capital Beltway.

LENGTH: 34.3 miles.

TERRAIN: Rolling hills. Mostly hard-packed dirt roads, with some gravel. *Mountain bike recommended.*

POINTS OF INTEREST: Hamilton at 12.3 miles. Goose Creek and Beaverdam Creek crossings at many places along the route.

FOOD: Market at 12.3 miles.

MAPS: Loudoun County, Va. road map.

MILES   DIRECTIONS & COMMENTS

0.0   **Straight** to go north on **VA 771** (The Woods Road) [unpaved].

1.9   **Right** on **VA 650** (Gleedsville Road) [unpaved].

2.5   **Left** on **VA 651** (Gap Road) [unpaved].

3.3   **Right** on **US 15** [paved].

3.5   **Left** on **VA 651** (Hogback Mountain Road) [unpaved].

5.5   **Left** on **VA 797** (Mount Gilead Road) [unpaved].

6.4   **Right** on **VA 662** (Loudoun Orchard Road) [unpaved, then becomes paved].

8.1   **Bear right** to remain on **VA 662** [paved].

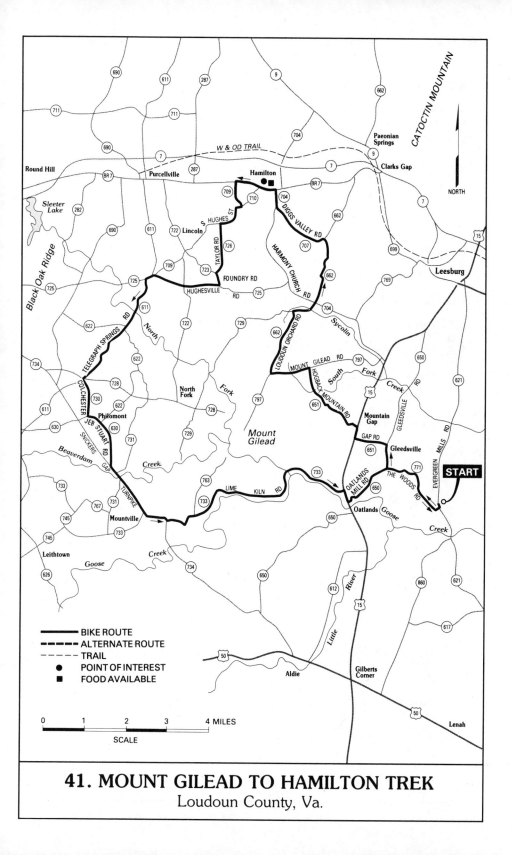

41. MOUNT GILEAD TO HAMILTON TREK
Loudoun County, Va.

8.7   Cross VA 704, continue **straight** uphill on **VA 662** [unpaved].

9.8   **Bear left** to remain on **VA 662** [unpaved].

10.3   **Left** on **VA 707** (Diggs Valley Road) [unpaved]. *Careful: thick gravel and steep downhill.* At unmarked intersection near bottom of hill, **bear right** instead of going straight uphill.

11.8   **Right** on **VA 704** (Harmony Church Road) [paved].

12.3   **Left** on **BUS VA 7** [paved] into Hamilton. General store (open Sundays).

13.2   **Left** on **VA 709** (South Hughes Street) [paved]. Street sign says "T709 S. Hughes."

13.9   **Right** on **VA 709** [unpaved] at T. Becomes **SANDS ROAD**.

14.6   **Left** on **VA 726** [unpaved].

15.8   **Left** on **VA 723** (Foundry Road).

16.1   **Right** on **VA 725** (Hughesville Road) [unpaved].

17.0   Cross VA 722 (Lincoln Road).

18.0   **Left** on **VA 611** (Telegraph Springs Road) [paved].

19.0   Pavement ends.

21.0   **Left** on **VA 730** (Colchester Road) [unpaved].

21.9   **Left** on **VA 630** (Jeb Stuart Road) [unpaved].

23.2   **Left** on **VA 734** (Snickers Gap Turnpike) [paved].

25.1   **Left** on **VA 733** (Lime Kiln Road) [paved, but watch for big potholes].

26.0   Pavement ends.

28.6   Pavement begins. Very nice riding here.

30.8   **Right** on **US 15** [paved]. *Caution: heavy traffic.*

31.0   **Left** on **VA 650** (Oatlands Mill Road) [unpaved].

32.4   **Right** on **VA 771** (The Woods Road) [unpaved].

34.3   **Return** to **PARKING AREA** on VA 711.

42. POINT OF ROCKS EXPLORER

A panorama of terrain and countryside, this tour loops through Waterford, Va. and Point of Rocks, Md. The first half in Virginia contains some long, steep hills, but the Maryland portion on the C&O Canal Towpath is level. The Towpath may be impassable with mud after heavy rains, so plan accordingly.

This tour includes a side trip to Balls Bluff National Cemetery. In October 1861, Union General George McClellan ordered a probe of Confederate defenses in Loudoun County. At Balls Bluff, the Union troops were trapped against the high banks of the Potomac River and forced to choose between deadly Confederate gunfire and a suicidal leap to the waters below. Nearly 1,000 died, a bloody omen of the coming years. The defeat was an enormous blow to the Union. For days afterward, blue-clad corpses were sighted downstream in Georgetown. Among the wounded was Oliver Wendell Holmes, Jr., a recent Harvard College graduate and future Supreme Court Justice. Today, the Balls Bluff site remains an undeveloped national cemetery and a quiet testimony to American history's most violent and emotional chapter.

START: Loudoun County High School on Dry Mill Road (VA 699) in Leesburg, Va. From the Capital Beltway, take VA 7 West for 28 miles to Leesburg. At the Leesburg city limits, continue straight to remain on BUS VA 7, and turn left on Catoctin Circle. At the third traffic light turn left on Dry Mill Road (VA 699) and continue 200 yards; school parking lot is on right. Leesburg is 31 miles northwest of the Capital Beltway.

LENGTH: 36.0 miles.

TERRAIN: Rolling hills on predominantly gravel and dirt roads. *Mountain bike recommended.*

POINTS OF INTEREST: Leesburg at start; Point of Rocks on the Potomac River at 17.7 miles, with restored 19th century railroad station; C&O Canal, from 17.8 to 30.6 miles; Whites Ferry (301-349-5200) at 30.6 miles, the only continually operating ferry on the Potomac River ($0.50 for bicycles, 7 days a week); Balls Bluff National Cemetery.

FOOD: Markets and restaurants in Leesburg, near start; markets at 14.9 and 17.7 miles.

MAPS: Loudoun County, Va. and Montgomery County, Md. road maps.

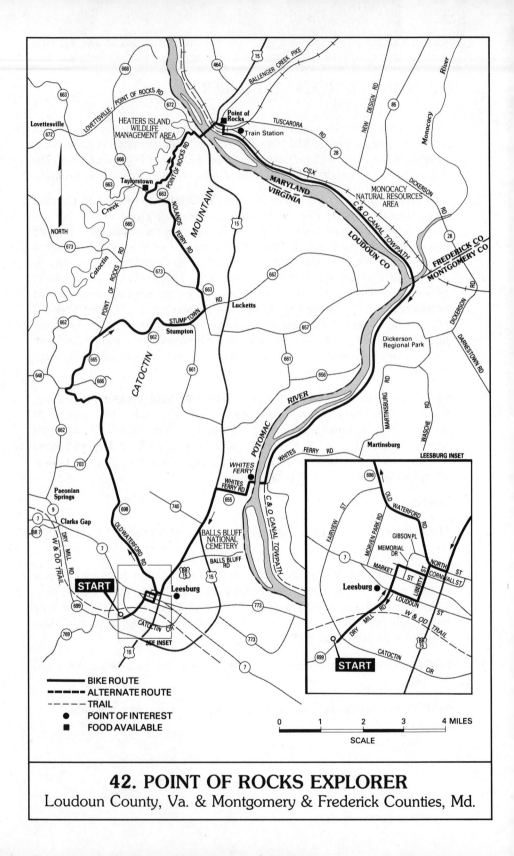

42. POINT OF ROCKS EXPLORER
Loudoun County, Va. & Montgomery & Frederick Counties, Md.

MILES   DIRECTIONS & COMMENTS

0.0   **Left** on **DRY MILL ROAD** (VA 699) [paved]. Cross W&OD Trail.

0.7   **Right** on **CORNWALL STREET** [paved].

0.9   **Left** on **LIBERTY STREET** [paved].

1.0   **Bear left** on **NORTH STREET** [paved].

1.1   **Bear right** on **OLD WATERFORD ROAD** (VA 698) [paved and unpaved].

6.9   **Right** on **VA 665** (Point of Rocks Road) [paved].

8.3   **Right** on **VA 662** (Stumptown Road) [paved].

11.4 **Left** on **VA 663** (Nolands Ferry Road) [paved and unpaved].

14.9 **Right** on **VA 665** (Point of Rocks Road) [unpaved]. [Note: store in Taylorstown, 0.2 miles ahead on VA 663.]

17.3 **Right** on **VA 672** (Lovettsville-Point of Rocks Road) [paved].

17.4 **Left** on **US 15**. Cross Potomac River into Maryland.

17.7 **Right** on **MD 28** (Tuscarora Road) [paved]. Point of Rocks. General store one block on left.

17.8 **Right** at first driveway to go **left** (downriver) on **C&O CANAL TOWPATH** [unpaved].

30.6 **Right** to **Whites Ferry.** Cross Potomac River on ferry. In Virginia, continue **straight** on **WHITES FERRY ROAD** (VA 655) [paved].

31.8 **Left** on **US 15** [paved]. Use road shoulder.

33.1 **Bear right** on **BUS US 15** [paved] to Leesburg. For SIDE TRIP to Balls Bluff, bear left here to stay on US 15 and turn left on Balls Bluff Road.

34.7 **Right** on **NORTH STREET** [paved].

34.9 **Left** on **LIBERTY STREET** [paved].

35.0 **Right** on **LOUDOUN STREET** [paved].

35.4 **Left** on **DRY MILL ROAD** (VA 699) [paved].

36.0 **Right** into **PARKING LOT.**

Farther Afield

43. CHESAPEAKE & DELAWARE CANAL RIDE

This ride is a treat for the senses — natural wonders are abundant and history is everywhere. You will travel through picturesque farm country as you cross from Maryland to Delaware to Maryland again. Most roads are lightly traveled and as you ride through two state wildlife management areas, you will see flocks of ducks, geese and swans.

The ride begins near Chesapeake City, Md. Formerly known as "The Village of Bohemia," Chesapeake City became a hub of activity in 1804 when construction began on the Chesapeake & Delaware Canal, which would connect the Delaware River and the Chesapeake Bay. The Canal reduced by nearly 300 miles the water route between Philadelphia and Baltimore. It is the sole major commercial navigation waterway in the United States built during the early 1800s that is still in use. Chesapeake City has many restored historic homes built in the distinctive style of the 19th century.

The ride also visits Odessa, Del. Known in the 18th century as Cantwell's Bridge, Odessa was once a busy commercial grain-shipping port. It is now known for its four historic houses, the Corbit-Sharp House, the Wilson-Warner House, the Brick Hotel Gallery (which houses the country's largest collection of Victorian furniture made in the style of J.H. Belter) and the Collins-Sharp House (a log and frame structure that is one of Delaware's oldest houses). An admission fee is charged for entrance to the houses.

START: Bohemia Manor High School on MD 213, one mile south of Chesapeake City in Cecil County, Md. From the Capital Beltway, take US 50 East, cross the Bay Bridge and continue north on US 301. Turn left on MD 313, at sign for Galena. This becomes MD 213 in Cecil County. The school is on the left, largely obscured by trees. Opposite is a Texaco station and Jack and Helen's Restaurant. Chesapeake City is 88 miles northeast of the Capital Beltway.

LENGTH: 48.1 miles.

TERRAIN: Level.

POINTS OF INTEREST: Historic town of Chesapeake City near start (410-885-2871); Chesapeake & Delaware Canal Museum at 1.9 miles; Port Penn Museum, Augustine State Wildlife Management Area at 24.3 miles; Silver Run State Wildlife Area at 27.3 miles; Town of Odessa at 32.0 miles (historic houses are owned and operated by Winterthur Museum which charges admission).

FOOD: Restaurants, markets near start in Chesapeake City; Berry's Market at 1.4 miles; market at 14.0 miles; grocery at 24.4 miles; many options in Odessa at 32.0 miles.

LODGING: Bed-and-breakfasts in Chesapeake City at start; camping at Lums Pond State Park (302-368-6989).

MAPS AND INFORMATION: Cecil County, Md. road map; New Castle County, Del. road map; Delaware and Maryland state highway maps; Cecil County Chamber of Commerce (800-232-4595).

MILES DIRECTIONS & COMMENTS

0.0 **Left** to go north on **MD 213**.

1.1 **Left** on **MD 286** just before bridge.

1.4 **Right** to stay on **MD 286**. Berry's Market.

1.9 **Right** to stay on **MD 286** at T. Chesapeake & Delaware Canal Museum and picnic area on left.

3.3 Cross Old Telegraph Road.

5.3 **Left** on **CHOPTANK ROAD** (DE 433) at T.

6.1 **Right** on **DE 896**. *Caution: traffic.*

6.8 **Left** on **ROAD 63**. Sign is before left-turn lane.

7.5 **Right** on **LOREWOOD GROVE ROAD** (Road 412), just past Summit United Methodist Church on left, in Summit Bridge. Summit railroad bridge (Conrail) visible to left from Road 412.

8.7 Cross railroad tracks.

9.5 **Right** on **ROAD 414**. Tree windbreaks, planted in lines to prevent wind erosion of soil, on both sides of road.

11.0 **Left** on **DE 896** at T. *Caution: busy road; use shoulder.*

14.0 **Straight** on **ROAD 420**, crossing US 13. *Caution: busy intersection.* Food market - open daily.

16.5 **Sharp left** on **ROAD 2** (unmarked) at stop sign (Road 2).

17.8 **Right** on **DUTCH NECK ROAD** (Road 417). Pass modern houses, then tidal marshes. Chesapeake & Delaware Canal on left.

21.5 **Right** on **SOUTH REEDY POINT ROAD** (unmarked).

22.3   **Right** on **DE 9** at stop sign. *Caution: 50 mph, two-lane road with no shoulder, but little traffic.*

24.3   **Left** on **MARKET STREET** at T to stay on DE 9. Port Penn Museum on right. Augustine State Wildlife Management Area on left.

24.4   **Right** on **CONGRESS STREET** at T to stay on DE 9. Grocery on left.

25.1   Augustine Beach and picnic area on left. Salem Nuclear Power Plant across Delaware River in New Jersey.

26.8   Road bends right.

27.3   **Left** to stay on **DE 9**, where Road 423 goes straight. Pass through Silver Run State Wildlife Area. Tall reed grasses abound. Cross bridge.

30.6   **Right** on **DE 424** at stop sign.

31.9   **Right** on **DE 299** (Main Street; unmarked) at T. Enter historic town of Odessa at 32.0 miles. Winterthur Museum on right at 2nd and Main Streets, provides directions to historic Corbit-Sharp House and Wilson-Warner House.

32.8   Cross US 13 and DE 1, north and south segments. **Straight on DE 299** for one-half block, then **right** on **CORBIT ALLEY** (unmarked).

32.9   **First left** on **MECHANIC STREET** (DE 429). Descend hill, cross bridge.

36.4   **Straight** on **ROAD 429**, crossing US 301 (DE 71, Road 39).

37.3   **Left** on **ROAD 435** (unmarked) at T. Pass horse farms.

39.1   **Right** on **ROAD 437** at T. More horse farms. Re-enter Maryland.

40.9   **Right** on **BUNKER HILL ROAD** at fork and stop sign. Cross creek.

41.8   **Bear left** on **ST. AUGUSTINE ROAD** at fork.

43.5   **Left** on **MD 310** (Mount Pleasant Road; unmarked) at T.

44.1   **Sharp right** on **MD 342.** Church on left.

46.9   **Left** on **GEORGE STREET** at stop sign.

47.0   **Right** to pass under Chesapeake City Bridge. **Straight** on **BASIL AVENUE.**

48.0   **Right** into High School at T.

48.1   **Arrive** at **BOHEMIA MANOR HIGH SCHOOL.**

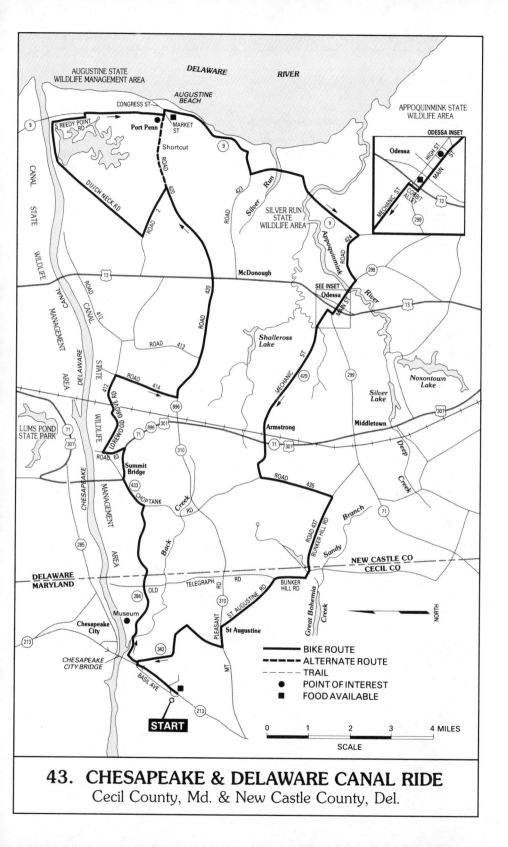

43. CHESAPEAKE & DELAWARE CANAL RIDE
Cecil County, Md. & New Castle County, Del.

44. ROCK HALL RAMBLE

Looping through two wildlife refuges, this tour is a must for the outdoor enthusiast and especially for bird-watching bicyclists. The Eastern Neck Island National Wildlife Refuge is home to herons and egrets year-round. You also can spot bald eagles, woodpeckers, osprey, quail and doves. Earthbound creatures include deer, rabbits and possum. Remington Farms, the other nature preserve, holds acres of ponds, marshes, fields and woodlands with over 20,000 waterfowl.

Between October and early April the region serves as a feeding and resting ground for migratory waterfowl, such as ducks, swans and geese, as they travel along the Eastern Shore flyway.

If you like this area, get a copy of Kent County Bicycle Tours, which includes rides from 11 to 81 miles in the county. Developed by the Baltimore Bicycling Club, it's available by calling 410-778-0416.

START: Waterfront at High and Water Streets in Chestertown, Md. From the Capital Beltway, take US 50 East, crossing the Bay Bridge to the Eastern Shore. Take US 301 North, and turn left on MD 213. Turn left on Cross Street in Chestertown, and left on Water Street to High Street. Chestertown is 73 miles northeast of the Capital Beltway.

LENGTH: 50.6 miles. **ALTERNATE ROUTE:** 33.1 miles (eliminates leg to Eastern Neck Island Wildlife Refuge).

TERRAIN: Level.

POINTS OF INTEREST: In Chestertown (410-778-0416) at start: Custom House, Buck-Bacchus Store Museum, Geddes Piper House, Bikeworks (410-778-6940), Washington College (1782), historic houses, Old St. Paul's Church (1692) with Tallulah Bankhead grave site (c.1778). Remington Farms at 10.4 miles; Eastern Neck Island National Wildlife Refuge at 22.7 miles, with trails and boat rentals; and Rock Hall at 15.0 and 32.6 miles, a maritime community with a rich history.

FOOD: Markets at start, 4.5, 13.0 and 32.6 miles. Snack bar and restaurant at start and 38.9 miles.

LODGING: In Chestertown, motels, bed-and-breakfasts and inns include the Imperial (410-778-5000), Mitchell House (410-778-6500) and the White Swan Tavern (410-778-2300). South of Chestertown, Duck Neck Campground (410-778-3070). In Rock Hall, Mariner's Motel (410-639-2291).

MAPS AND INFORMATION: Kent County, Md. road map. Kent County Chamber of Commerce, 400 High Street, Chestertown (410-778-0416).

MILES   DIRECTIONS & COMMENTS

0.0   Go **northwest** away from river on **HIGH STREET**. Custom House at corner.

0.2   **Left** on **CROSS STREET** (MD 289).

1.6   Pass Chester River Yacht and Country Club on right, and go **straight** on **QUAKER NECK ROAD.**

4.5   **Right** on **POMONA ROAD** at T. Grocery just before intersection. Becomes **LANGFORD ROAD.**

6.0   **Left** to stay on **LANGFORD ROAD.**

7.9   **Straight** on **RICAUDS BRANCH LANGFORD ROAD,** crossing Broad Neck Road (MD 446).

10.2 Pass Old St. Paul's Episcopal Church and Tallulah Bankhead grave site on right.

10.4 Remington Farms.

11.0 **Left** on **MD 20** (Rock Hall Fairlee Road) at T.

13.0 Store (closed Sundays). Fruit stand across from Edesville Community Park.

15.0 **Left** on **MAIN STREET** (MD 445) in Rock Hall.

15.1 **Right** on **SHARP STREET**. 0.5 miles to docks and restaurant. **Reverse direction**. Turn **right** on **MD 445** to continue south to Eastern Neck. ALTERNATE ROUTE begins here (see end of cues).

21.9 Cross Eastern Neck Island Bridge.

22.7 Observation Trail on right. Toilets.

23.2 **Left** on **BOGLES WHARF ROAD.**

24.0 **Arrive** at landing. Views of lower Chester River. **Reverse direction** on **BOGLES WHARF ROAD.**

24.8 **Right** on **MD 445**.

32.6 **Straight** on **MD 445** (Main Street), crossing MD 20 in Rock Hall. Groceries available.

38.0 **Left** on **MD 21** (Tolchester Beach Road).

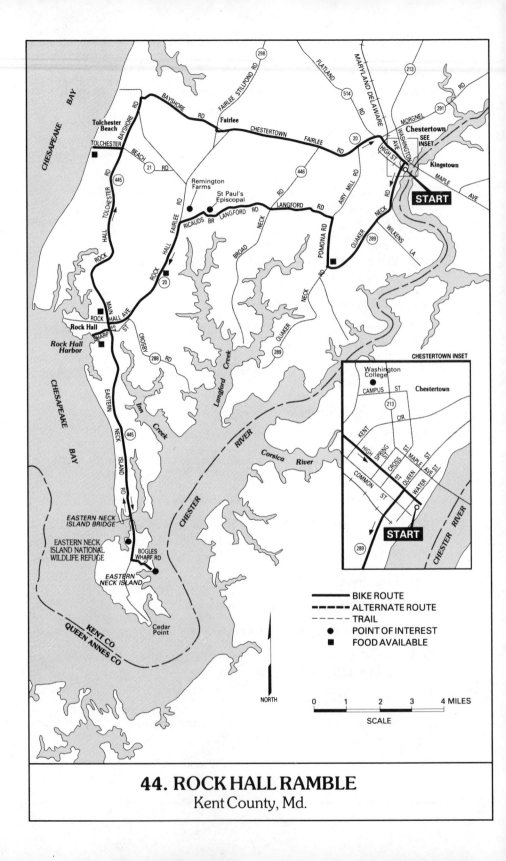

44. ROCK HALL RAMBLE
Kent County, Md.

38.9   Tolchester Beach on Chesapeake Bay. Snack bar, restrooms, marina. **Reverse direction.**

39.8   **Left** on **BAYSHORE ROAD.**

44.0   **Right** on **MD 298** (unmarked) at T in Fairlee. Go 100 yards, then **first left** on **PARSONS ROAD.**

44.3   **Left** on **OLD FAIRLEE ROAD** in Fairlee.

44.5   **Left** on **MD 20** (Chestertown Fairlee Road).

49.5   **Straight** on **HIGH STREET** in Chestertown. *Caution: grates in road.*

50.6   **Arrive** at **WATER STREET.**

ALTERNATE ROUTE

At approximately 15.1 miles, turn **left** instead of right on **MD 445** for shorter tour. Pick up cues at 32.6 miles.

Queen Anne County Courthouse in Centreville, the oldest courthouse in Maryland (1792).

45. CHESTERTOWN TO BETTERTON LOOP

Almost anywhere you ride in Kent County on Maryland's Eastern Shore, you'll find that George Washington was there first. From Chestertown to Betterton Beach, the region is bustling with activity and growth, yet steeped in history and lifestyles gone by.

Chestertown is the Kent County seat, founded in 1706, and its location on the Chester River made it an excellent port of entry during colonial times. It was a bustling place until cars and railroads replaced the river as the predominant means of transportation. Stop by the Chamber of Commerce office on Cross Street and pick up a walking tour guide with excellent descriptions of the town's historical sites. A plaque at Cannon and Queen Streets identifies historic Worrell's Tavern as a place where George Washington slept during one of the eight documented times that he passed through Kent County. Chestertown's Washington College was founded in 1782 with George Washington providing his name and financial support.

Twelve miles outside of town, you'll come to Turner's Creek. Here you can picnic on a waterfront bluff overlooking the creek, a tributary of the Sassafras River. Buy your picnic at the Kennedyville Market as there are no stores in Turner's Creek.

Further on, you'll come to Betterton, a small fishing village founded in the 1700s. Located across the Chesapeake Bay from Baltimore, Betterton (originally named Crew's Landing) was a frequent calling point for boats exchanging cargo for Kent County's agricultural exports. Excursion steamers filled with tourists came to the town in the late 1800s. There were hotels, restaurants, dance halls, bowling alleys, beer gardens and amusement arcades. Things began to decline in the 1930s when a large amusement pier burned. Gas rationing restricted tourist travel during the Second World War, and the Bay Bridge in the 1950s shuttled beach-bound travelers to ocean rather than bay resorts.

The town has brought back the beach, though, and it's a beautiful setting for a relaxing break. Bring your bathing suit: it's the only nettle-free beach on the Chesapeake.

START: Waterfront at High and Water Streets in Chestertown, Md. From the Capital Beltway, take US 50 East, crossing the Bay Bridge to the Eastern Shore. Take US 301 North, and turn left on MD 213. Turn left on Cross Street in Chestertown, and left on Water Street to High Street. Chestertown is 73 miles northeast of the Capital Beltway.

LENGTH: 36.6 miles.

TERRAIN: Level.

POINTS OF INTEREST: Many attractions in the historic town of Chestertown at start (farmers market on Saturdays 9 a.m. - noon); Turners Creek landing at 11.7 miles; the mouth of the Sassafras River at 20.9 miles; Betterton Beach at 21.4 miles.

FOOD: Restaurants, markets in Chestertown at start; Kennedyville Market at 8.2 miles; Still Pond Market at 17.8 miles.

LODGING: Hotels, motels, bed-and-breakfasts in Chestertown, and Duck Neck Campground nearby (see Tour 44 for details). For more information, call the Kent County Chamber of Commerce at 410-778-0416.

MAPS: Kent County, Md. road map.

MILES   DIRECTIONS & COMMENTS

0.0   From the High & Water Streets Park, proceed **north** on **HIGH STREET**.

0.2   **Right** on **SPRING AVENUE.**

0.4   **Left** on **MD 213.**

0.7   Campus of Washington College.

1.3   Cross MD 291.

6.1   Pass Urieville Lake (nice stop for a break).

8.2   Enter Kennedyville. Food available at Kennedyville Market, open Monday - Saturday 7 a.m. - 9 p.m.; Sunday 9 a.m. - 6 p.m.

8.7   **Left** on **KENNEDYVILLE ROAD.**

10.0 Stop sign. Cross MD 298.

11.3 Pass Bloomfield Road. Kennedyville Road becomes **TURNERS CREEK ROAD** (MD 448).

12.3 Kent County Farm Museum. Open the first and third Saturdays of each month, 10 a.m. - 4 p.m., from April to September.

12.7 **Arrive** at Turner's Creek Landing. Picnic facilities on the right, restrooms and phone on the left. **Reverse direction.**

14.1 **Right** on **BLOOMFIELD ROAD.**

16.6 **Right** on **MD 566** (use shoulder).

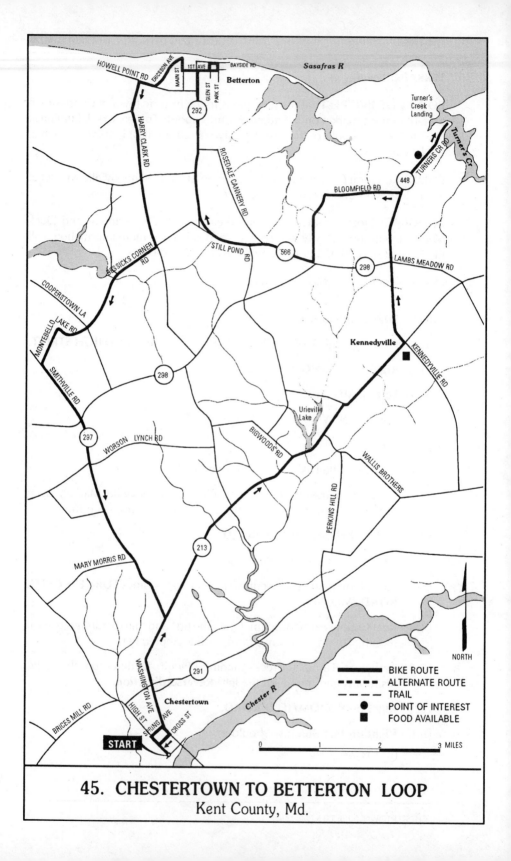

45. CHESTERTOWN TO BETTERTON LOOP
Kent County, Md.

17.8   Enter Village of Still Pond. Still Pond Market open Monday - Saturday 6 a.m. - 9 p.m.; Sunday 8 a.m. - 6 p.m. **Continue straight** through Still Pond on **MD 292**.

20.5   Betterton. Continue straight.

21.3   **Right** on **FIRST AVENUE**. Views of Chesapeake Bay.

21.6   **Left** on **PARK STREET**.

21.7   **Left** on **BAYSIDE**. To the right is the mouth of the Sassafras River. Across the Chesapeake Bay, you can see the U.S. Army Aberdeen Proving Ground.

21.8   **Left** on **GLEN STREET**.

21.9   **Right** on **FIRST AVENUE**.

22.1   **Right** on **MAIN STREET**.

22.2   **Left** on **ERICSSON AVENUE** at the Bay. Restroom facilities on the right as you turn. Also on the right is a picnic pavilion.

22.8   **Right** on **HOWELL POINT ROAD**.

23.6   **Left** on **CLARK ROAD**.

25.2   Stop sign. Coleman's Corner. **Straight** to remain on **CLARK ROAD**.

26.3   **Right** on **BESSICKS CORNER ROAD**.

27.2   **Bear left** across the bridge at the head of Still Pond Creek.

28.2   Cross Cooperstown Lane. **Straight** on **MONTEBELLO LAKE ROAD**. *Use caution in this area. Sharp curves and blind corners.*

29.4   **Left** on **SMITHVILLE ROAD** (MD 297).

30.6   Cross MD 298.

34.2   **Right** on **MD 213** (use shoulder).

35.3   Cross MD 291.

36.3   **Right** on **CROSS STREET** (MD 289).

36.4   **Left** on **HIGH STREET**.

36.6   **Arrive** at **HIGH & WATER STREET PARK**.

46. ST. MICHAELS - OXFORD LOOP

This delightful, popular ride loops through the quaint towns of Oxford and St. Michaels and takes you through some of the mid-Atlantic's best cycling and bird watching territory. Most of the Delmarva Peninsula is worth exploring by bicycle, so use this route as a base to discover the area on your own.

In St. Michaels you will enjoy parks, antique shops and the Chesapeake Bay Maritime Museum. The Oxford-Bellevue ferry, established in 1683, departs every 20 minutes from Oxford (it does not operate from mid-December to February). Oxford also has a nice park, beach and shops, including a unique hardware-gourmet-bicycle shop that should not be missed.

If you continue past St. Michaels, you reach the fishing community of Tilghman Island. Seemingly cut off from the 20th century, Tilghman Island is the home of the Chesapeake Skipjack Fleet.

START: YMCA on MD 333 (Peach Blossom Road) in Easton, Md. From the Capital Beltway, take US 50 East, cross the Bay Bridge and continue to Easton on Maryland's Eastern Shore. In Easton, bear right on MD 322, and continue 3.5 miles. Turn left on MD 333. The YMCA is on the right. Do not turn on MD 33! Easton is 74 miles east of the Capital Beltway.

LENGTH: 28.9 miles.

TERRAIN: Level, with signed, on-road bike lanes most of the way.

POINTS OF INTEREST: Easton at start, with waterfowl festival in early November, and Historic District (410-822-0773) with museum and tours; Oxford at 8.7 miles, with beach, park, shops and Oxford-Bellevue ferry, America's oldest privately owned ferry, established 1683 (410-745-9023; $1.50 for bicycles); St. Michaels at 17.0 miles, with parks, shops, the famous Crab Claw Restaurant (410-745-2900) and the Chesapeake Bay Maritime Museum (410-745-2916) at 17.4 miles. Fishing and sailing areas along the route.

FOOD: Markets at start, 5.3, 9.2, 12.8 and 17.0 miles. Restaurants at start, 9.6 and 17.0 miles.

LODGING: In Easton, four motels, a tourist home and the Tidewater Inn (410-822-1300). In Royal Oak, Pasadena Conference Center (410-745-5053), with bountiful home-cooked food and special care for bicyclists. In Oxford, Robert Morris Inn (410-226-5111). In St. Michaels, inns include Tarr House (410-745-3419), Kemp House (410-745-2243), Two Swan Inn (410-745-2929) and Wades Point Inn (410-745-2500).

MAPS AND INFORMATION: Talbot County, Md. road map; Maryland state highway map. St. Michaels Visitor Center (800-736-6965).

MILES DIRECTIONS & COMMENTS

0.0   **Left** out of YMCA parking lot, to go southwest on **MD 333** (Peach Blossom Road). Bike lane on road.

5.3   Trappe Station Country Store.

8.7   Enter Oxford. Bike shop (open 9 a.m. - 5 p.m. every day but Wednesday), delicatessen (open 7 a.m. - 8 p.m. daily) and restaurant on right at 9.2 miles, and park and beach on left. Stay on **MD 333** (Morris Street) to Oxford-Bellevue ferry across Tred Avon River.

9.8   In Bellevue, take **BELLEVUE ROAD** toward Royal Oak.

12.8 **Left** on **MD 329** at T. General store (open 6 a.m. daily), antiques shop. Pass Pasadena Conference Center on right.

The harbor at St. Michaels.

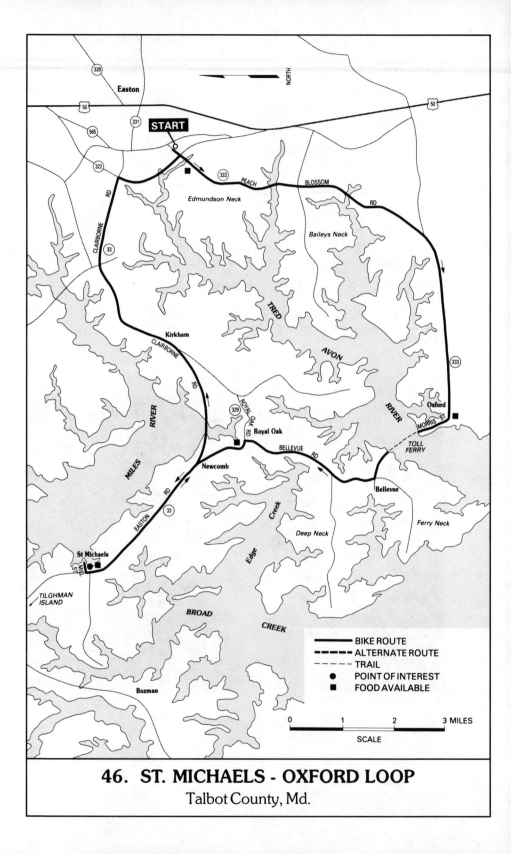

46. ST. MICHAELS - OXFORD LOOP
Talbot County, Md.

13.8 **Left** on **MD 33** at T. *Caution: fast-moving traffic.* Signed on-road bike lane.

17.0 Enter St. Michaels. Inns, restaurants, antique shops.

17.3 **Right** on **MILL STREET**. Pass historic homes.

17.4 **Arrive** at maritime museum, gift shops and the famous Crab Claw restaurant near end of street. **Reverse direction.**

17.5 **Left** on **MD 33.** (A right turn here will take you to Tilghman Island, at the end of MD 33 in 13 miles.)

27.4 **Right** on **MD 322** in Easton.

28.8 **Left** on **MD 333** (Peach Blossom Road). *Caution: traffic.*

28.9 **Right** into **YMCA PARKING LOT.**

47. RIDE TO WYE OAK

This ride is in memory of former WABA Board Member Doug Farnsworth, who loved to ride to the Wye Oak.

Before you start this ride, take some time to explore historic Easton, Md., once known as Talbot Court House and the "East Capital" of Maryland. It had the Eastern Shore's first bank, first newspaper, first federal offices and first brick hotel. English settlers first made their homes in Easton in the 1650s. Visit the Talbot County Historical Society Museum for a walking tour and don't miss No Corner for the Devil, a hexagon-shaped church, built in 1881 by four different denominations and designed so that "the devil would have no corner in which to sit and hatch evil."

You won't leave civilization behind on this ride, but you will get an excellent sense for what the country was like in colonial times. Historic landmarks pop up around every corner, from the Little Red Schoolhouse to Wye Oak State Park. The terrain is suitable for beginners and entertaining for everyone.

The Wye Oak, for which the ride is named, is 450 years old. The largest white oak tree in the United States, its trunk is 374 inches in circumference!

START: YMCA on MD 333 (Peach Blossom Road) in Easton, Md. From the Capital Beltway, take US 50 East, cross the Bay Bridge and continue to Easton on Maryland's Eastern Shore. In Easton, bear right on MD 322, and continue 3.5 miles. Turn left on MD 333. The YMCA is on the right. Do not turn on MD 33! Easton is 74 miles east of the Capital Beltway.

LENGTH: 41.4 miles.

TERRAIN: Level.

POINTS OF INTEREST: Easton at start with many historical sites including the Third Haven Friends Meeting, the oldest religious building still in use in the U.S., and the Historical Society of Talbot County at 25 South Washington Street (410-822-0773). Little Red Schoolhouse (built in 1868) at 16.2 miles. Wye Oak State Park at 24.4 miles. (The Wye Oak is the largest white oak tree in America and it stands in the smallest state park in America.)

FOOD: Restaurants and markets in Easton at start; Rainbow Farms Fruit Stand at 17.5 miles (open summer and fall); Wye Mills Store at 24.3 miles.

LODGING: Bed-and-breakfasts and hotels in Easton. Call the Talbot County Tourism Bureau at 410-822-4606.

MAPS: Talbot County, Md. road map; Maryland state highway map.

The Wye Oak.

MILES   DIRECTIONS & COMMENTS

0.0   **Right** on **PEACH BLOSSOM ROAD** out of the YMCA parking lot.

0.6   **Left** on **HARRISON STREET.**

0.9   **Left** on **DOVER STREET** at traffic light.

1.0   **Right** on **SOUTH WASHINGTON STREET.**

1.1   **Left** on **BAY STREET.**

1.6   **Straight** across traffic light at MD 322. Becomes **MD 33** — use bike trail.

3.4   **Right** on **MD 370.**

4.2   Bridge over the Miles River.

5.0   **Left** on **MILES RIVER ROAD.**

5.3   **Right** on **MORENGO ROAD.**

7.2   **Bear right** at the Y intersection on **GREGORY ROAD.**

8.4   **Left** on **TUNIS MILL ROAD** at stop sign.

8.9   Road bends left. **Turn right** (not to Leeds Landing).

9.0   Wooden bridge over Leeds Creek.

9.4   **Right** on **COOPERVILLE ROAD.**

10.6 **Right** on **unmarked road** at T.

11.3 **Bear left** on **BRUFFS ISLAND ROAD** at the intersection with Gregory Road.

11.7 Continue **straight** on **TODDS CORNER ROAD.**

12.8 **Right** on **LITTLE PARK ROAD** (sign says "To Route 50").

14.8 **Left** on **FOREST LANDING ROAD.**

16.1 **Left** on **MD 662** at stop sign.

16.2 Little Red Schoolhouse.

17.5 Stop sign. Straight across US 50. *Use extreme caution when crossing this busy highway.* (Rainbow Farms fruit stand open summer and fall. Drinks, restrooms, fruit.)

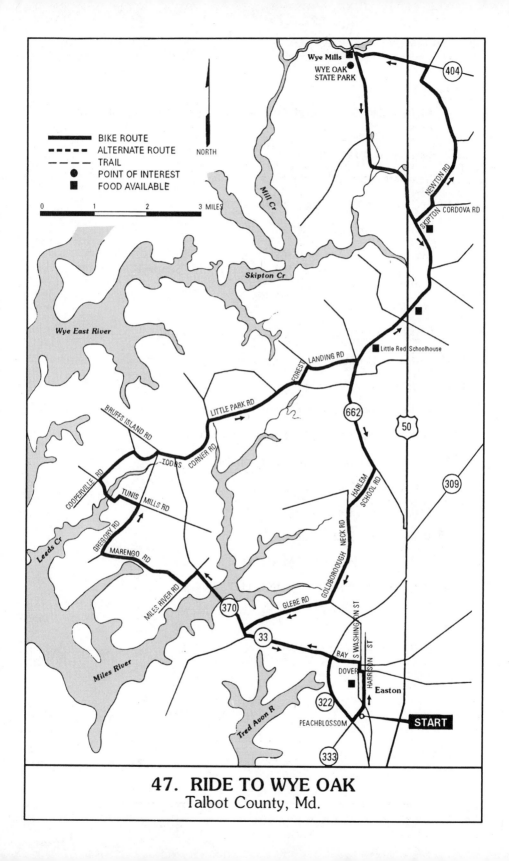

47. RIDE TO WYE OAK
Talbot County, Md.

19.3   Skipton Store. General store open 7:30 a.m. - 7 p.m. Closed Sundays.

19.4   **Right** on **SKIPTON CORDOVA ROAD** (just before the Sealtest plant on the left).

20.0   **Left** on **NEWTOWN ROAD.**

21.2   **Bear left** at the fork in the road.

22.9   **Left** on **MD 404** at stop sign (*use caution*).

23.3   **Straight** across US 50 at traffic light.

24.3   **Left** on **MD 622** at stop sign. Wye Mills Store open 7:30 a.m. - 6 p.m. Monday - Saturday; 8 a.m. - 5 p.m. Sundays (sandwiches, drinks).

24.4   Wye Oak State Park.

27.3   **Right** on **US 50** at stop sign. *Caution: use shoulder.*

27.8   **Left** on **MD 622.** *Caution: traffic.*

30.0   Cross US 50 at stop sign.

33.5   **Right** on **HARLEM SCHOOL ROAD.**

34.4   **Left** on **GOLDSBOROUGH NECK ROAD** at stop sign.

36.3   **Right** on **GLEBE ROAD** at stop sign.

38.1   **Left** on **MD 370** at stop sign.

38.2   **Left** on **MD 33** at stop sign.

39.9   **Right** on **MD 322** at traffic light.

41.3   **Left** on **PEACH BLOSSOM ROAD** at traffic light.

41.4   **Right** into the **YMCA PARKING LOT.**

48. BRIDGES OF DORCHESTER COUNTY

This ride over quiet country roads on Maryland's Eastern Shore passes farms and wetlands in southern Dorchester County. The route crosses six bridges.

Dorchester County has more marshland than any county on the Chesapeake Bay. As a result, it abounds in wildlife, particularly bird life.

The ride is one of 10 rides, ranging in length from 12 miles to 86 miles, developed for Wingate Manor, a bed-and-breakfast in Wingate, Md., that caters to cyclists. Wingate Manor can be reached at 410-397-8717.

Thanks to Dan Schaller who developed this ride and allowed us to use it.

START: Corner of Greenbrier Road and Bucktown Road in Dorchester County, Md. From the Capital Beltway, take US 50 East across the Bay Bridge to Cambridge. After crossing the Choptank River, continue on US 50 about two miles to a right turn on Bucktown Road. Continue south on Bucktown Road for 7.5 miles to the intersection of Bucktown and Greenbrier Roads. Park on the shoulder of Bucktown Road far enough off the road to be safe from traffic traveling south around the curve.

LENGTH: 31.3 miles.

TERRAIN: Level.

POINTS OF INTEREST: Cambridge, off the route at 5.9 miles, is a picturesque town with High Street Historical District, beachfront and fishing pier, and a bike shop at Race and Elm Streets. The Cambridge Visitor Center (410-228-3234) has more information.

FOOD: Food is scarce on this route, so bring lunch. Many choices in Cambridge, off the route at 5.9 miles.

LODGING: Wingate Manor, a bed-and-breakfast that caters to cyclists, is located about 15 miles south of the starting point in Wingate (410-397-8717). In Cambridge, Quality Inn (410-228-6900) at US 50 and Crusader Road. The Cambridge Visitor Center (410-228-1000) has more information.

MAPS AND INFORMATION: Dorchester County, Md. road map. Cambridge Visitor Center (410-228-1000).

MILES   DIRECTIONS & COMMENTS

   0.0   Go **north** on **BUCKTOWN ROAD.**

   1.1   Pass Decoursey Road on right.

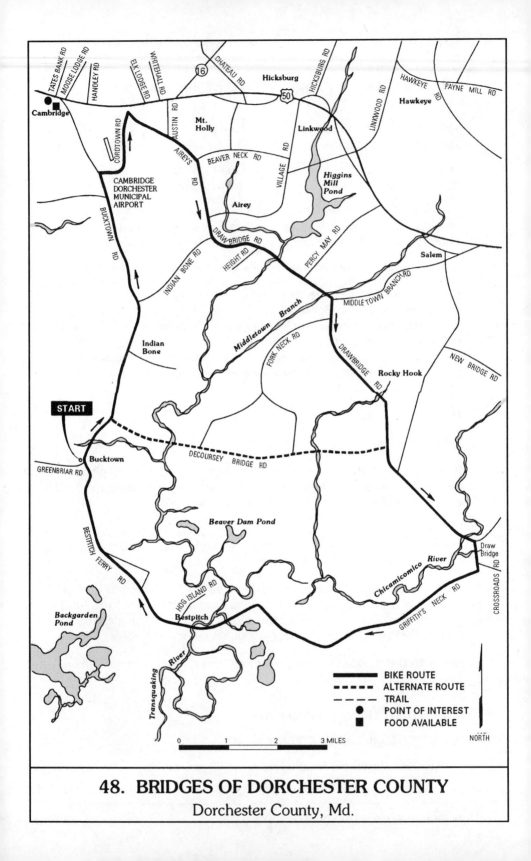

48. BRIDGES OF DORCHESTER COUNTY
Dorchester County, Md.

5.9   **Right** on **CORDTOWN ROAD.** (To reach Cambridge, continue straight on Bucktown Road rather than turning right.)

7.5   **Right** on **AIREYS ROAD.**

10.6 **Bear left** on **DRAWBRIDGE ROAD.**

12.1 Cross bridge over Higgins Mill Pond.

14.6 Cross bridge over Middletown Branch.

14.7 **Bear right** at intersection with unpaved Middletown Branch Road to remain on **DRAWBRIDGE ROAD.**

16.9 Cross bridge over Chickamicomico River.

20.2 Cross second bridge over Chickamicomico River.

20.4 **Bear right** at Steels Neck Road to remain on **DRAWBRIDGE ROAD.**

20.6 Cross third bridge over Chickamicomico River.

20.8 **Bear right** on **GRIFFITH'S NECK ROAD.**

25.9 Griffith's Neck Road becomes **BESTPITCH FERRY ROAD**.

27.1 Cross bridge over Transquaking River.

31.3 **Arrive** at **INTERSECTION** of Bucktown Road and Greenbrier Road.

The bridge over the Transquaking River.

49. BLACKWATER WILDLIFE REFUGE RIDE

Starting from the town of Cambridge, Md., this ride swings through Blackwater National Wildlife Refuge. Famous for its flocks of geese and ducks, the refuge also is home for bald eagles, osprey, muskrat, deer and many other animals. A visit in fall, winter or early spring avoids the hot summer months when flying insects can be a nuisance.

Historic High Street in Cambridge features old Victorian homes. For extended touring, try MD 343, which travels west of Cambridge and has a bike lane. So does MD 16, which takes you to Taylors Island. Or you may want to take MD 335 west from mile 24.9 to Hooper Island, with its fishing villages and splendid views of the Chesapeake Bay. Many bicycling opportunities exist in this area — stay off US 50 and you won't go wrong!

START: South Dorchester High School at the corner of Church Creek Road (MD 16) and Maple Dam Road (Race Street) in Cambridge, Md. From the Capital Beltway, take US 50 East across the Bay Bridge to Cambridge. Turn right in town on Washington Street, then left on Race Street. School is just past Church Creek Road on the right. Cambridge is 90 miles southeast of the Capital Beltway.

LENGTH: 42.1 miles.

TERRAIN: Level.

POINTS OF INTEREST: Picturesque town of Cambridge (410-228-3234) at start, with High Street, museums, Meredith House (1760), beachfront areas and a bike shop at Race and Elm Streets; Blackwater National Wildlife Refuge Visitor Center at 33.2 miles, with 20-minute movie and exhibits, observation tower and two-mile Wildlife Drive (15 mph speed limit).

FOOD: Markets at 23.0 miles. Best to bring lunch with you.

LODGING: In Cambridge, Quality Inn (410-228-6900) at US 50 and Crusader Road.

MAPS AND INFORMATION: Dorchester County, Md. road map. Cambridge Visitor Center (410-228-1000). The Dorchester County Visitor Guide also includes information on three bike loops (from six to 41 miles) through Blackwater Refuge (800-522-TOUR).

MILES   DIRECTIONS & COMMENTS

0.0   **Right** out of parking lot, to go south on **MAPLE DAM ROAD.** Pass through Blackwater National Wildlife Refuge.

18.1   **Right** on **MD 336** (Crapo Road) at T.

23.0   **Straight** on **MD 335** (Hooper Island Road) at Golden Hill Road. Marina with food available (snacks and vending machines). Open 7:30 a.m. - 5 p.m. weekdays, 7:30 a.m. - 4 p.m. Saturdays, closed Sundays.

24.9   **Right** on **SMITHVILLE ROAD.** (Go straight here instead for Hooper Island, 4.6 miles. Food available at the Waterman's Cafe and at Old Salty's.)

25.4   **Right** on **HIP ROOF ROAD.**

28.3   **Left** on **MD 335** (Church Creek Road) at T.

29.0   MD 335 becomes **GOLDEN HILL ROAD.**

32.2   **Right** on **KEY WALLACE DRIVE.**

33.2   **Right** into **BLACKWATER NATIONAL WILDLIFE REFUGE.** Visitors Center, with water. Closed weekends, Memorial Day to Labor Day. Exit Refuge, **right** on **KEY WALLACE DRIVE.**

34.5   **Left** on **EGYPT ROAD.** (Go straight here instead for beginning of Wildlife Drive in 0.2 miles, with Observation Tower.)

41.7   **Right** on **MD 16** (Church Creek Road).

42.1   **Right** into **SOUTH DORCHESTER HIGH SCHOOL.**

Abandoned church in Blackwater Refuge.

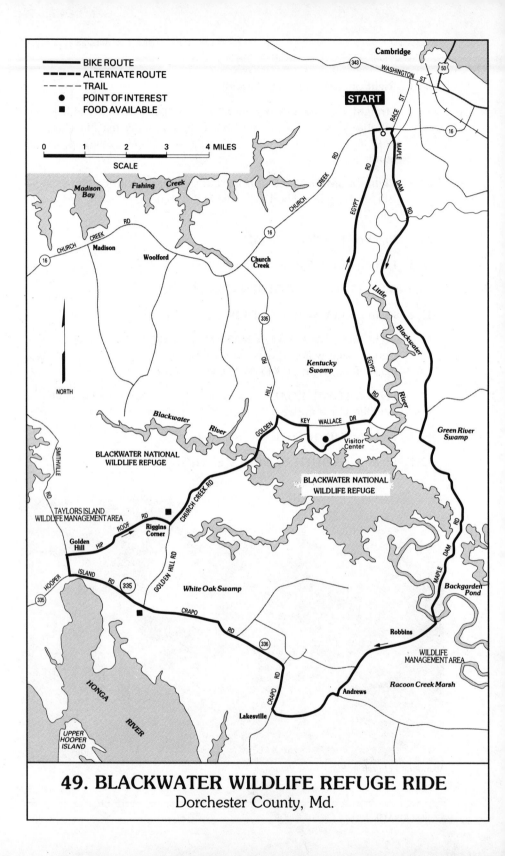

49. BLACKWATER WILDLIFE REFUGE RIDE
Dorchester County, Md.

50. PRINCESS ANNE/SNOW HILL

There is virtually no traffic on this easy and interesting ride through Somerset and Worcester Counties, on Maryland's Eastern Shore. The roads are tree-lined and surrounded by farms and cornfields. The town of Princess Anne was founded officially in 1773; a Presbyterian meeting house was located there as early as 1685. Located at the headwaters of the Manokin River, Princess Anne is a charming place, offering a great variety of historical Eastern Shore architecture.

Snow Hill became the county seat of Worcester County in 1742. Though a disastrous fire in 1983 destroyed Snow Hill's original downtown area, many other historic homes and public buildings remain, including several pre-Revolutionary War structures. The Julia Purnell Museum on Market Street includes a remarkable exhibit of area artifacts, memorabilia, costumes, tools and machinery dating from pre-historic ages through the early 20th century.

This ride can be combined with Tour 51 for a weekend packed with great cycling and fascinating sights. In addition, Worcester County publishes View Trail 100, a guide to 100 miles of bike routes in the county (800-852-0335).

START: Manokin River Park on Somerset Avenue (MD 675) in Princess Anne, Md., just north of Broad Street. From the Capital Beltway, take US 50 East over the Bay Bridge and continue on US 50 to Salisbury. Turn south on US 13 and continue 11 miles to the Princess Anne turn-off (MD 362, on the left). Make a right on Somerset Avenue. The park is 0.5 miles on the right. Princess Anne is 130 miles southeast of the Capital Beltway.

LENGTH: 47.0 miles.

TERRAIN: Level.

POINTS OF INTEREST: Historic sites in Princess Anne at start; Snow Hill at 19.6 miles; Julia Purnell Museum at 19.8 miles, with exhibits of area artifacts, memorabilia, costumes, tools and machinery.

FOOD: Restaurants in Princess Anne; Snow Hill Inn and Tastee Freez in Snow Hill at 19.6 miles; Buck's Store at 38.4 miles.

LODGING: Choices in Princess Anne include Washington Hotel (410-651-2525) and bed-and-breakfasts on Prince William Street. Snow Hill Inn in Snow Hill (410-632-2102). Princess Anne Campground on US 13 (410-651-1520).

MAPS AND INFORMATION: Somerset and Worcester Counties, Md. road maps; Princess Anne Chamber of Commerce (800-521-9189); Snow Hill Area Chamber of Commerce (410-632-0809).

MILES DIRECTIONS & COMMENTS

0.0 With Manokin River Park at your back, **turn right**.

0.3 **Left** on **MD 388** (East Antioch Avenue). *Caution: railroad tracks just after turn.* Becomes **WEST POST OFFICE ROAD**.

6.7 **Left** on **PETE'S HILL ROAD** at stop sign (sign says "Snow Hill").

7.0 **Right** on **MEADOWBRIDGE ROAD** at stop sign. Old Friendship United Methodist Church.

8.6 **Straight** on **OLD FURNACE ROAD** at stop sign.

15.5 **Right** on **MD 12** at stop sign. *Caution: busy road; use shoulder.* Enter Snow Hill.

19.2 Tastee Freez.

19.6 Snow Hill. **Right** on **MD 394** (Market Street) at traffic light.

19.8 Julia Purnell Crafts Museum. Open Monday - Friday 10 a.m. - 4 p.m.; Saturday and Sunday 1 p.m. - 4 p.m. Admission charged. **Reverse direction.**

20.0 **Left** on **MD 12** (Washington Street) at traffic light.

Whitehaven Ferry, near Princess Anne.

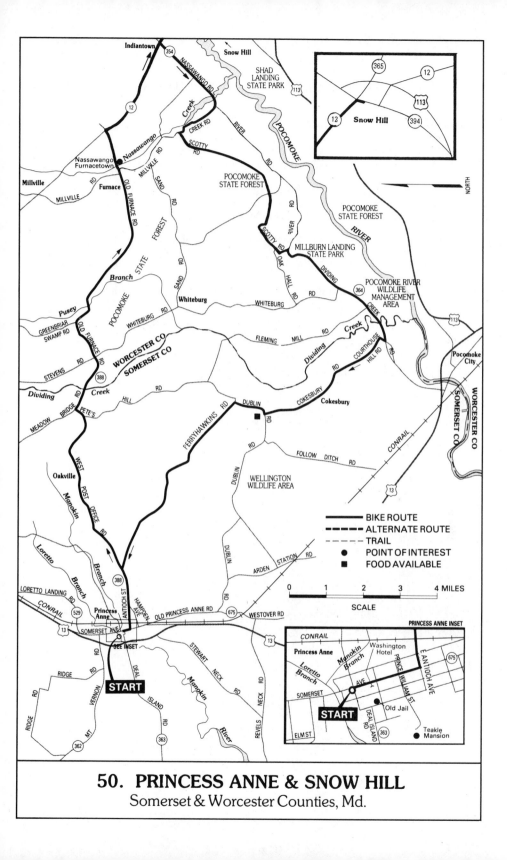

50. PRINCESS ANNE & SNOW HILL
Somerset & Worcester Counties, Md.

21.2   **Left** on **NASSAWANGO ROAD** at blinking light, toward Milburn Landing.

23.6   **Right** on **CREEK ROAD** just after bridge.

25.2   **Left** on **SCOTTY ROAD.** (This is the first paved road on the left, and it is unmarked at a sharp angle.)

30.4   **Right** on **unmarked road** at yield sign.

31.0   Road bends right and becomes **MD 364**.

34.2   **Right** on **COURTHOUSE HILL ROAD** (to Cokesbury).

36.7   Becomes **COKESBURY ROAD.**

38.4   **Right** on **unmarked road** at stop sign. T. Buck's Store makes sandwiches and is open Monday - Thursday 8 a.m. - 10 p.m.; Friday and Saturday 8 a.m. - midnight; Sunday noon - 5 p.m.

39.3   **Left** on **PERRYHAWKIN ROAD.**

45.0   **Left** on **MD 388** at stop sign.

46.7   **Right** on **MD 675** at stop sign.

47.0   **Arrive** at **MANOKIN RIVER PARK** (on left).

51. PRINCESS ANNE TO DEAL ISLAND

Another very flat ride, this combines well with the other Princess Anne ride (Tour 50) for an excellent weekend of cycling. There is very little traffic.

Deal Island was once known as Devil's Island, a place noted for its pirates, including the famous Edward Teach, better known as Blackbeard. Piracy began on the bay around 1610 and flourished until the mid-1700s. Blackbeard blockaded the mouth of the Bay in 1717, demanding payment from all who passed, and plundered the seas from Maine to Florida. Legend is that some of his treasure is still hidden on Deal Island. The "v" was dropped from Devil Island after Methodism was spread throughout the Chesapeake Bay Islands. A charismatic man on the other end of the spectrum, Joshua Thomas, became known as "parson of the islands."

Deal Island is the home of men and women who make their living from the Chesapeake Bay — this is watermen's country. You can see local watermen unload their day's catch, observe a soft crab shedding operation, see how an oyster hatchery works, watch crab pickers' fingers fly, and sample soft crab sandwiches or crab cakes at the local deli. Soft crabs from Deal Island and Wenona are shipped all over the world.

Each church you pass has its own cemetery with concrete slabs covering the graves. Because of the high water table on the island, graves cannot be dug to the standard depth.

START: Manokin River Park on Somerset Avenue (Route 675) in Princess Anne, Md., just north of Broad Street. From the Capital Beltway, take US 50 East over the Bay Bridge to Salisbury. Turn south on US 13 and continue 11 miles to the Princess Anne turn-off (MD 362, on the left). From MD 362, turn right on Somerset Avenue. The park is 0.5 miles on the right. Princess Anne is 130 miles southeast of the Capital Beltway.

LENGTH: 38.7 miles.

TERRAIN: Level.

POINTS OF INTEREST: Princess Anne at start with historical sites; Deal Island Wildlife Management Area at 9.8 miles; Deal Island at 15.5 miles; Wenona at 17.6 miles.

FOOD: Many choices in Princess Anne; White's Market at 8.2 miles; Chance's Market at 14.0 miles; Island Seafood Deli at 18.6 miles.

LODGING: Choices in Princess Anne include Washington Hotel (410-651-2525) and bed-and-breakfasts on Prince William Street. Princess Anne Campground on US 13 (410-651-1520).

MAPS AND INFORMATION: Somerset and Wicomico Counties, Md. road maps. Princess Anne Visitors Center (410-651-2968). Somerset County Tourism (800-521-9189). The Wicomico County Tourism Office has ride maps and publishes *Cycling on Maryland's Southern Eastern Shore* (800-332-8687).

MILES   DIRECTIONS & COMMENTS

0.0   With the park at your back, **right** on **SOMERSET AVENUE.**

0.1   **Right** on **PRINCE WILLIAM STREET.**

0.3   **Right** on **MANSION STREET.**

0.4   **Left** on **MD 363** (Deal Island Road) at stop sign.

0.5   **Straight** across US 13 at traffic light.

8.2   White's Market. Open daily 6 a.m. - 10 p.m.

9.8   Enter Deal Island Wildlife Management Area.

10.8   Dames Quarter Creek.

11.3   Dames Quarter.

14.0   Chance One-Stop Store, open daily 6 a.m. - 11 p.m.

14.8   Deal Island Bridge. Arrive at Deal Island.

15.5   Bank Building (opened in 1912 and closed after the crash of 1929).

16.0   Josh Thomas Chapel. Site of many camp meetings. Family tragedies are recorded in the historic cemetery.

17.6   Wenona. Small harbor.

18.6   Fishing pier. Road ends. Island Seafood Deli with portable toilets. Closed Mondays April - September, closed Mondays and Tuesdays October - March. **Reverse direction**, following **MD 363.**

29.6   **Left** on **FITZGERALD ROAD.**

32.2   **Left** on **unmarked road** at T.

33.0   **Right** on **BLACK ROAD.**

35.2   **Right** on **MD 362** at stop sign.

38.0   **Straight** across US 13 at traffic light.

38.2   **Right** on **SOMERSET AVENUE** at stop sign.

38.7   **Arrive** at **MANOKIN RIVER PARK** on the right.

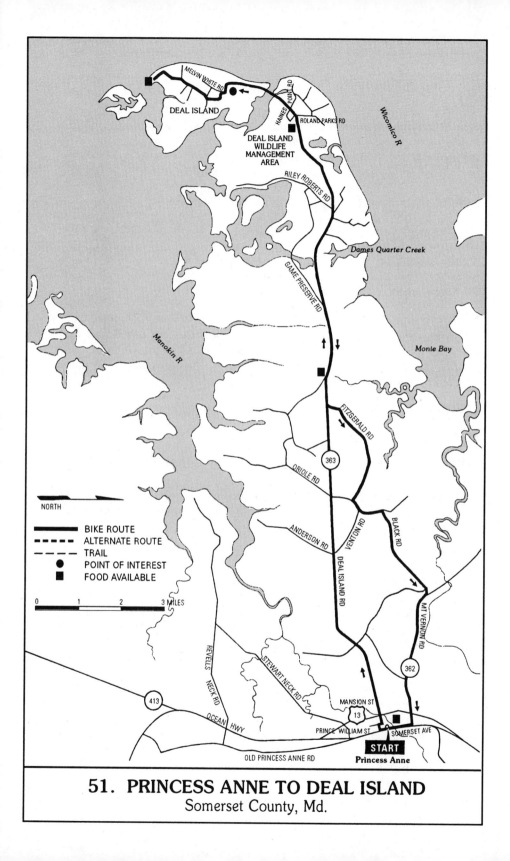

51. PRINCESS ANNE TO DEAL ISLAND
Somerset County, Md.

52. GHOST TOWN GAMBOL

Passing through wildlife refuges, open countryside and desolate swamps, this tour explores the picturesque Delmarva Peninsula. A good place to stay is the fishing/resort town of Chincoteague, Va., famous for its wild ponies (Misty of Chincoteague), fresh seafood and abundant birdlife. (A National Wildlife Refuge on Assateague Island, accessible from Chincoteague by bike trail, offers a nice, short side trip.)

The tour visits Greenbackville, a charming town of retired farmers, and the ghost town of Franklin City, established in 1876 as the terminus of the Eastern Shore Railroad. For 40 years, Chincoteague Bay oysters were shipped north by rail to urban "foreigners." Franklin City's prosperity abruptly ended with the construction of the Chincoteague causeway.

START: Bank at the intersection of VA 679 and VA 175 near Chincoteague, Va. From the Capital Beltway, take US 50 East across the Bay Bridge and continue to Salisbury, Md. Turn on US 13 South into Virginia, and then turn left on VA 175. Continue five miles to VA 679. Chincoteague is 168 miles southeast of the Capital Beltway.

LENGTH: 39.9 miles.

TERRAIN: Level.

POINTS OF INTEREST: Chincoteague National Wildlife Refuge (757-336-6161), approximately 12 miles from start, and adjacent Assateague Island National Seashore (both with famous wild ponies) connected by bicycle trail to the town of Chincoteague; Greenbackville at 10.4 miles; Franklin City at 11.5 miles; Vaughn Wildlife Management Area at 14.8 miles.

FOOD: Markets near start, 19.4 miles and 34.5 miles.

LODGING: In Chincoteague, numerous motels, campgrounds and four bed-and-breakfasts: Year of the Horse Inn, 3583 Main Street (757-336-3221); Channel Bass Inn, 6228 Church Street (757-336-6148); Island Manor House, 4160 Main Street (800-852-1505); Miss Molly's Inn, 4141 Main Street (757-336-6686). For general bed-and-breakfast information, call 757-627-1983.

MAPS AND INFORMATION: Accomack County, Va. and Worcester County, Md. road maps; *ADC's Chesapeake Bay Regional Map*. For information on Chincoteague and Assateague, call 757-336-6161. For information on a 100-mile Worcester County loop, contact: Worcester County Extension Service, P.O. Box 219, Snow Hill, MD 21863-0219 (410-632-1972). Worcester County Tourism (410-632-3617).

MILES   DIRECTIONS & COMMENTS

0.0   **North** on **VA 679.**

5.5   **Bear right** to stay on **VA 679.**

8.5   **Right** on **STATE LINE ROAD.**

10.4   Enter Greenbackville.

10.7   **Left** on **BAYFRONT STREET** to remain on VA 679.

11.1   **Right** at T (unmarked street).

11.5   **Arrive** at **FRANKLIN CITY,** end of road. **Reverse direction.**

11.9   **Left** on **VA 679** (Bayfront Street).

12.0   **Right** on **VA 3002** (Stockton Avenue). Pass Post Office on right.

12.8   **Bear right** on **GREENBACKVILLE ROAD** at fork. Enter Maryland.

14.8   **Right** on **GEORGE ISLAND LANDING ROAD** (MD 366). Vaughn Wildlife Management Area on left.

Franklin City, ghost town.

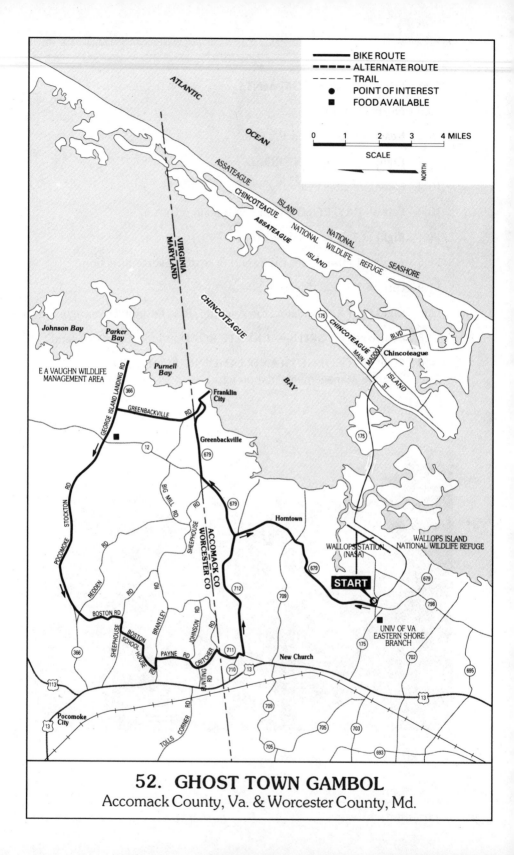

52. GHOST TOWN GAMBOL
Accomack County, Va. & Worcester County, Md.

16.6 Arrive at **PARKER BAY**, end of road. **Reverse direction.**

18.4 **Straight** on **MD 366** at intersection with Greenbackville Road.

18.7 Enter Stockton.

19.4 **Straight** on **POCOMOKE STOCKTON ROAD**, crossing MD 12. Grocery on left.

24.4 **Left** on **BOSTON ROAD**.

25.7 **Right** on **SHEEPHOUSE ROAD** (may be unmarked).

26.1 **Left** on **BUCK HARBOR ROAD** (Boston Schoolhouse Road).

27.6 **Left** on **BRANTLEY ROAD** (may be unmarked).

27.8 **Right** on **PAYNE ROAD**.

29.1 **Bear left** on **CRITCHER ROAD** (may be unmarked).

29.9 **Right** on **MD 711** (may be unmarked). Re-enter Virginia.

30.4 **Left** on **VA 710** at T.

30.8 **Left** on **VA 712**.

34.5 **Right** on **VA 679.** Grocery store.

39.9 **Arrive** at starting point (**VA 175**).

53. BETHANY BEACH BACKROADS

Bethany Beach is an excellent spot to leave your car and the crowds behind to explore the rural nature of the Delaware shore. Within a mile of the busy ocean beach, you can be on lightly-traveled, flat country roads that weave among cornfields, pine trees and chicken farms.

The ride takes you to Assawoman Wildlife Area, created from nine farms lost during the Great Depression and bought by the U.S. Forest Service. The area is managed primarily for migrating and wintering waterfowl, white-tailed deer and bobwhite quail. A dirt road within the park takes you past sunflower fields, small wooded ponds, marshes and an observation tower.

Further on, you'll encounter Holt's Landing State Park. The Holt family maintained a farm with a bayshore boat landing on this site until 1957, when the property was sold to the State Highway Department. On a clear day, you'll have a grand view of Indian River Bay, from the Indian River Inlet bridge on the east to the river coves on the west.

START: Bethany Bandstand, at the intersection of DE 26 (Garfield Parkway) and the Atlantic Ocean. From the Capital Beltway, take US 50 East, cross the Bay Bridge, and follow the signs to the ocean beaches. Bethany Beach is located between Rehoboth Beach, Del. and Ocean City, Md., 130 miles from the Capital Beltway.

LENGTH: 27.5 miles.

TERRAIN: Level.

POINTS OF INTEREST: Atlantic Ocean at Bethany Beach at start and finish, with many recreational opportunities; Bethany Beach Museum, with maritime memorabilia, open noon to 3 p.m. Sundays (10 a.m. to 4 p.m. June through August), 1 p.m. to 3 p.m. Tuesdays - Thursdays; Assawoman Wildlife Area at 6.6 miles; Blackwater Presbyterian Church at 14.0 miles; Holt's Landing State Park at 16.7 miles.

FOOD: Restaurants and markets in Bethany Beach at start; Millville Service Center at 20.8 miles.

LODGING: Contact the Chamber of Commerce of the Bethany-Fenwick Area at 302-539-2100.

MAPS: Sussex County, Del. road map; Delaware state road map.

MILES DIRECTIONS & COMMENTS

0.0 Start at Bethany Bandstand. With the ocean at your back, go **straight** west on **DE 26** (Garfield Parkway).

0.2 Cross DE 1 at traffic light. *Caution: traffic.*

0.3 **Left** on **KENT AVENUE** (DE 361) at first intersection after DE 1. Pass South Coastal Regional Library.

1.7 **Left** on **DE 363** (unmarked) after bridge across Assawoman Canal. Note sign for Camp Barnes.

5.0 **Left** on **DE 364.** Sign says Camp Barnes/Assawoman.

6.1 **Bear left** to continue on **DE 364**. Another sign saying Camp Barnes/Assawoman.

6.4 Stop for interpretive brochure on Assawoman. Continue on DE 364 to Assawoman.

6.6 **Right** into the park, following dirt paths through the park to points of interest. **Reverse direction** to return to **DE 364. Left** on **DE 364.**

7.2 **Left** on **DE 364A** (unmarked) at stop sign.

7.5 **Bear right** to remain on **DE 364A.** Cross small bridge.

8.5 **Right** on **DE 381** at T.

9.4 **Right** on **DE 384** at T.

10.3 **Left** on **DE 84** at Y intersection.

10.6 **Left** on **DE 365**.

12.1 Cross DE 52 at stop sign.

12.7 **Bear left** on **DE 374.** This is a soft left at the intersection of DE 365, DE 373 and DE 374.

14.0 Cross DE 54 and continue **straight** on **DE 346.** Blackwater Presbyterian Church is just to the left on DE 54, and is worth a look.

14.7 Cross DE 26 at stop sign.

16.7 **Left** to continue on **DE 346** to Holt's Landing State Park.

17.7 **Arrive** at **PARK.** No entrance fee for bikes. Nice place for picnics, clamming and views of Indian River Bay. No drinking water. Restrooms closed in winter. After visiting the park, **return to DE 346.**

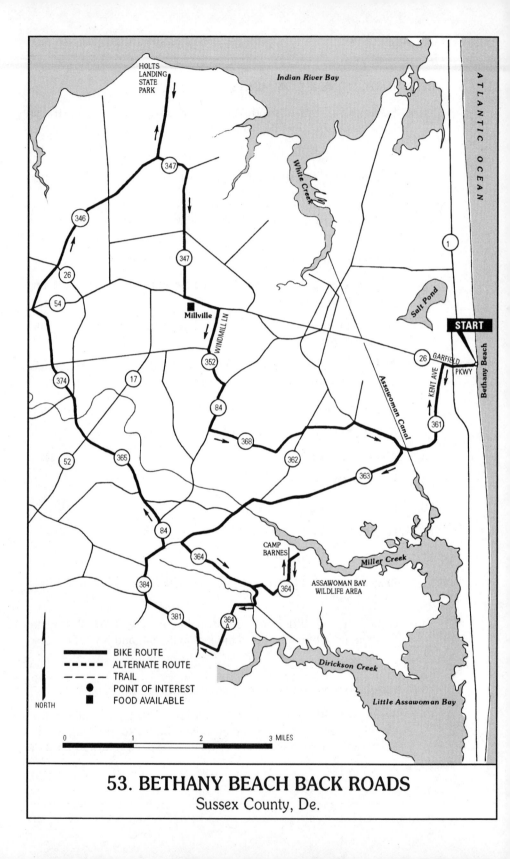

HOLTS
LANDING
STATE
PARK

Indian River Bay

White Creek

ATLANTIC OCEAN

347

346

26

54

347

Salt Pond

Millville

WINDMILL LN

26

GARFIELD

START

Bethany Beach

374

17

352

84

KENT AVE

PKWY

Assawoman Canal

361

52

365

368

362

363

84

364

CAMP
BARNES

Miller Creek

384

364

ASSAWOMAN BAY
WILDLIFE AREA

381

364
A

Dirickson Creek

NORTH

—— BIKE ROUTE
----- ALTERNATE ROUTE
– – TRAIL
● POINT OF INTEREST
■ FOOD AVAILABLE

Little Assawoman Bay

0   1   2   3 MILES

53. BETHANY BEACH BACK ROADS
Sussex County, De.

18.8 **Left** on **DE 347** at stop sign.

20.8 **Left** on **DE 26.** Millville Service Center. Open daily. Drinks, sandwiches. *Caution: traffic and no shoulder.*

21.2 **Right** on **DE 352** (Windmill Lane).

22.3 **Right** on **DE 84** at T.

23.0 **Left** on **DE 368.**

24.3 **Jog left**, then take an **immediate right** to stay on **DE 368.** Cross DE 362.

25.0 **Right** on **DE 361** (unmarked) at T. Continue on DE 361, crossing Assawoman Canal at 25.8 miles.

27.1 **Right** on **DE 26** at T.

27.2 Cross DE 1. *Caution: traffic.*

27.5 **Arrive** at **BETHANY BEACH BANDSTAND.**

Assawoman Canal.

54. AMISH COUNTRY RIDE

St. Mary's County, Md., about an hour's drive southeast of the Capital Beltway, features quiet roads and beautiful, gently rolling countryside. The county, which occupies the southern end of a peninsula between the Patuxent and Potomac Rivers, includes the oldest settled areas in Maryland.

This ride over scenic (and for the most part lightly-traveled) highways passes through Amish communities and past farms where tobacco has been grown for generations. The length and relatively low level of traffic make this a good ride for the beginning cyclist.

This ride was developed by Patuxent Area Cycling Enthusiasts (PACE), P.O. Box 1318, Solomons, MD 20688-1318. Thanks to Tom Roberts of PACE for sharing it with us.

START: Park and Ride lot across from the Halfway House Restaurant at the MD 5/235 split in St. Mary's County, Md. From the Capital Beltway, take MD 5 south, merge with US 301 and continue south to Waldorf, where MD 5 and US 301 split. Follow MD 5 another 16 miles south to Mechanicsville. Starting point is two miles south of Mechanicsville and 33 miles south of the Capital Beltway.

LENGTH: 26.4 miles.

TERRAIN: Generally level, with some rolling hills and one long, steep hill.

POINTS OF INTEREST: Amish farms near Mechanicsville and Thompson Corner. Amish Market on MD 5 in Mechanicsville, open Wednesdays and Saturdays, with auction on Saturdays at 2 p.m.

FOOD: Markets at 13.2 miles and 17.3 miles. Restaurants near start.

LODGING: Charlotte's Hall Motel in Mechanicsville, 301-884-3172. For other choices, call the St. Mary's Chamber of Commerce, 301-884-5555.

MAPS AND INFORMATION: St. Mary's County, Md. road map. *Southern Maryland Bicycle Map* from the St. Mary's Chamber of Commerce, 301-884-5555.

MILES   DIRECTIONS & COMMENTS

0.0   **Right** to go north on **OLD ROUTE 5** (Old Village Road).

0.5   Pass Baptist Church Road on left.

1.9   Mechanicsville.

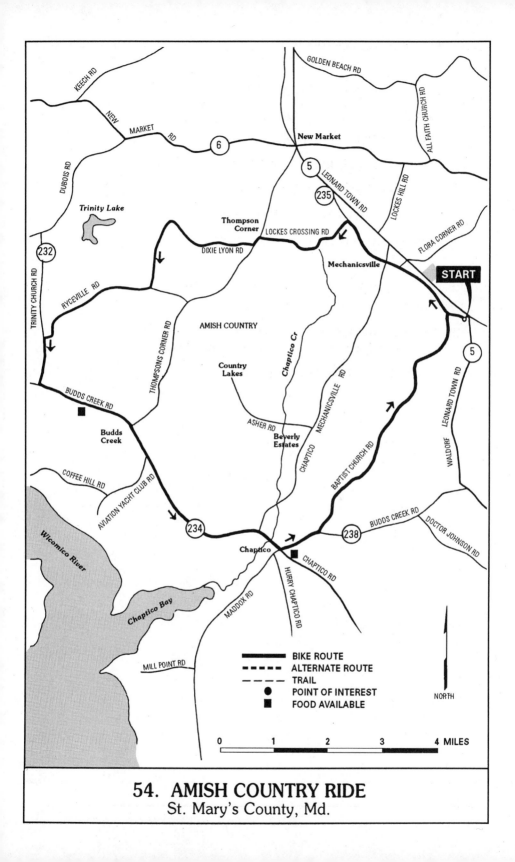

54. AMISH COUNTRY RIDE
St. Mary's County, Md.

3.5 **Left** on **LOCKE'S CROSSING ROAD.**

5.6 **Left** on **THOMPSON'S CORNER ROAD** (unmarked) at T.

5.9 **Right** on **DIXIE LYON ROAD.**

7.1 Becomes **NORTH RYCEVILLE ROAD.**

9.3 **Right** on **RYCEVILLE ROAD.**

11.5 **Left** on **TRINITY CHURCH ROAD** at T.

12.6 **Left** on **MD 234** at T, a major road with fast traffic, but wide shoulders.

13.2 Start of biggest hill on route.

13.7 Stone's Store. Drinks, snacks.

19.9 **Left** on **CHAPTICO-HELEN ROAD** (MD 238 North). At intersection, Chaptico Market/Deli and Citgo gas station with restrooms.

21.8 **Left** on **BAPTIST CHURCH ROAD.**

25.9 **Right** on **OLD VILLAGE ROAD** (Old Route 5).

26.4 **Left** into **PARK AND RIDE LOT.**

Tobacco fields.

55. ST. MARY'S CITY TO POINT LOOKOUT

Historic St. Mary's City, the fourth permanent settlement in British North America and first capital of Maryland, is the starting point for this flat ride over quiet roads to Point Lookout State Park.

A national historic landmark, St. Mary's City boasts a replica of the Dove (one of the two ships that brought Maryland's first settlers), reconstructed 17th century buildings, a tobacco plantation and an active archaeological dig. The ride proceeds to Point Lookout State Park, where the Potomac River meets the Chesapeake Bay. The park features camping, swimming, fishing, picnic areas and a Civil War Museum.

Thanks to Tom Roberts and the Patuxent Area Cycling Enthusiasts, who developed this ride and allowed us to use it.

START: Parking lot on Mattapany Road, 0.5 miles east of MD 5, near St. Mary's City, Md. From the Capital Beltway, take MD 5 south, merge with US 301 and continue south to Waldorf, where MD 5 and US 301 split. Follow MD 5 another 18 miles south to MD 235. Continue south on MD 235 approximately 24 miles to Mattapany Road. Go right (west) toward St. Mary's College. Parking lot is 1.9 miles west of MD 235 on the right hand side. Starting point is 59 miles south of the Capital Beltway.

LENGTH: 27.3 miles.

TERRAIN: Level roads, generally with shoulders and very little traffic.

POINTS OF INTEREST: Historic St. Mary's City, near start, open daily from Memorial Day to Labor Day, and weekends from March to November (800-762-1634) — admission $6.50; St. Michael's Manor and Vineyard at 9.7 miles; Point Lookout State Park and lighthouse at 10.4 miles (301-872-5688).

FOOD: Markets at 7.7, 19.9 and 25.4 miles. Restaurants at Historic St. Mary's City near start and at 6.3 miles.

LODGING: Camping at Point Lookout State Park (301-872-5688). For other choices, call the St. Mary's Chamber of Commerce, 301-884-5555.

MAPS: St. Mary's County, Md. road map. *Southern Maryland Bicycle Map* from the St. Mary's Chamber of Commerce, 301-884-5555.

MILES   DIRECTIONS & COMMENTS

0.0   Exit parking lot **right** on **MATTAPANY ROAD.**

0.5   **Left** on **MD 5.** (Historic St. Mary's City straight ahead.)

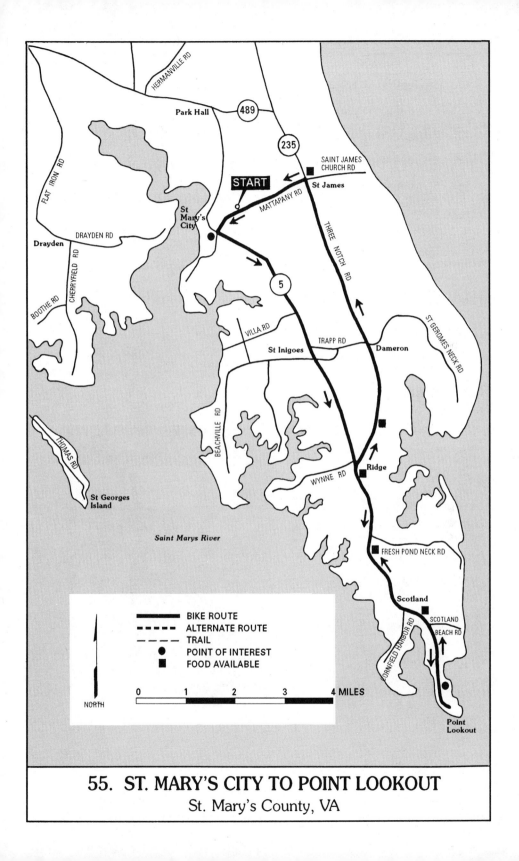

HERMANVILLE RD

Park Hall (489)

(235)

SAINT JAMES
CHURCH RD

START

St James

FLAT IRON RD

DRAYDEN RD

St Mary's City

MATTAPANY RD

Drayden

CHERRYFIELD RD

THREE NOTCH RD

BOOTHE RD

5

VILLA RD

TRAPP RD

St Inigoes

Dameron

ST GEROMES NECK RD

BEACHVILLE RD

THOMAS RD

St Georges Island

WYNNE RD

Ridge

Saint Marys River

FRESH POND NECK RD

Scotland

SCOTLAND BEACH RD

CORNFIELD HARBOR RD

BIKE ROUTE
ALTERNATE ROUTE
TRAIL
● POINT OF INTEREST
■ FOOD AVAILABLE

0   1   2   3   4 MILES

NORTH

Point Lookout

55. ST. MARY'S CITY TO POINT LOOKOUT
St. Mary's County, VA

6.0   **Straight** on **MD 5** at intersection with MD 235.

6.3   Old Ridge Restaurant.

7.7   Buzzy's Country Store.

9.0   Produce stand.

9.7   St. Michael's Manor and Vineyard.

10.4 Enter Point Lookout State Park (entrance fee of $2 per person on summer weekends and holidays).

12.7 Road ends at lighthouse. **Reverse direction.**

16.0 Rick's Marina (coffee, ice cream).

19.4 **Bear right** on **MD 235.**

19.9 Ann and Tony's Sandwiches.

25.4 **Left** on **MATTAPANY ROAD.** St. James Store, deli and gas station at intersection.

27.3 **Right** into **PARKING LOT**.

Roadside scene.

56. NORTHERN CENTRAL RAILROAD TRAIL

An exemplary rails-to-trails conversion, the Northern Central Railroad Trail offers you a bicycle tour with few cross streets in a pastoral off-road setting. Canopied by trees and following the meandering Gunpowder Falls, the trail promises a relaxing excursion into the Baltimore County countryside, separated from the traffic of nearby roads.

The Northern Central Railroad once transported both passengers and freight between Baltimore and York, Pa. One of the oldest rail lines in the country, it ran for 134 years, beginning in 1838. Abraham Lincoln traveled on the Northern Central on his way to deliver the Gettysburg Address in 1863, changing trains in Hanover Junction. After his assassination, his body was transported via the same rails on its long journey home to Illinois.

In 1972, the railroad ceased operations, when Hurricane Agnes dealt a last destructive blow to its financially unstable owner. Later, the Maryland Department of Natural Resources converted the corridor into a trail which opened to the public in 1984. Today, hundreds of people enjoy the trail daily by bicycle, foot and horse. The trail also provides boating and fishing access to the popular Gunpowder River and Loch Raven watershed.

In 1996, the trail was extended from the Maryland line 10.7 miles north to Hanover Junction, Pa. This section, called the York County Heritage Rail Trail, features railroad tracks and a parallel trail. Cyclists can bike both ways or one way and return on the Liberty Limited Dinner Train. The train (with bike racks) stops at five locations along the route. For information, call 800-94TRAIN.

The trail will eventually extend another 11 miles to York, Pa. The new section will pass through Howard Tunnel, the oldest railroad tunnel in the United States. Completion is tentatively scheduled for fall 1998.

START: Parking lot on Ashland Road in Ashland, Md. From the Baltimore Beltway, take I-83 North and exit on Shawan Road (exit 20). Go east 1.0 miles and turn right on York Road. After 0.3 miles, turn left on Ashland Road and continue 0.5 miles to parking lot (do not bear left on Paper Mill Road). Ashland is approximately 40 miles northeast of the Capital Beltway. **ALTERNATE START:** Trailside parking lot in Phoenix at mile 2.0 avoids a dangerous highway crossing between Ashland and Phoenix. To reach Phoenix, turn left at the intersection of Shawan Road and York Road; after 1.3 miles, turn right on Phoenix Road and proceed 1.6 miles to trailside parking.

LENGTH: 29.0 miles.

TERRAIN: Level, smooth crushed stone surface in Maryland; DER sand (a hard surface, suitable for all kinds of bicycles) in Pennsylvania.

POINTS OF INTEREST: Villages of Corbett and Monkton at 6.2 and 6.8 miles, both on the National Register of Historic Places. Restored Monkton train station at 6.8 miles, now a visitor center with concessions, bike rental, first-aid station and restrooms. Historic railroad structures and numerous pre-Civil War buildings along the trail, as well as scenic rock outcrops, spring wildflowers, Gunpowder Falls, Beetree Run and other natural beauties. In Pennsylvania, town of New Freedom offers rail sidings with restored locomotives and rail cars of bygone eras.

FOOD: Markets at 6.8, 20.2 and 22.3 miles. Drinks and snack foods at 12.3 miles. Restaurants at 20.2 and 25.2 miles.

LODGING: Glen Rock Mill Inn in Glen Rock, Pa. (717-235-5918).

MAPS AND INFORMATION: *Baltimore Area Bike Map;* Baltimore County, Md. road map; York County, Pa. road map. Free trail maps available at Whistlestop Bike Shop in New Freedom, Pa. (717-227-0737).

Along the Northern Central Railroad Trail.

MILES   DIRECTIONS & COMMENTS

0.0   Go **north** out of parking lot on **TRAIL.**

2.0   Community of Phoenix. Parking, portable toilet and phone on left.

3.5   Town of Sparks. Parking, portable toilet, water and phone.

6.2   Victorian village of Corbett at crossroads.

6.8   Town of Monkton. General store and bike shop on right. Restored train station with parking on left. Restroom, telephone, food.

8.8   Community of Bluemont.

10.2   Community of White Hall. Parking lot, portable toilet and telephones.

12.3   Town of Parkton. Hunting store on left, with drinks and snacks.

15.1   Bentley Springs. Portable toilet.

15.7   Community of Beetree. Look for interesting 19th century brick viaducts at intervals along Beetree Run.

17.7   Community of Freeland. Parking at trail intersection with Freeland Road. Restrooms.

19.0   Maryland-Pennsylvania State Line (the Mason-Dixon Line). Farms and rural countryside. Look for hex signs on barns. *Watch road crossings carefully. Cars are not required to stop for the trail.*

20.2   Town of New Freedom. New Freedom is the "continental divide" of the trail: a barely perceptible grade down in both directions makes for an easy ride. Convenience stores and restaurants. Terminus of the York County Heritage Railroad offers rail sidings with restored locomotives and railroad cars. Whistlestop Bike Shop has free maps of the trail and is a good source of information. Parking at New Freedom station.

22.3   Town of Railroad. General store. Parking.

25.5   Town of Glen Rock. The largest town on the trail, Glen Rock offers restaurants, Glen Rock Mill Inn, Momma's Pizza (trailside, with picnic tables for customers) and a trailside chiropractor!

29.7   **Arrive** in **HANOVER JUNCTION**. Trail will be extended 11 miles further to York, Pa. Tentative completion in fall 1998.

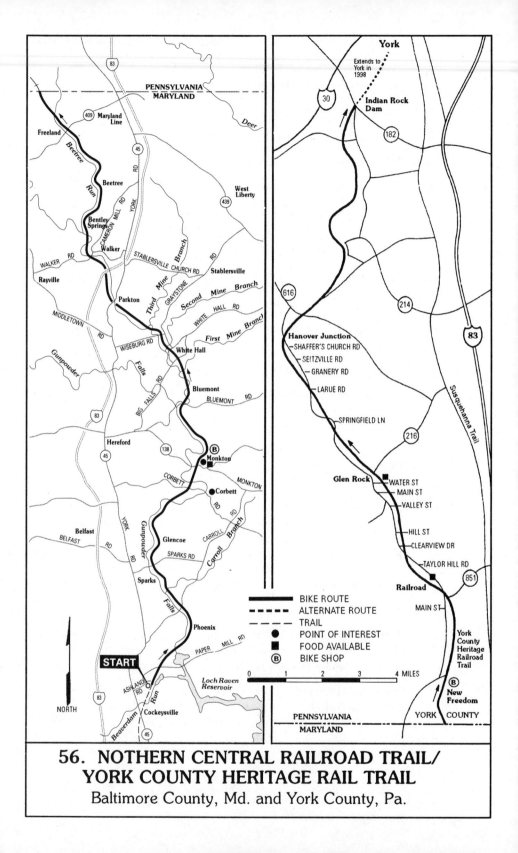

56. NOTHERN CENTRAL RAILROAD TRAIL/ YORK COUNTY HERITAGE RAIL TRAIL
Baltimore County, Md. and York County, Pa.

57. LOCH RAVEN LOOP

The rolling hills, quaint farmland and scenic woodland watershed of Loch Raven Reservoir set the tone of this tour. Created for novice bicyclists, the tour offers two routes for exploring the area over low-traffic roads.

START: Loch Raven Dam parking lot on Loch Raven Road in Baltimore County, Md. From the Baltimore Beltway, take Cromwell Bridge Road (exit 29) east for two miles and turn left on Loch Raven Drive, just after Sanders Corners. Continue one mile to parking lot. The starting point is approximately 40 miles northeast of the Capital Beltway.

LENGTH: 31.4 miles. **ALTERNATE ROUTE:** 19.4 miles.

TERRAIN: Rolling hills.

POINTS OF INTEREST: Loch Raven Reservoir at 3.4 miles. Gunpowder Falls State Park at 18.2 miles.

FOOD: Markets at 9.0, 14.8, 18.2, 22.1 and 30.4 miles. Restaurant (Peerce Plantation) with outside dining and sandwiches at 3.4 miles.

MAPS: *Baltimore Area Bike Map;* Baltimore and Harford Counties, Md. road maps.

MILES   DIRECTIONS & COMMENTS

0.0   **Left** out of parking lot to go northwest on **LOCH RAVEN ROAD** (closed to motor vehicles on weekends!).

3.4   **Right** on **DULANEY VALLEY ROAD.** Pass Peerce Plantation (food).

5.6   **Left** on **MANOR ROAD** at T.

6.0   Straight on Manor Road. ALTERNATE ROUTE begins here (see end of cues).

7.6   **Left** on **SWEET AIR ROAD.**

9.0   Cross Jarretsville Pike at traffic light. Food.

9.7   **Right** on **OLD YORK ROAD.** Scenic rest stop.

12.2   **Merge left** to remain on **OLD YORK ROAD.**

12.5   **Right** on **HESS ROAD.**

14.8   Cross Jarretsville Pike (MD 146). Country stores, food.

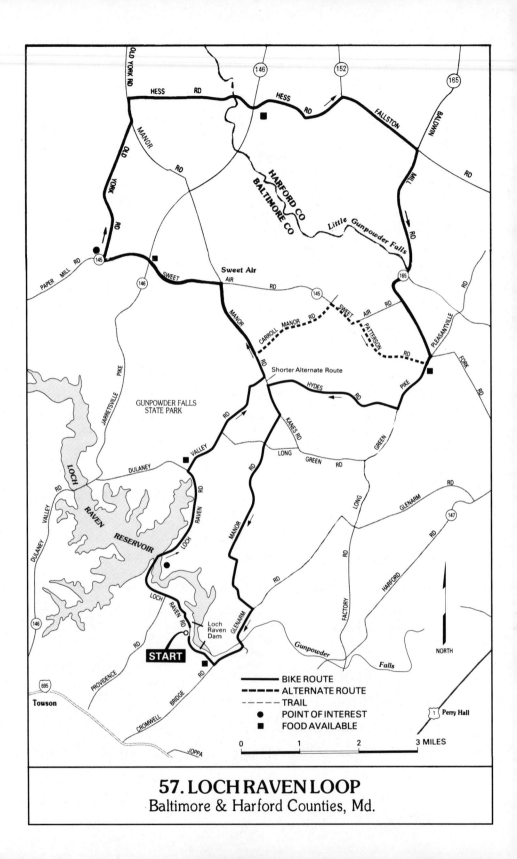

57. LOCH RAVEN LOOP
Baltimore & Harford Counties, Md.

16.6   **Right** on **FALLSTON ROAD** (MD 152).

18.2   **Right** on **BALDWIN MILL ROAD.** Water, convenience store. Pass Gunpowder Falls State Park on left.

22.1   **Right** on **LONG GREEN PIKE.** Deli and Italian gourmet market.

23.2   **Right** on **HYDES ROAD.**

25.5   **Left** on **MANOR ROAD** at T.

26.2   **Bear right** to stay on **MANOR ROAD.**

29.2   **Right** on **GLENARM ROAD.**

29.9   **Right** on **CROMWELL BRIDGE ROAD.**

30.4   **Right** on **LOCH RAVEN ROAD.** Food.

31.4   **Arrive** at **PARKING LOT.**

ALTERNATE ROUTE

At 6.0 miles, turn **right** on **CARROLL MANOR ROAD.** Continue 1.6 miles to T. Go **right** on **SWEET AIR ROAD** (MD 145) at T. After 0.6 miles, **bear right** on **PATTERSON ROAD.** After 1.5 miles, go **right** on **LONG GREEN PIKE** at T, and pick up cues at mile 22.1 for a 19.4-mile ride.

Don't forget your sugar cubes.

58. PRETTYBOY RESERVOIR CHALLENGE

If you are in search of hills, this tour is for you. The route follows old, narrow roads bordered by cornfields as it circles the Prettyboy Reservoir.

The reservoir, which supplies water to Baltimore County, has many inlets that pop up along the loop. Steep declines lead to panoramas of sparkling water and tall pines. It's a case of, "Water, water everywhere, and not a drop to drink," however. Bring your own food and drink, because there's no sustenance along the way. The reservoir dam, shortly before the 10-mile ride back to the start, offers a good lunch stopping point.

START: Commuter parking lot on corner of Shawan Road and Western Run Road in Baltimore County, Md. From the Baltimore Beltway, take I-83 North for six miles and exit west on Shawan Road (exit 20). Continue west for 0.6 miles. Lot is on the left, just west of I-83. The starting point is 51 miles north of the Capital Beltway. **ALTERNATE START:** At 9.4 miles. Park at intersection of Yeoho Road and Mount Carmel Road, and just loop the reservoir.

LENGTH: 36.8 miles. **ALTERNATE START:** 18.0 miles.

TERRAIN: Steep hills. Several short stretches of bad surfaces.

POINTS OF INTEREST: Scott's Quarry on Tanyard Road (at 4.4 and 32.4 miles); marble from this quarry was used to build Baltimore's Washington Monument — the first monument to George Washington. Prettyboy Reservoir with Prettyboy Dam at 23.2 miles. Scenic countryside along the route.

FOOD: Markets near start, but none along the route. No water or food available at the reservoir. Friendly Farm Restaurant (410-239-7400) on Foreston Road, after mile 10.0, open noon to 8 p.m. seven days a week, serves American style dinners, family style.

MAPS: *Baltimore Area Bike Map;* Baltimore County, Md. road map.

MILES   DIRECTIONS & COMMENTS

0.0   **Right** on **WESTERN RUN ROAD.**

3.7   **Right** on **TANYARD ROAD.** Very narrow old road.

5.1   **Left** on **BELFAST ROAD** at T.

5.3   **Right** on **YEOHO ROAD.**

9.4   **Left** on **MOUNT CARMEL ROAD** at T (unmarked). ALTERNATE START begins here.

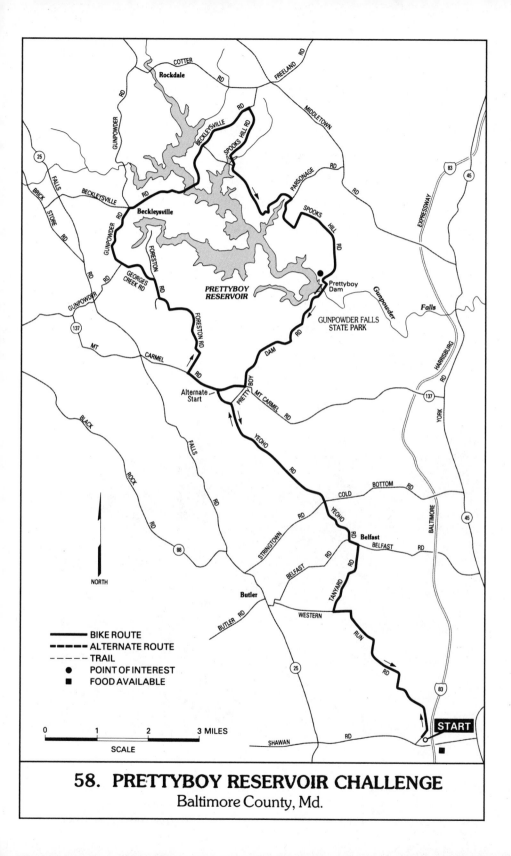

58. PRETTYBOY RESERVOIR CHALLENGE
Baltimore County, Md.

10.0   **Right** on **FORESTON ROAD.** Friendly Farm Restaurant right after turn.

12.4   **Bear left** on **GEORGES CREEK ROAD.**

13.2   **Right** on **GUNPOWDER ROAD** at T.

14.8   **Right** on **BECKLEYSVILLE ROAD.**

18.2   **Right** on **SPOOKS HILL ROAD.** Steep downhill to reservoir.

23.2   **Right** on **PRETTYBOY DAM ROAD** at T.

24.4   Cross Prettyboy Dam.

26.9   **Right** on **MOUNT CARMEL ROAD.** Church straight ahead.

27.5   **Left** on **YEOHO ROAD.**

31.5   **Left** on **BELFAST ROAD** at T.

31.7   **Right** on **TANYARD ROAD.**

33.1   **Left** on **WESTERN RUN ROAD** at T.

36.8   **Arrive** at **COMMUTER PARKING LOT.**

Prettyboy Reservoir.

59. WESTMINSTER TO GETTYSBURG LOOP

On the way out, this ride runs from historic Westminster through Uniontown and Taneytown, old towns dating from the early settling of western Maryland. The ride follows the route that Union General George Meade took to Gettysburg to reinforce outnumbered Federal forces on July 1, 1863.

In Gettysburg, you have the opportunity to see monuments, battlefields and historic buildings of the famous battle, the turning point of the Civil War. Here, over a four-day period, more men fell than in any other battle fought in North America before or since.

The return trip picks its way among rural Adams County and Carroll County farm roads, some one lane, some two lanes. Although these roads mostly have no shoulders, they also have little traffic, making the riding delightful.

Thanks to Dan Schaller, who developed this ride and allowed us to use it. If you enjoy this ride and want to do more in Carroll County, contact the Carroll County Visitor Center, 210 East Main Street, Westminster, MD 21157-5225 (800-272-1933), for a free packet of 10 bicycle tours in the county. The tours range from eight to 33 miles over scenic country roads, with varying terrain.

START: Intersection of Main Street and MD 27 in Westminster (Carroll County), Md. From the Capital Beltway, take I-270 north to MD 27 (Exit 15). Follow MD 27 north for 34 miles to the town of Westminster. Public parking is available in several locations within a few blocks of the starting point, including a large lot north of Main Street, behind the shops. Avoid the library parking lot, which is patrolled and ticketed, except on Sunday. Westminster is approximately 50 miles north of the Capital Beltway.

LENGTH: 58.9 miles.

TERRAIN: Moderately hilly.

POINTS OF INTEREST: Westminster historic district (southeast of starting point on Main Street) includes historic buildings and antique shops; Gettysburg National Military Park at mile 25.8; Eisenhower National Historic Site (home of President Dwight D. Eisenhower) is adjacent to Gettysburg — visitors must have tickets and board shuttle buses at the Visitor Center in Gettysburg.

FOOD: Restaurants and markets at start and in Gettysburg. Also, markets at 13.0, 17.9, 35.9 and 49.5 miles.

LODGING: Both Westminster and Gettysburg offer a variety of accommodations, including bed-and-breakfasts and motels. For information, contact the Carroll County Office of Tourism (800-272-1933) in Westminster or the Gettysburg Travel Council (717-334-6274).

MAPS: Carroll County, Md. and Adams County, Pa. road maps.

MILES   DIRECTIONS & COMMENTS

0.0   **West** on **MAIN STREET.** Sam's Bagels on the right.

0.5   **Bear left** on **UNIONTOWN ROAD.**

6.5   Historic Uniontown.

7.3   **Right** on **TREVANION ROAD** (MD 84).

10.0   Cross bridge over Meadow Branch.

13.0   **Left** on **BALTIMORE ROAD** (MD 140) at T in Taneytown. Services.

13.1   *Caution: railroad crossing.*

13.7   **Right** on **HARNEY ROAD.**

17.9   Town of Harney. Grocery store.

18.4   Maryland-Pennsylvania state line (the Mason-Dixon Line). Harney Road becomes **TANEYTOWN ROAD** (PA 134).

23.3   Cross over US 15 to remain on **TANEYTOWN ROAD.**

25.8   **Left** to enter **GETTYSBURG NATIONAL MILITARY PARK.** From this point, tour the battlefields (on the Park Service bicycle route) or continue on Taneytown Road to the town of Gettysburg. To return: from parking lot, **right** on **TANEYTOWN ROAD.**

26.6   **Left** on **SCHOOLHOUSE ROAD** (unmarked), opposite monument to Battery C Third Artillery. *Note: This turn is easy to miss. It is 0.1 miles past the Park Service Maintenance Building.*

27.3   **Right** on **BLACKSMITH SHOP ROAD** at stop sign.

27.7   **Bear left** on **HOSPITAL ROAD** at stop sign.

28.7   **Left** on **SACHS ROAD** (unmarked) at T.

28.8   Cross over US 15 to remain on **SACHS ROAD.**

30.1   **Right** on **WHITE CHURCH ROAD** (unmarked) at T.

31.2   Cross Solomon Road to remain on **WHITE CHURCH ROAD.**

31.9   Becomes **FURNEY ROAD** at Barlow-Two Taverns Road.

32.6   **Left** on **ORPHANAGE ROAD** at T.

32.7   **Right** on **DAGUE ROAD.**

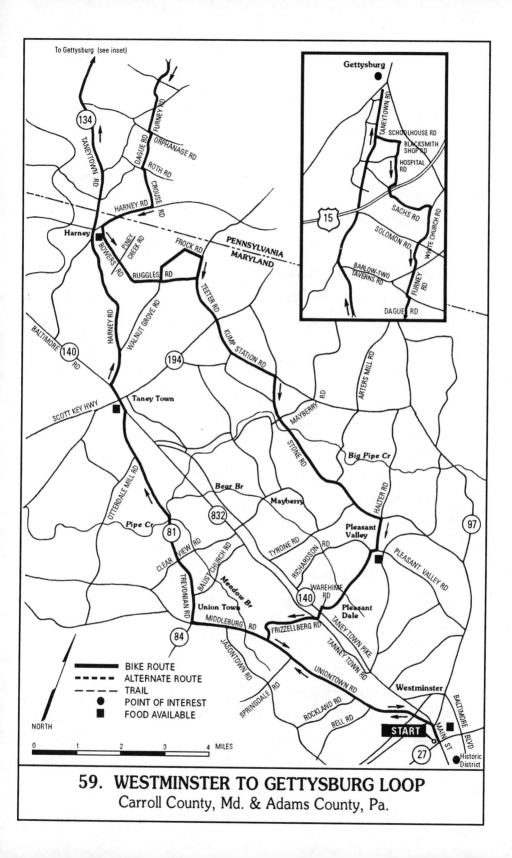

59. WESTMINSTER TO GETTYSBURG LOOP
Carroll County, Md. & Adams County, Pa.

33.1   Road is unpaved (but rideable) for 0.5 miles.

33.6   **Left** on **ROTH ROAD** (unmarked) at T. Then **right** after 200 feet on **CROUSE ROAD** (unmarked).

34.5   **Right** on **HARNEY ROAD** (unmarked) at T.

35.5   Cross Pennsylvania/Maryland state line. Becomes **CONOVER ROAD.**

35.9   **Left** on **BOWERS ROAD.** Grocery store in Harney.

37.0   Cross Piney Creek Road.

38.2   **Left** on **WALNUT GROVE ROAD** at T.

38.8   **Right** to remain on paved road.

39.4   **Right** on **FROCK ROAD.**

39.7   **Right** on **TEETER ROAD** at T.

40.5   Cross Ruggles Road.

41.4   **Cross** MD 194 onto **KUMP STATION ROAD.**

43.7   **Right** to remain on **KUMP STATION ROAD**.

43.8   **Bear right** on **STONE ROAD**, uphill.

45.0   Cross Mayberry Road at stop sign.

48.7   **Right** on **HALTER ROAD.**

49.5   **Right** on **PLEASANT VALLEY ROAD** at T. Grocery to left.

49.6   **Left** to remain on **PLEASANT VALLEY ROAD** at stop sign.

51.8   **Left** on **WAREHIME ROAD** at stop sign.

51.9   Becomes **SOUTH PLEASANT VALLEY ROAD** at MD 140.

52.0   Becomes **FRIZZELBURG ROAD** (unmarked) at Old Tanleytown Road.

53.7   **Left** on **UNIONTOWN ROAD** at stop sign.

57.9   Cross MD 31 at traffic light.

58.4   **Straight** on **MAIN STREET** at stop sign.

58.9   **Arrive** at intersection of **MAIN STREET** and **MD 27.**

60. SOUTH MOUNTAIN - SHARPSBURG TOUR

One of seven bicycle tours developed by the Washington County Planning Department and the county tourism office, this tour passes over rolling hills in the Great Valley, Maryland's continuation of Virginia's Shenandoah Valley. The valley was the site of the National Road, a major route carrying settlers west to the Ohio Valley in the 1820s and 1830s. Now a country road, in the early 1800s it was the busiest highway in the nation.

The ride follows the National Road to Boonsboro, then climbs to Gathland State Park and South Mountain, a good picnic spot. On the return, you pass Antietam Battlefield, site of the bloodiest single-day battle in U.S. history.

START: Sharpsburg Pike Park and Ride Lot, off Interstate 70, one mile south of Hagerstown, Md. From the Capital Beltway, take I-270 north. At Frederick, take I-70 west to Hagerstown. Take Exit 29 and go south on MD 65, Sharpsburg Pike. Pass underneath I-70. Park and Ride Lot is on the left just past the exit ramps. Hagerstown is 58 miles northwest of the Capital Beltway.

LENGTH: 38.3 miles.

TERRAIN: Rolling hills with a climb to Gathland State Park near mile 16.5.

POINTS OF INTEREST: Boonsborough Museum, with Indian artifacts and Civil War relics, at mile 8.5 (301-432-5151); Gathland State Park, estate of Civil War correspondent George Townsend and "the only park in the world dedicated to the free press," at mile 17.5; Antietam Battlefield (301-432-5124) at mile 29.2, where 23,000 Americans died on September 17, 1862.

FOOD: Many choices in Hagerstown; markets at 14.8 and 35.0 miles.

LODGING: Many choices in Hagerstown; camping at Gathland State Park. For information, call Washington County Tourism (800-228-7829).

MAPS: Washington County Bicycle Tour Map; *ADC's Washington, D.C. 50-mile Radius Map.*

MILES   DIRECTIONS & COMMENTS

0.0   **Left** to go south from parking lot on **SHARPSBURG PIKE** (MD 65).

0.6   **Left** on **POFFENBERGER ROAD.**

2.2   **Right** on **ALT US 40** (Boonsboro Pike). *Traffic. Use shoulder.*

8.5   Enter Boonsboro. Boonsborough Museum, open Sundays, May to September, 1 p.m. - 5 p.m. **Right** on **MD 34** (Shepherdstown Pike).

9.0 **Left** on **KING ROAD.**

11.0 **Right** on **MD 67.**

16.2 **Left** on **TOWNSEND ROAD.** Begin climb.

17.5 **Arrive** at Gathland State Park. After visiting park, **reverse direction, bearing left** on **GAPLAND ROAD.** Steep descent.

18.6 **Right** on **MD 67 NORTH**.

20.0 **Left** on **TREGO ROAD.** Becomes **MOUNT BRIAR ROAD**, and then becomes **EAKLES MILL ROAD.**

21.0 Trego Mountain Road. Do *not* turn left here!

24.3 **Left** on **DOG STREET ROAD**, **bearing right** at top of steep hill.

25.1 Descent. Enter Keedysville. **Left** on **MAIN STREET** at stop sign.

25.5 **Left** on **MD 34.**

28.2 Enter Sharpsburg. **Right** on **MD 65** (Sharpsburg Pike).

29.2 **Right** on **DUNKER CHURCH ROAD** to Antietam Battlefield Visitor Center, open 8:30 a.m. to 6 p.m. (5 p.m. in winter). $2 per person. Restrooms. Continue on Dunker Church Road to return to MD 65.

30.3 **North** to **MD 65.**

38.3 **Arrive** at **SHARPSBURG PIKE PARK AND RIDE LOT.**

Antietam National Battlefield.

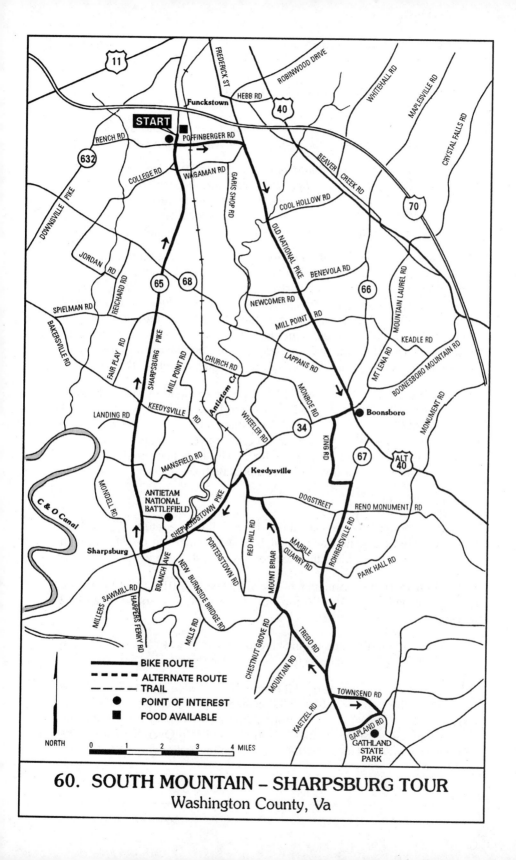

60. SOUTH MOUNTAIN – SHARPSBURG TOUR
Washington County, Va

61. ANTIETAM BATTLEFIELD LOOP

Encompassing mountainous inclines, rolling farmlands and scenic canal roads, this ride rolls through the heart of Civil War Maryland.

A tour of Antietam National Battlefield highlights the trip. On September 17, 1862, the bloodiest day of the Civil War, 12,400 Union and 10,300 Confederate soldiers fell on the Antietam fields, slightly less than half of the number of U.S. casualties during the entire Vietnam War. More than 4,770 Confederate soldiers are buried at Antietam National Cemetery.

The Battle of Antietam was the first major attempt by the South to attack in the North. Led by General Robert E. Lee, the Confederates were vastly outnumbered by Union armies under General George McClellan. After his bloody victory at Antietam, McClellan missed an opportunity to crush Lee's army, which slipped across the Potomac River the day after the battle. Despite direct orders from President Lincoln, McClellan failed to pursue Lee. Exasperated, Lincoln removed McClellan from command. Most historians agree that an aggressive attack by McClellan would have ended the Civil War.

START: Harpers Ferry Lodge at 19123 Sandy Hook Road in Knoxville, Md. From the Capital Beltway, take I-270 North to Frederick and exit on US 340 West (toward Charles Town, W.Va.). Continue 16 miles west on US 340 and turn left on MD 180 (Keep Tryst Road) at blinking yellow light. Continue 0.8 miles and turn right on Sandy Hook Road. Hostel is first building on left. Knoxville is 48 miles northwest of the Capital Beltway.

LENGTH: 32.1 miles.

TERRAIN: Very hilly up to Sharpsburg. Downhill on the return. The **ALTER-NATE ROUTE** avoids the C&O Canal Towpath, which can be difficult with narrow tires or impassable if the weather has recently been wet.

POINTS OF INTEREST: Antietam National Battlefield (301-432-5124) at 13.8 miles (open daily 8:30 a.m. to 5 p.m.); Antietam Creek Aqueduct at 22.2 miles; and C&O Canal at 22.3 miles.

FOOD: Markets and restaurants in Sharpsburg. Grocery at start and a 24-hour restaurant less than 0.5 miles before reaching start/finish.

LODGING: Near Harpers Ferry, HI-Harpers Ferry Lodge, 19123 Sandy Hook Road, Knoxville, Md. (301-834-7652) at start; and Hilltop House (800-338-8319), on Ridge Street, 10 blocks from C&O Canal Towpath. Near Antietam, inns include Gilbert House (301-725-0637), Antietam Overlook Farm (800-878-4241) and Piper House (301-797-1862) in the National Battlefield Park.

MAPS: Washington County, Md. road map.

MILES   DIRECTIONS & COMMENTS

0.0   **Left** to go south out of Harpers Ferry Lodge driveway, on **SANDY HOOK ROAD.** This becomes **HARPERS FERRY ROAD.** Steep hills.

5.4   **Bear left** at Chestnut Road to remain on **HARPERS FERRY ROAD.**

6.3   **Bear right** to remain on **HARPERS FERRY ROAD.**

8.8   **Right** on **MILLS ROAD.**

10.5   **Left** on **BURNSIDE BRIDGE ROAD**, which becomes **EAST CHURCH STREET.** This passes but does not cross Burnside Bridge, where 400 Georgians held for three decisive hours against Union General Ambrose Burnside's 12,500 troops.

12.9   In Sharpsburg, cross East Main Street (MD 34), proceeding **straight** on **MD 65.**

13.8   **Right** into **ANTIETAM NATIONAL BATTLEFIELD** to Visitor Center. Follow battlefield tour in National Park Service brochure (at Visitor Center) as far as Branch Avenue.

20.2   From Branch Avenue, turn **left** on **HARPERS FERRY ROAD** to begin return trip.

22.2   **Right** on **CANAL ROAD** (on downhill, easy to miss). Follow markers to C&O Canal. ALTERNATE ROUTE begins here (see end of cues).

22.3   **Left** at Antietam Creek Aqueduct, and **left** on **C&O CANAL TOWPATH.** Camping. *Caution: fat tires recommended! Avoid C&O Canal Towpath when wet or snowy.*

30.1   **Left** at **LOCK 34** to leave C&O Canal Towpath. (Canal condition deteriorates south of here.) **Right** on **HARPERS FERRY ROAD** which becomes **SANDY HOOK ROAD.**

32.1   **Arrive** at **HARPERS FERRY LODGE.**

ALTERNATE ROUTE

At 22.2 miles, to avoid C&O Canal Towpath, stay on **HARPERS FERRY ROAD** all the way back to **HARPERS FERRY LODGE.**

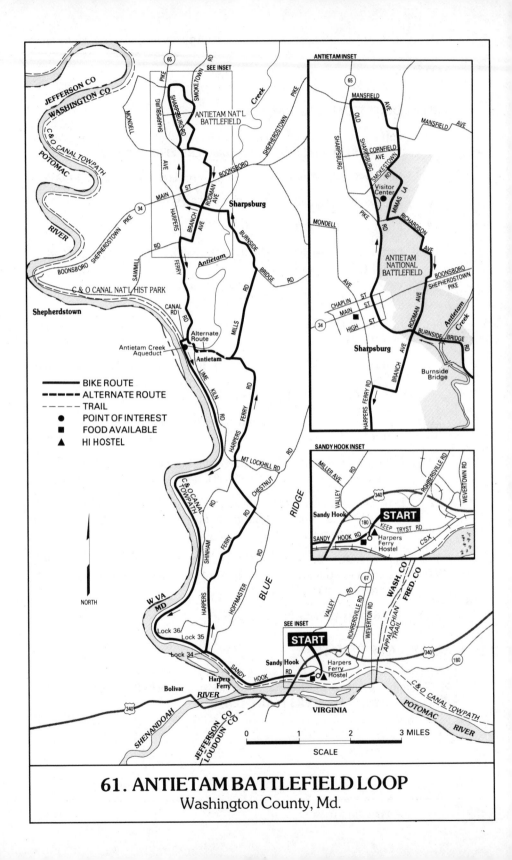

61. ANTIETAM BATTLEFIELD LOOP
Washington County, Md.

62. SHENANDOAH VALLEY VENTURE

Traversing scenic farmland and picturesque small towns, this tour explores the Shenandoah River Valley. Highlights include the Burwell-Morgan Mill on Spout Run Creek. The 1782 stone and clapboard mill once ground grain into meal and flour and served as the commercial outlet for the wheat-growing region. Its wooden gears date to the mid-1700s, and the building remains a notable example of 18th century architecture and technology. Today, the Clarke County Historical Society maintains the mill, and meal and whole wheat flour are still ground and sold there.

Winchester, just west of the tour, was central to Civil War control of the fertile Shenandoah Valley. The town changed hands 72 times over the course of the war, including 13 times in one day. In 1862 Stonewall Jackson routed a much larger Union force commanded by Nathaniel Banks, alarming Federal officials who feared Jackson would wheel east to Washington. In 1864, Union forces under General Philip Sheridan were ordered into the Shenandoah to strip it so clean that "crows flying over it will have to carry their provender." Sheridan smashed Jubal Early's army at Winchester on September 19, driving the Confederates from the valley forever and ensuring Lincoln's reelection.

START: Cooley Elementary School at the intersection of BUS VA 7 and VA 636 in Berryville, Va. From the Capital Beltway, take VA 7 West and bear left at Berryville on BUS VA 7. Continue to Berryville; school is on the left at the far end of town. Berryville is 46 miles west of the Capital Beltway. **ALTERNATE START:** At Millwood. From Berryville, follow tour directions to mile 11.9. Park at mill. This allows a complete loop.

LENGTH: 45.7 miles. From **ALTERNATE START:** 33.8 miles, including northern loop. The ride could also be divided into two separate rides, a northern loop of 23.8 miles and a southern loop of 21.9 miles.

TERRAIN: Rolling hills.

POINTS OF INTEREST: Hope Center, headquarters of Project Hope, at 11.9 miles; and the Burwell-Morgan Mill (540-837-1799) at 33.9 miles.

FOOD: Berryville (at start) has many choices. Markets at 11.9, 24.5 and 33.4 miles. Burwell-Morgan Mill at 33.9 miles makes a good lunch stop.

LODGING: In Winchester, many choices including Travelodge (540-665-0685) at the junction of I-81 and US 17, and Holiday Inn East (540-667-3300) at the junction of US 50 and I-81. In Berryville, bed-and-breakfasts include the Battletown Inn, 102 West Main Street (540-955-4100). In Boyce, River House (540-837-1476). In White Post, L'Auberge Provencale (540-837-1375). In Paris, Ashby Inn (540-592-3900).

MAPS: Clarke and Warren Counties, Va. road maps.

MILES   DIRECTIONS & COMMENTS

0.0   **Right** out of school parking lot to go south on **VA 636.**

1.4   **Right** on **VA 657** at T.

5.1   **Left** on **VA 634**.

5.6   **Bear left** on **VA 655.**

6.8   **Left** on **VA 620.**

9.7   Cross US 340. *Caution: traffic.*

11.0   **Bear right** on **VA 255.** *Caution: traffic.*

11.9   **Left** on **VA 723** in Millwood. Hope Center (Carter Hall) and grocery store (closed Sunday) on left. ALTERNATE START begins here.

12.1   **Bear right** on **VA 255.**

12.6   **Straight** on **VA 624**, crossing US 17/50. *Caution: traffic.*

13.2   **Bear left** to stay on **VA 624**.

21.0   Cross Shenandoah River on low water bridge. *Caution: uneven joints.*

21.3   **Left** on **VA 643.**

22.3   **Straight** on **VA 603.**

24.5   **Left** on **VA 638** at T. General store on right, open daily.

30.5   **Left** on **US 17/50** at T. *Caution: heavy traffic.*

31.4   **Bear right** on **VA 723.**

33.4   **Bear right** to stay on **VA 723**. Millwood Grocery (closed Sunday).

33.9   Burwell-Morgan Mill on left (open Wednesday - Sunday).

35.4   Cross US 340. *Caution: traffic.*

37.7   **Right** on **VA 655.**

40.1   **Bear right** on **VA 634.**

40.6   **Right** on **VA 657** at T.

44.4   **Left** on **VA 636.**

45.7   **Left** into **COOLEY ELEMENTARY SCHOOL.**

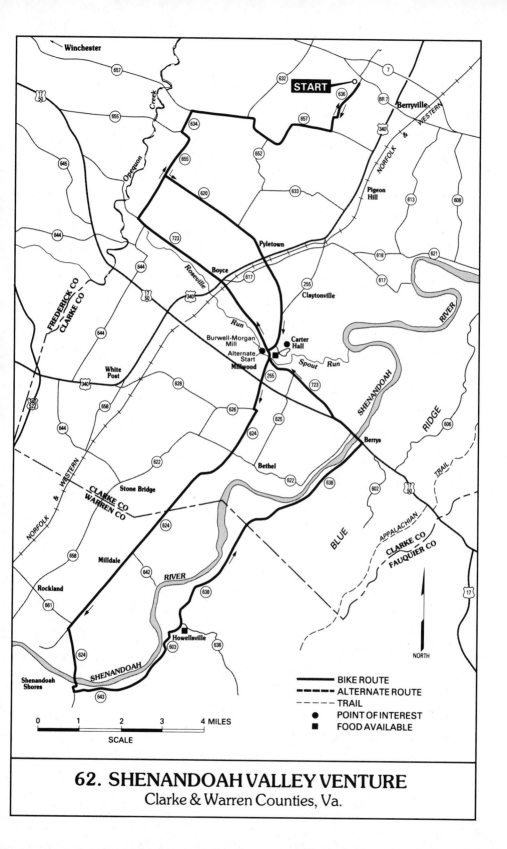

62. SHENANDOAH VALLEY VENTURE
Clarke & Warren Counties, Va.

63. BEAR'S DEN TO HARPERS FERRY

Presenting you with a view of the Blue Ridge Mountains on the left and Short Hill on the right, this tour runs through an area of hilly farms and abundant wildlife. If you succeeded in climbing to Bear's Den Lodge (Tour 6), you are rewarded with downhill wheeling to the Harpers Ferry Lodge in Knoxville, Md., across the river from Harpers Ferry.

While in Harpers Ferry, take a side trip to Harpers Ferry National Historical Park, off US 340 in West Virginia. The park surrounds the town, which was captured in September 1862 by Confederate forces under Stonewall Jackson. Over 2,700 Union troops surrendered in the battle, the largest mass surrender in U.S. military history until World War II. The park also memorializes John Brown's famous 1859 raid on Harpers Ferry's arsenals.

The route in western Loudoun County uses fairly low-traffic roads, but they are narrow, without shoulders, and hedged with foliage. The tour is recommended for bicyclists with good nerves and experience on narrow roads.

For a direct route back to Washington, D.C. from Harpers Ferry, see Washington to Harpers Ferry (Tour 19) or the C&O Canal Towpath (Tour 7).

START: Bear's Den Lodge on VA 601 (Blue Ridge Mountain Road) near Bluemont, Va. From the Capital Beltway, take VA 7 West. Continue 18 miles beyond Leesburg, then turn left on VA 601. Continue 0.5 miles; hostel is on the right. Bluemont is 48 miles west of the Capital Beltway. (The ride can also be started in Purcellville, using the cues from mile 45.0 to 49.5 of Tour 6 and picking up this route with a right turn at mile 5.5.)

LENGTH: 23.2 miles.

TERRAIN: Mostly level or downhill. Narrow roads.

POINTS OF INTEREST: Bear's Den, at the start, a mountaintop mansion built in the 1930s by Wagnerian diva Francesca Caspar Lawson; Bluemont at 2.3 miles, with fall fair and picnic grounds; Round Hill at 8.2 miles; Mechanicsville at 14.6 miles, named after a blacksmith and wheelwright who repaired wagons that broke down on the badly rutted roads; Old St. Paul's Church at 18.3 miles; and Harpers Ferry National Historical Park (304-535-6223) at end.

FOOD: Markets at 2.3 (open Sundays), 8.2 (open Sundays), 14.6 and 21.2 miles. Restaurant at 22.7 miles.

LODGING: At start, HI-Bear's Den Lodge (540-554-8708) on Blue Ridge Mountain Road (VA 601). Near Harpers Ferry, HI-Harpers Ferry Lodge, 19123 Sandy Hook Road, Knoxville, Md. (301-834-7652); and Hilltop House (800-338-8319), on Ridge Street, 10 blocks from C&O Canal Towpath.

MAPS: Loudoun County, Va. road map.

MILES   DIRECTIONS & COMMENTS

0.0   Leave Bear's Den Lodge by **GRAVEL ROAD.**

0.4   **Left** on **VA 601** at T.

0.8   **Right** on **VA 7,** and descend mountain.

1.5   **Right** on **VA 734.**

2.3   Bluemont, with general store and historical buildings. **Continue** on **VA 734.**

5.5   **Left** on **VA 719** (Airmont Road) in Airmont.

The old train station (now a private home) in Round Hill.

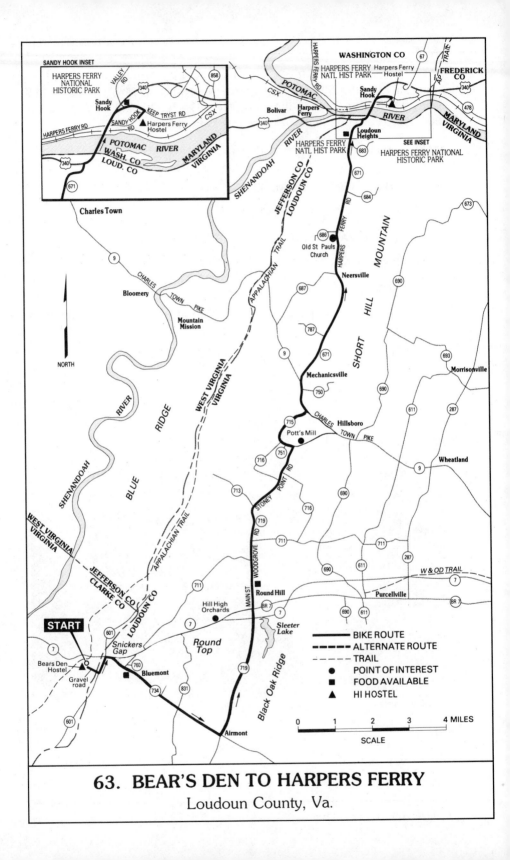

63. BEAR'S DEN TO HARPERS FERRY
Loudoun County, Va.

8.0   Cross VA 7 and BUS VA 7, continuing **straight** on **VA 719.** Round Hill at BUS VA 7 has diner and two general stores.

10.3   **Bear right** to stay on **VA 719** (Woodgrove Road), where gravel VA 713 goes straight.

12.2   **Left** on **VA 751** at T.

12.6   **Right** on **VA 715** (Cider Mill Road).

13.8   **Left** on **VA 9** (Charles Town Pike) *Caution: fast traffic.*

14.6   **Bear right** on **VA 671** (Harpers Ferry Road) in Mechanicsville. Junction's Market (closed before noon and after 6 p.m. Sundays).

18.3   Old St. Paul's Church on left.

21.2   Butts Grocery on left, as downhill to Potomac River begins.

21.9   **Right** on **US 340** at T. Cross bridge over Potomac River on walkway.

22.7   **Bear right** on **MD 180** (Keep Tryst Road). Pass Cindy Dee Diner on left (large menu, reasonable prices, good pie).

23.0   **Right** on **SANDY HOOK ROAD.**

23.2   **First left** up hill to **HARPERS FERRY LODGE** parking lot.

64. PENN DUTCH TREAT

Pennsylvania Dutch Country, a region of cultural contrasts and beautiful cycling opportunities, offers some of the best cycling in the mid-Atlantic area. The misnomer "Dutch" finds its roots in the early settlement of the area by German-speaking Amish immigrants, who described their heritage as "Deutsche." The religious and social customs of the large Amish population include a rejection of modern technology and a devotion to a simpler agrarian lifestyle. For the bicycle tourist, the Amish countryside offers a unique excursion into the past.

In addition to the route described here, develop your own tours to places like the Ephrata Cloister, Green Dragon Farmers Market, Lancaster and Bird in Hand.

START: HI-Bowmansville on PA 625 in Bowmansville, Pa. (13 miles south of Reading). From the Baltimore Beltway, take I-83 North to York, Pa. and exit on US 30 East (toward Lancaster). Take PA 23 East (toward New Holland) and turn left on PA 625 North. Continue four miles; hostel is on right. Bowmansville is 152 miles north of the Capital Beltway.

LENGTH: 40.1 miles.

TERRAIN: Easy hills. Ruts in the road caused by buggy wheels are a unique, endearing, and sometimes challenging aspect of this ride.

POINTS OF INTEREST: Lancaster Cheese Factory at 13.2 miles; Hayloft Candles at 15.6 miles, with ice cream and gift shop; and Ebersol's Chair Shop at 21.1 miles. Picturesque Amish farmlands and communities, grist mills, hex signs (to frighten evil spirits), and horses and buggies along the route.

FOOD: Restaurant at 21.8 miles (closed Sundays). Penn Dutch dinners are served to groups at the following farms: Amos King, 229 Hammertown Road, Narvon, PA 17555-9781, 215-445-6005 (near Churchtown, six miles from hostel, no weekend service); Paul Stoltzfus, 2747 Main Street, Morgantown, PA 19543-9454, 215-286-5609 (in Berks County, service by appointment only and no Sunday service).

LODGING: In Geigertown, HI-Geigertown (610-286-9537). In Bird in Hand, Greystone Manor (717-393-4233). In Ephrata, Historic Smithton Inn (717-733-6094). In Lancaster, Whitmer's Tavern (717-299-5305). In Lititz, Sutter Inn (717-626-2115). In Mount Joy, Cameron Estate (717-653-1773).

MAPS AND INFORMATION: *Lancaster County Bicycle Tours,* available for $8.50 (postpaid) from the Lancaster Bicycle Club, P.O. Box 535, Lancaster, PA 17603-0535 (717-394-8220). Pennsylvania Dutch Visitors Bureau (717-299-8901).

MILES   DIRECTIONS & COMMENTS

0.0   **Straight** out of hostel to go west on **MAPLE GROVE ROAD**.

0.6   **Bear left** to stay on **MAPLE GROVE ROAD. Bear left again** at School Road to continue on **MAPLE GROVE ROAD** up the hill.

2.3   **Left** on **PA 897** (Dry Tavern Street). This is a five-road intersection. Stay on **PA 897** to Terre Hill.

3.2   **Bear left** to stay **on PA 897** (up big hill).

4.2   Arrive Terre Hill. **Left** on **MAIN STREET,** then **first right** on **LANCASTER AVENUE**. Becomes **MARTINDALE ROAD**.

6.2   **Left** on **GRIST MILL ROAD** in Martindale (road may be unmarked). Becomes **LINDEN GROVE ROAD**.

7.5   Cross US 322.

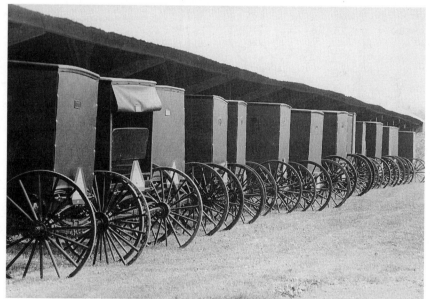

Amish parking lot.

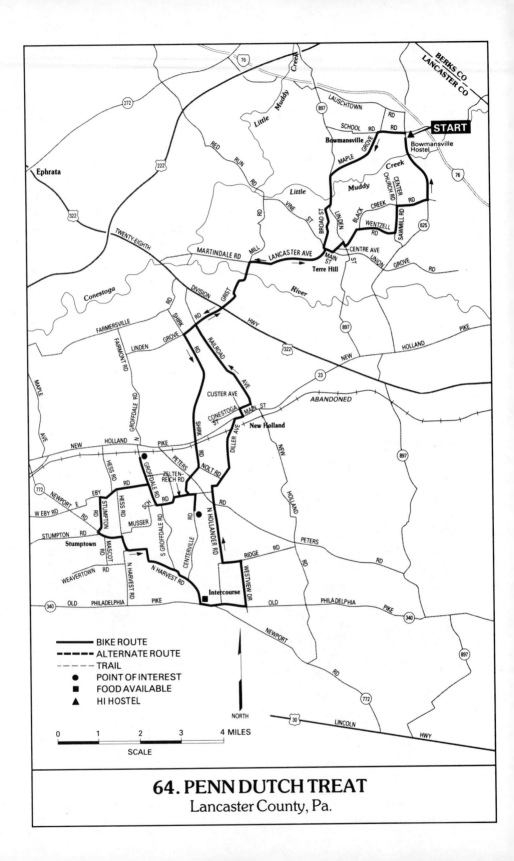

LEGEND

— BIKE ROUTE
--- ALTERNATE ROUTE
-- TRAIL
● POINT OF INTEREST
■ FOOD AVAILABLE
▲ HI HOSTEL

0 1 2 3 4 MILES

SCALE

NORTH

64. PENN DUTCH TREAT
Lancaster County, Pa.

8.6   **Left** on **SHIRK ROAD**. *Caution: no shoulder, heavy traffic.*

11.3 Cross PA 23, then railroad tracks. *Caution: heavy traffic.* **Bear right** to stay on **SHIRK ROAD,** where Nolt Road goes left at mile 11.9.

12.2 **Straight** at stop sign **at PETERS ROAD.** *Caution: hard to see traffic from left.*

12.8 **Left** on **ZELTENREICH ROAD,** then **first right** on **CENTERVILLE ROAD,** to Lancaster County Cheese Factory (open Monday - Friday 8 a.m. - 5 p.m., Saturday 9 a.m. - 3 p.m., closed Sundays). **Reverse direction** to **ZELTENREICH ROAD,** turning **left** to continue.

14.1 **Left** on **MUSSER SCHOOL ROAD.**

14.6 **Right** on **GROFFDALE ROAD.** (Do not take South Groffdale Road, which precedes Groffdale Road and goes left.) Pass East Eby Road and go 0.5 miles to Hayloft Candles on right (closed Sundays).

16.1 **Reverse direction. Right** on **EAST EBY ROAD.** Pass Hess Road and cemetery on right.

17.4 **Left** on **STUMPTON ROAD.**

18.3 **Left** on **NEWPORT ROAD** (PA 772).

18.9 **Right** on **HESS ROAD** at T to stay on PA 772.

19.3 **Left** on **NORTH HARVEST ROAD** to stay on PA 772 East.

21.1 **Bear right** to stay on **PA 772.** Pass Ebersol's Chair Shop at junction with Centerville Road. *Caution: traffic heavy into Intercourse.*

21.8 Kitchen Kettle Restaurant (closed Sundays) on left. **Left** on **OLD PHILADELPHIA PIKE** (PA 340) in Intercourse. *Caution: heavy traffic for 0.5 miles.*

22.0 **Bear left** to stay on **PA 340** (Old Philadelphia Pike) at fork.

22.8 **Left** on **WEST VIEW DRIVE.**

23.8 **Left** on **RIDGE ROAD.**

24.4 **Right** on **NORTH HOLLANDER ROAD.**

26.2 **Bear left** to stay on **HOLLANDER ROAD.**

27.3 Becomes **DILLER AVENUE** by New Holland plant.

27.7 Cross railroad tracks and enter New Holland.

27.9 **Right** on **MAIN STREET** (PA 23).

28.1   **Left** on **CUSTER ROAD** (bank on corner).

28.3   **Right** on **CONESTOGA STREET.**

28.6   **Left** on **RAILROAD AVENUE.**

30.9   **Right** on **LINDEN GROVE ROAD** (old school house on left, wooden post street sign on right). Becomes **GRIST MILL ROAD.**

31.7   Cross PA 322.

33.0   **Right** on **MARTINDALE ROAD** (may be unmarked).

34.6   Becomes **LANCASTER AVENUE.**

35.0   **Right** on **MAIN STREET** in Terre Hill.

35.2   **Left** on **CENTRE AVENUE** (bank on corner).

35.5   **Right** on **LINDEN STREET** at T. Go 200 feet, then **left** on **WENTZELL ROAD**.

36.9   **Left** on **SAW MILL ROAD.**

37.6   **Right** on **BLACK CREEK ROAD**.

38.3   **Left** on **READING ROAD** (PA 625) at T to Bowmansville.

40.1   **Right** into **BOWMANSVILLE HOSTEL.**

65. BERKELEY SPRINGS LOOP

Berkeley Springs has been a well-known gathering spot since Indian times, when Shawnee, Tuscarora and other Indians from along the Appalachian range were attracted to its warm springs. White settlers arrived as early as 1730. Among the early visitors was George Washington, who helped survey the area for Lord Fairfax in 1748, and later returned many times. Washington purchased some of the original lots in the town of Bath in 1776, and established the first "summer White House" here in the 1790s. The town has been famous as a mountain resort ever since.

The ride begins at the State Park and Baths and traverses steep roads over largely forested areas. It is hard work, but it rewards the experienced cyclist with beautiful vistas of mountains, forests and clear streams.

START: Berkeley Springs State Park and Baths on US 522 in Berkeley Springs, W. Va. From the Capital Beltway, take I-270 North 33 miles to Frederick, Md. From Frederick, continue on I-70 West 52 miles to the junction of I-70, I-68 and US 522 in Hancock, Md. Exit on US 522 south. Proceed five miles to Berkeley Springs. Starting point is 90 miles northwest of the Capital Beltway.

LENGTH: 36.2 miles.

TERRAIN: Steep hills.

POINTS OF INTEREST: Berkeley Springs State Park and Baths at start, open seven days a week, with public swimming pool open in summer. Dawson House and historic walking tour of the town of Bath (Berkeley Springs) near start. Colonel Suit's Castle at 35.6 miles.

FOOD: There's not much to eat or drink on this route, particularly on Sundays, so bring liquids and food. Markets and restaurants near the start. Unger Store (closed Sundays) at 17.8 miles. Coolfont Resort at 31.3 miles.

LODGING: The Country Inn, an historic inn adjacent to the springs and spa in Berkeley Springs (304-258-2210).

MAPS AND INFORMATION: Berkeley Springs Chamber of Commerce (304-258-3738).

MILES   DIRECTIONS & COMMENTS

0.0   **Right** on **US 522** from State Park.

0.3   **Left** on **JOHNSON'S MILL ROAD (WV 38/3).** Immediate steep hill. Road is occasionally unmarked — follow double yellow line.

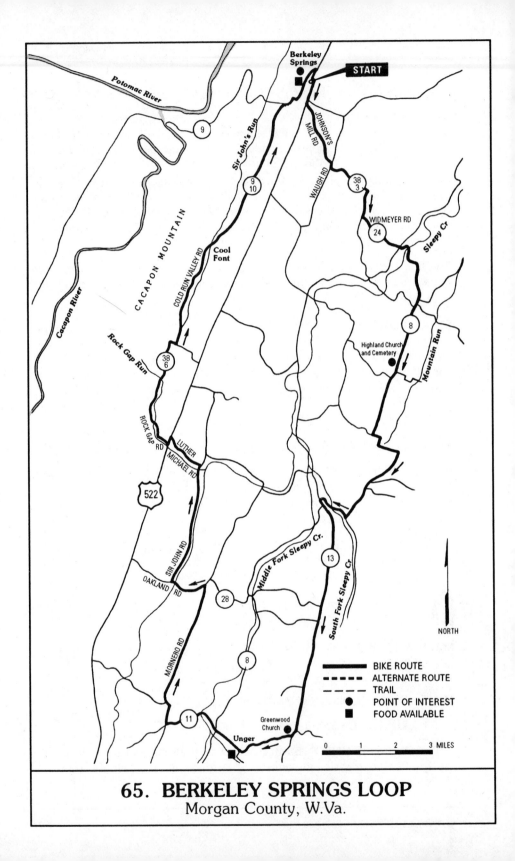

65. BERKELEY SPRINGS LOOP
Morgan County, W.Va.

1.8   Pass Waugh Road (WV 15/1). Continue to follow double yellow line.

3.0   Continue on road with double yellow line. (Don't take road to the right.)

4.0   Double yellow line ends. Becomes **WIDMYER ROAD** (WV 24).

4.5   One-lane iron suspension bridge over Sleepy Creek. Becomes **WV 8.**

7.7   Highland United Methodist Church and the Highland Cemetery.

11.0 **Right** on **WV 8/4** at T. Cross small, one-lane bridge.

11.3 Cross one-lane bridge.

11.6 Steep hill. **Left** on **WV 13** at stop sign. *Caution: traffic.*

16.5 **Bear right** at fork towards Greenwood United Methodist Church. Stay on road with double yellow line.

17.8 Unger Store (Mobil sign), closed Sundays.

18.5 **Continue straight** (not up the hill to the right).

18.9 Cross one-lane bridge.

19.8 **Sharp right** at stop sign.

20.3 **Straight** on **MORNERO ROAD.** Don't take left or right.

22.9 **Left** on **OAKLAND ROAD** (WV 28) at stop sign.

23.6 Cross one-lane bridge.

23.8 **Sharp right** on **SIR JOHN ROAD.** Very steep hill.

26.3 **Right** on **LUTHER MICHAEL ROAD** at stop sign.

27.1 **Left** on **US 522** at stop sign. *Caution: traffic.*

27.2 **Quick right** on **ROCK GAP ROAD.**

29.7 **Left** on **COLD RUN VALLEY ROAD**, toward Coolfont.

31.3 Pass Coolfont.

35.1 **Right** on **WV 9** at stop sign. *Caution: traffic.*

35.6 Colonel Suit's Castle on left. Open daily.

35.9 **Right** on **US 522** at traffic light.

36.2 **Arrive** at **STATE PARK.**

66. CHARLOTTESVILLE CIRCUIT

A challenge for the ambitious cyclist, this tour runs through almost mountainous terrain north of Charlottesville, Va. Take time to enjoy the many scenic vistas, with the Blue Ridge Mountains looming majestically in the distance.

For a full two-day ride, include the steeply ascending side trip to Skyline Drive and the Shenandoah Mountains. Lodging is available at Rockfish Gap.

An alternate route, avoiding traffic entering and exiting Charlottesville, begins in Earlysville.

START: Rotunda of the University of Virginia in Charlottesville, Va. From the Capital Beltway, take I-66 West and exit on US 29 South (toward Charlottesville). In Charlottesville, BUS US 250 leads to the university. Charlottesville is 120 miles southwest of the Capital Beltway. **ALTERNATE START:** From US 29, turn west on VA 743 before entering Charlottesville and proceed to Earlysville.

LENGTH: 54.5 miles. **ALTERNATE START:** 46.3 miles. **SIDE TRIP** to Skyline Drive adds 34 miles, mostly up steep hills (see end of cues).

TERRAIN: Hilly. No shoulders, but good country roads.

POINTS OF INTEREST: Charlottesville and the University of Virginia at start, with historic structures designed by Thomas Jefferson. Near Charlottesville, but not on route, Mitchie Tavern, a restored 18th century inn; Monticello, Jefferson's 35-room home (804-295-8181); and Ash Lawn, home of President James Monroe, designed by Jefferson in 1799 (804-293-9539); Rivanna Reservoir at 11.6 miles. Scenic views of the Blue Ridge Mountains along the route. Bike shop near start.

FOOD: Markets at start, 4.3, 15.0, 15.6 and 41.0 miles. Restaurants in Charlottesville.

LODGING: In Charlottesville, numerous bed-and-breakfasts and hotels. For information on bed-and-breakfasts, call 804-979-7264. Holiday Inn at Rockfish Gap (side trip).

MAPS AND INFORMATION: Charlottesville, Va. and Albemarle County, Va. maps, available in city stores and from the Chamber of Commerce (open weekdays, 804-295-3141).

MILES   DIRECTIONS & COMMENTS

0.0   Go **south** on **McCORMICK ROAD.** Exit university campus.

0.7   **Right** on **ALDERMAN ROAD** at traffic light.

1.3   **Left** on **IVY ROAD** (US 250) at traffic light.

1.5   **Bear right** on **OLD IVY ROAD** at next traffic light. Pass under railroad bridge. **Continue** on **OLD IVY ROAD** (VA 754), crossing over US 29. *Caution: traffic.* Becomes **VA 601.**

2.3   **Left** on **VA 601.** *Caution: traffic.*

4.3   **Right** on **VA 601** (Garth Road) at Hunt Country Corner Store.

8.2   **Right** on **VA 676.**

10.6   **Left** on **VA 660.** Cross Rivanna Reservoir.

15.0   **Left** on **VA 743** at stop sign. Supermarket and Comfort Cafe, with down home comfort food across street. ALTERNATE START for 46.3 mile loop.

15.6   **Bear left** on **VA 663.** Earlysville General Store on right.

17.0   **Straight** on **VA 664,** where VA 663 bears right.

17.4   **Straight** on **VA 665,** where VA 664 bears right. (For a less hilly alternate, bear right on VA 664 and follow to intersection with VA 810. Go left on VA 810, and pick up cues at mile 28.9.)

22.0   **Bear right** on **VA 601** in Free Union.

28.9   **Left** on **VA 810** at T.

34.7   **Left** to stay on **VA 810** at T, at the bottom of a big hill.

41.0   **Left** on **VA 614/810.** White Hall. Groceries.

41.1   **Straight** to stay on **VA 614** (Garth Road). Gas station on left. For SIDE TRIP to Skyline Drive, turn right on VA 810 and see cues below.

50.2   Becomes **VA 601. Right** to stay on **VA 601** at bottom of big hill. ALTERNATE ROUTE (to return to Earlysville), left on VA 601, picking up cues at mile 8.2 above.

52.2   **Straight** on **OLD IVY ROAD** (VA 754), crossing over US 29. *Caution: traffic.*

53.0   **Bear left** on **IVY ROAD** (US 250) at stop sign. Enter Charlottesville.

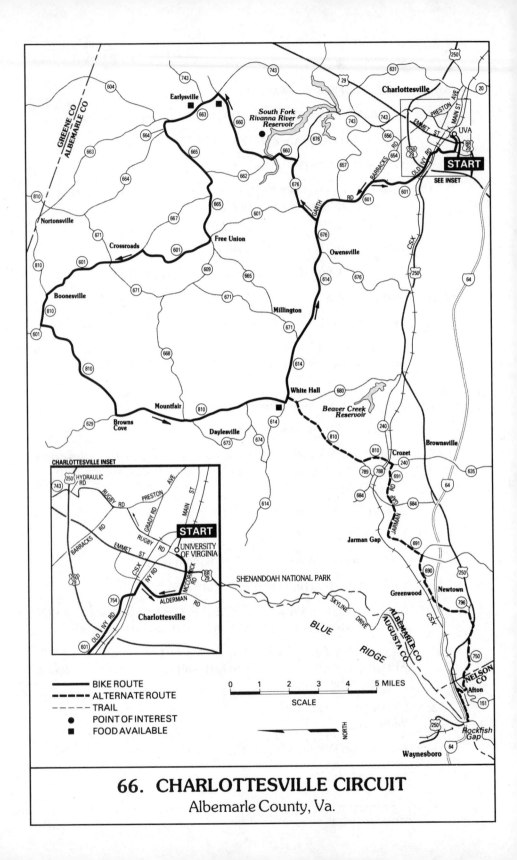

66. CHARLOTTESVILLE CIRCUIT
Albemarle County, Va.

53.2 **Right** on **ALDERMAN ROAD** at traffic light.

53.8 **Left** on **McCORMICK ROAD** at traffic light. Enter university campus.

54.5 **Right** into **ROTUNDA.**

SIDE TRIP TO SKYLINE DRIVE

41.1 **Right** on **VA 810** (unmarked) in White Hall.

45.6 **Straight** on **VA 240** in Crozet.

45.8 **Right** on **VA 691** (Jarmon Gap Road).

49.8 **Right** on **VA 690.** Begin steep incline.

53.3 **Right** on **VA 796** at T.

53.7 **Right** on **US 250** at T.

54.3 **Left** on **VA 750.** Steep incline.

56.2 **Right** on **VA 151.** Keep climbing.

56.8 **Left** on **US 250.** *Caution: fast traffic.*

58.0 **Arrive** at **ROCKFISH GAP.** Skyline Drive to north, Blue Ridge Parkway to south. Motels. Appalachian Trail. **Reverse direction** for return to main route.

67. WILLIAMSBURG - JAMESTOWN LOOP

Explore the famed "Colonial Triangle" and an important part of early American history on this loop between Williamsburg and Jamestown Island. Little remains on the island (the first permanent English settlement in the United States) today except the Old Church Tower (1639). The island features a variety of historical displays and a network of short nature loops open to bicycles. The Visitors Center provides water and restrooms. Jamestown Festival Park lies west of Jamestown Island and features a reconstructed fort, ships and other attractions. (There are entrance fees to the island and park.)

The Williamsburg Information Center offers a brochure of bicycle tours in the Colonial Triangle (Williamsburg, Yorktown, Jamestown). In addition, a 20-minute ferry ($0.15 for bicycles) takes you from Jamestown to Scotland on the south bank of the James River — a nice place for a picnic.

START: Williamsburg Information Center on VA 132Y in Williamsburg, Va. From the Capital Beltway, take I-95 South (to Richmond), then I-295 East (to Norfolk), then I-64 East to VA 132 (to Williamsburg). VA 132Y is a spur of VA 132. Williamsburg is 160 miles south of the Capital Beltway.

LENGTH: 23.2 miles (does not include a 5.2-mile loop on Jamestown Island).

TERRAIN: Rolling hills. Cobblestone surface on the Colonial Parkway makes for slow going. Bike lanes on some roads.

POINTS OF INTEREST: Williamsburg at start; James River Ferry at 13.9 miles; Jamestown Island (757-229-1733) at 14.1 miles, with nature loops, information center and Glasshouse (c.1608), Old Church Tower, craft exhibits; and College of William and Mary (1693) at 22.1 miles, the second oldest college in the country with Sir Christopher Wren building and Sunken Garden. Jamestown Festival Park (757-229-1607) west of Jamestown Island.

FOOD: Markets in Williamsburg and Jamestown, and at 6.6 miles.

LODGING: Colonial Williamsburg Chamber of Commerce (757-229-1000) and Colonial Williamsburg Foundation (757-229-2141) have information.

MAPS AND INFORMATION: *Bike Map: Historic Triangle* available from Williamsburg Information Center at the start.

MILES DIRECTIONS & COMMENTS

0.0 **Right** out of Information Center, and **right** on **VA 132** (Henry Street).

0.4 **Left** on **US 60.**

1.6   **Right** on **BUS US 60.** *Caution: heavy traffic.*

1.9   **Left** on **IRONBOUND ROAD** (VA 615), then immediate **right** on **LONGHILL ROAD** (VA 612). Pleasant, shady road.

3.1   **Right** to stay on **LONGHILL ROAD.**

6.6   **Left** on **VA 614.** Grocery.

11.7   **Right** on **VA 5** (John Taylor Highway).

11.8   **Left** on **VA 614.**

13.9   **Straight** on **VA 359.** (Right on VA 31 to Jamestown-Scotland Ferry.)

14.1   **Right** on **COLONIAL PARKWAY** to Jamestown Island. [Note: the cues do not include Jamestown Island, which should not be missed!] **Reverse direction** and take **left** on **COLONIAL PARKWAY** for return.

21.8   **Right** on **RAMP,** following signed bike route.

21.9   **Right** on **NEWPORT AVENUE.**

22.1   **Right** on **HENRY STREET.** College of William and Mary.

23.0   **Right** on **VA 132Y.**

23.2   **Left** at **WILLIAMSBURG INFORMATION CENTER.**

Along the Colonial Parkway.

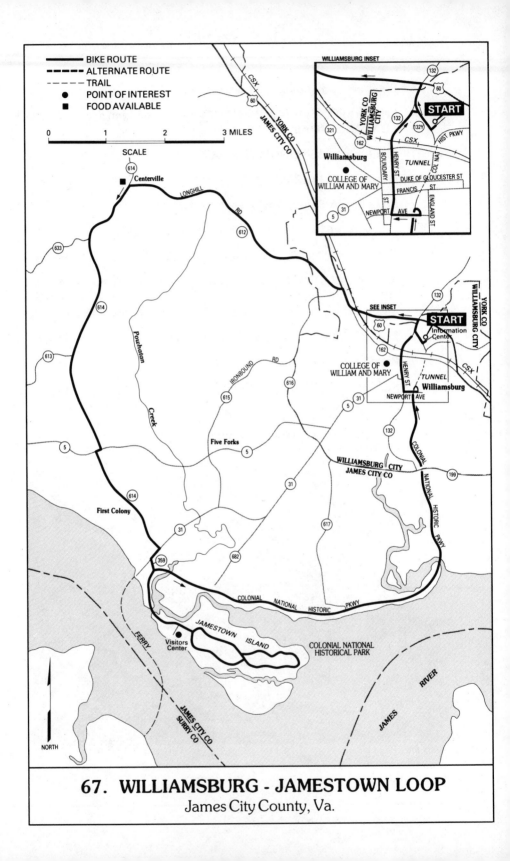

67. WILLIAMSBURG - JAMESTOWN LOOP
James City County, Va.

Appendix ·

A. BICYCLE AND RELATED ORGANIZATIONS

The Washington area is home to many active bicycling organizations, from touring clubs to advocacy groups to racing clubs to mountain bike clubs. Many of these groups, particularly the touring clubs, sponsor rides. These groups can benefit from your active support, and, as a cyclist, you benefit from their efforts to organize the cycling community and work for safer and better conditions.

In addition to the local and regional groups, several national cycling organizations are working to improve bicycling facilities and conditions. What follows is a selected list of these organizations.

Regional

Washington Area Bicyclist Association
1511 K Street NW #1015
Washington, DC 20005-1401
202-628-2500
Web: http://www.waba.org; e-mail: waba@waba.org
Co-publisher of this Atlas, WABA is one of the nation's oldest, largest and most effective local bicycle advocacy groups. A non-profit membership organization, WABA works with volunteers and community and government agencies and officials to improve bicycling conditions for transportation and recreation. WABA's programs range from facility creation and improvement to policy and planning. WABA's Bicycle Helmet Safety Institute is internationally renowned for providing reliable and current information on helmet safety and testing.

Mid-Atlantic Off-Road Enthusiasts
P.O. Box 2662
Fairfax, VA 22031
703-502-0359
MORE promotes regional mountain biking opportunities through weekly off-road rides, social events, maintenance, advocacy and education.

Potomac Pedalers Touring Club
P.O. Box 23601
Washington, DC 20026-3601
202-363-TOUR
The nation's largest local bicycle touring club, with nearly 5,000 members, offers rides for all ages and abilities. Ride schedule: http://blueridge/infomkt.ibm.com/bikes.

Maryland

Annapolis Bicycle Club
P.O Box 224
Annapolis, MD 21404-0224
410-721-9151
A recreational cycling group.

Atlantic Cycling
P.O. Box 2772
Gaithersburg, MD 20886-2772
301-774-6839
Provides information on 39 rides from New York State to North Carolina.

Baltimore Bicycling Club
P.O. Box 5894
Baltimore, MD 21282-5894
410-628-1554
A large touring club (2,500 members) sponsoring rides at all levels in Maryland.

Capybara Mountain Bike Club
P.O. Box 3932
Crofton, MD 21114-3932
Off-road in central Maryland.

College Park Area Bicycle Coalition
P.O. Box 1035
College Park, MD 20740-1035
301-441-2740
An active bicycle advocacy group focusing on north Prince Georges County.

Frederick Pedalers Bicycle Club
P.O. Box 1293
Frederick, MD 21702-0293
Sponsors recreational rides in Frederick County.

Greenbelt Bicycle Coalition
108 Ridge Road
Greenbelt, MD 20770-1664
301-474-7280
Works to make Greenbelt a bicycle friendly city.

Oxon Hill Bicycle and Trail Club
P.O. Box 81
Oxon Hill, MD 20750-0081
301-839-9398
Sponsors scheduled rides.

Patuxent Area Cycling Enthusiasts
P.O. Box 1318
Solomons, MD 20688-1318
Sponsors club rides in Charles County and St. Mary's County.

Salisbury Bicycle Club
708 Walnut Street
Pocomoke City, MD 21851-1525
410-957-3089

WB&A Trail Association
9430 Lanham-Severn Road
Seabrook, MD 20706-2642
410-459-7090
An advocacy group promoting the establishment of a bicycle trail on the abandoned Washington Baltimore & Annapolis Railroad right-of-way.

Virginia

Bicycle Organization of South Side (BOSS)
P.O. Box 36458
Richmond, VA 23235-8458
804-276-0934

Blue Ridge Bicycle Club
P.O. Box 13383
Roanoke, VA 24033-3383

Central Virginia Bicycle Club
P.O. Box 4344
Lynchburg, VA 24502-0344

Emporia Bicycle Club
P.O. Box 631
Emporia, VA 23847-0631
540-634-2222

Fredericksburg Cyclists
P.O. Box 7844
Fredericksburg, VA 22404-7844
540-371-0398

Peninsula Bicycling Association
P.O. Box 5639
Newport News, VA 23605-0639

Prince William Bicycle Association
14420 Bristow Road
Mannassas, VA 20112-3932

Rappahannock Bicycle Club
P.O. Box 682
Bowling Green, VA 22427-0682
540-633-6500

Reston Bicycle Club
P.O. Box 3389
Reston, VA 20195-1389
703-904-0900
A fast-growing, active touring club.

Richmond Area Bicycling Association
c/o Betsy Blevins
409-H North Hamilton Street
Richmond, VA 23221-2025

Shenandoah Valley Bicycle Club
P.O. Box 1014
Harrisonburg, VA 22801-1014

Tidewater Bicycle Association
P.O. Box 12254
Norfolk, VA 23502-0254
757-425-9301

Virginia Bicycling Federation
P.O. Box 5621
Arlington, VA 22205-0621
703-237-8967
An advocacy and education group for bicycling in the Commonwealth.

Williamsburg Bicycle Association
P.O. Box 713
Williamsburg, VA 23187-0713

Winchester Wheelmen
1609 Van Couver Street
Winchester, VA 22601-3228
540-667-6703

National

Adventure Cycling Association
P.O. Box 8308
Missoula, MT 59807-8308
406-721-1776
www.adv-cycling.org
A national member-supported service organization for recreational bicycling. Formerly known as Bikecentennial, Adventure Cycling established the TransAmerica Bicycle route, and has since mapped additional long-distance routes through all sections of the country.

International Mountain Biking Association
P.O. Box 7578
Boulder, CO 80306-7578
303-545-9011

League of American Bicyclists
1612 K Street NW #401
Washington, DC 20006-2802
202-822-1333
A national membership organization of individuals, state and local bicycle clubs, and advocacy groups founded in 1880 to protect the rights and promote the interests of bicyclists.

Rails-to-Trails Conservancy
1100 17th Street NW, 10th floor
Washington, DC 20036-4637
202-331-9696
A national membership organization to promote the conversion of abandoned railroad corridors into recreational and commuter greenways.

B. ADDITIONAL TOURING INFORMATION

If you want additional detail on the areas where you are touring, state, regional and local maps complement the maps in this atlas. This section of the Appendix begins by listing sources of maps and guides, following which we list state tourism offices, which can provide more general information.

A listing of area hostels is also provided in this section. Several of the rides start or end near hostels, which generally provide facilities supportive of cycling tourists at very reasonable prices.

Bike Maps and Guides

Regional

ADC's Washington Area Bike Map (1995). A table-sized map showing trails and on-road bikeways in the Washington area. Alexandria Drafting Company, 6440 General Green Way, Alexandria, VA 22312-2447, 703-750-0510. $9.50, available in bike shops and in many convenience stores, including most 7-Elevens.

Delaware

Delaware Maps for Bicycle Users. Delaware DOT, P.O. Box 778, Dover, DE 19903-0778, 302-739-4318. Very comprehensive.

District of Columbia

Getting Around Washington By Bicycle (1983). Eight section maps covering Washington, D.C. in fine detail. D.C. Office of Documents, 441 4th Street NW #520, Washington, DC 20001, 202-727-5090. $3 postpaid.

Rock Creek Park Official Guide. A map of the NPS portion of the Rock Creek Park and Trail. National Park Service, 5000 Glover Road NW, Washington, DC 20015-1098, 202-426-6829. Free; send a self-addressed stamped business-size envelope.

Maryland

Beach to Bay Indian Trail. Runs through Worcester and Somerset Counties on the southern Eastern Shore, on roads marked for cyclists. 800-521-9189 or 800-852-0335.

Bicycle Tours of Frederick County, Maryland. Nine tours in Frederick County. Tourism Council of Frederick County, 19 East Church Street, Frederick, MD 21701-5401, 301-663-8687. $5.70 postpaid.

Bike Trails Through Maryland and *Bicycling in Maryland: A Quick Reference Guide*. Published by the Maryland Department of Transportation (800-252-8776).

C&O Canal Official Guide. A map of the 185-mile C&O Canal. C&O Canal National Park, P.O. Box 4, Sharpsburg, MD 21782-0004, 301-739-4200. Free; send a self-addressed stamped business-size envelope.

Carroll County Classic Country Bicycle Tours. Ten loops of varying difficulty through farms, small towns and back roads. Published by Carroll County Tourism Office (800-272-1933).

Cycling Historical Landscapes: Sugarloaf Regional Trails, Maryland National Capital Parks and Planning Commission (MD-NCPPC), 8787 Georgia Avenue, Silver Spring, MD 20910-3760. $2. Thirteen short routes in historic areas of Montgomery and Frederick Counties.

A Frederick Cycling Guide. Frederick County Tourism Council, 19 East Church Street, Frederick, MD 21701-5401, 301-663-8687. $5.70 postpaid.

Guide to the Northern Central Rail Trail. Hoffman-Williams Systems, 1428 Fenwick Lane, Silver Spring, MD 20910-3328, 301-589-9460. $6.50 postpaid.

Have Bike, Will Tour, Baltimore Bicycling Club, P.O. Box 5894, Baltimore, MD 21282-5894. $5 postpaid. Over 40 tours in the Baltimore area.

Kent County Bicycle Tour. Rides from 11 to 81 miles from the Baltimore Bicycling Club (410-778-0416).

Rivers and Trails, Outdoor Press, P.O. Box 266, Knoxville, MD 21758-0266. $4.95. Maps of bike routes, hiking trails and rivers in the mid-Atlantic region.

Rock Creek Hiker-Biker Trail. A map of the Montgomery County portion of the Rock Creek Trail. MNCPPC Community Relations, 9500 Brunett Avenue, Silver Spring, MD 20901, 301-495-2503.

Southern Maryland Bicycle Map. A fantastic map of Calvert, Charles and St. Mary's Counties, including points of interest, bike shops, trails, routes and much more. Produced by the Southern Maryland Travel and Tourism Committee and the Patuxent Area Cycling Enthusiasts. St. Mary's Chamber of Commerce, 28290 Three Notch Road, Mechanicsville, MD 20659, 301-844-5555.

View Trail 100. A guide to 100 miles of bike routes in Worcester County on the Eastern Shore. 800-852-0335.

Pennsylvania

Guide to Bicycle Touring Routes Between Hostels in Eastern Pennsylvania and New Jersey. Detailed strip maps. Delaware Valley Council, 38 South 3rd Street, Philadelphia, PA 19106-2701, 215-925-6004. $6 postpaid.

Pennsylvania Biking Directories. 22"x36" color state map. PennDOT Map Sales, P.O. Box 2028, Harrisburg, PA 17105-2028, 717-787-6746. Free. More detailed quadrants are $1.25 each.

Scenic Lancaster County Bicycle Tours. A 35-map series (including many in Amish areas) and a county map. Lancaster Bicycle Club, P.O. Box 535, Lancaster, PA 17603-0535. $12 postpaid. Or contact Bike World, 747 South Broad Street, Lititz, PA 17543-2808, 717-626-0650.

Virginia

Arlington County Bikeway Map and Guide (1991). Extensive detail of Arlington's bikeway system, plus safety tips, mileage charts and bicycle laws. Arlington County DPW, 1 Courthouse Plaza, Suite 717, Arlington, VA 22201-5430, 703-358-3681. Free with self-addressed stamped envelope.

Historic Triangle Bike Map: Yorktown, Jamestown, Williamsburg. Four recommended tours in the Colonial Triangle. Virginia DOT, 1401 East Broad Street, Richmond, VA 23219-2040, 804-786-2964. Free.

Mount Vernon Trail Guide. Map of the 19-mile trail. National Park Service, Turkey Run Park, McLean, VA 22101, 703-285-2601. Free; send a self-addressed stamped business-size envelope.

TransAmerica Trail Guide (BC-1543). Adventure Cycling's 370-mile easternmost segment (from Yorktown to Christianburg) of the historic Bikecentennial transcontinental route. Adventure Cycling Association, P.O. Box 8308, Missoula, MT 59807-8308, 406-721-1776. $6.95.

Virginia Loop Bicycle Trail. Strip maps of 600-mile loop tour through hilly Virginia, beginning in D.C. Adventure Cycling, P.O. Box 8308, Missoula, MT 59807, 406-721-1776. $8.95.

W&OD Railroad Regional Park Trail Guide (1996). Trail guide and strip maps. NVRPA, 5400 Ox Road, Fairfax Station, VA 22039, 703-352-5900. $5.75 postpaid.

State and County Road Maps

Delaware DOT, P.O. Box 778, Dover, DE 19903-0778, 302-739-4318. $2 per county.

D.C. DPW Maps, 2000 14th Street NW, 6th floor, Washington, DC 20009-4484, 202-929-8115. Free with a self-addressed 7x10 envelope with $1.24 postage.

Maryland Maps Distribution, 2323 West Joppa Road, Brooklandville, MD 21022, 410-321-3518. $2 per county plus postage.

Pennsylvania DOT Sales Store, P.O. Box 2028, Harrisburg, PA 17105-2028, 717-787-6746. $1.25 per county, or $2.50 for large scale.

Virginia DOT, 1401 East Broad Street, Richmond, VA 23219-2040, 804-786-2963. County maps are $0.25 or $2.50 (for large scale) plus postage. $26 for a book of county maps.

West Virginia DOT, Planning Division, Map Sales, 1900 Kanawha Boulevard East, Charleston, WV 25305-0440, 304-558-2868. Variable prices for county maps.

State Tourism Offices

Delaware Tourism Office, P.O. Box 1401, Dover, DE 19903-1401, 800-441-8846 or 800-282-8667 in Delaware.

Washington D.C. Visitor Association, 1212 New York Avenue NW, Washington, DC 20005-3992, 202-789-7000.

Maryland Office of Tourism Development, 217 East Redwood Street, Baltimore, MD 21202-3316, 800-543-1036 or 410-333-6611.

Pennsylvania Bureau of Travel Development, 400 Forum Building, Harrisburg, PA 17120, 717-787-5453.

Virginia Tourism Corporation, 901 East Byrd Street, Richmond, VA 23219, 804-786-4484; also 1629 K Street NW, Washington, DC 20006, 202-659-5530, 800-VISITVA.

West Virginia Tourism Division. State Capitol Complex. Building 17. 2101 Washington Street East, Charleston, WV 25305-2216, 800-CALL-WVA.

Area Hostels

Hostelling International has a network of more than 150 hostels across the United States. You can vacation at a former lifesaving station on Nantucket Island, a dude ranch in Colorado or two converted lighthouses on the California coast. Most major American cities have HI/AYH hostels as well. Please visit our web site on the Internet at http://www.hiayh.org for more information.

Here in the mid-Atlantic, Hostelling International manages numerous hostels. Many are near tours in this atlas, and have special features and attractions for bicyclists. All of them offer friendly, low-cost overnight lodging — a place to relax after an active day. Here are some hostels you might want to consider. Be sure to call ahead for availability, check-in hours and other details. Hostels have separate dormitory facilities for men and women, secure bicycle storage, laundry rooms and kitchens. Ask about private accommodations.

HOSTELLING INTERNATIONAL — BALTIMORE is in a 19th century brownstone within walking distance of the Inner Harbor and Camden Yards, home of the Baltimore Orioles. Explore the depths at the National Aquarium, or take in any of the 100 shops and restaurants at Harbor Place. Cost: $13-16 per night. Information and reservations, call 410-576-8880. Address: 17 West Mulberry Street, Baltimore, MD 21201-4440.

HOSTELLING INTERNATIONAL — BEAR'S DEN LODGE stands high on the Appalachian Trail in the Blue Ridge Mountains. Located near extensive roads and trails for hiking and biking, visitors also can head to the nearby Shenandoah River for rafting, swimming, canoeing or fishing. Cost: $12-15 per night. For information and reservations: 540-554-8708. Address: Virginia Highway 601, RR 1, Box 288, Bluemont, VA 20135-9502.

HOSTELLING INTERNATIONAL – GEIGERTOWN is conveniently located for both bikers and hikers. The Adventure Cycle Maine-to-Virginia Route and the Horseshoe Trail pass close by. Glimpse into the past when you visit Pennsylvania Dutch Country, or ride the 150-year old Strasburg Railway. Cost: $10-13 per night. Information and reservations: 610-286-9537. Address: 1410 Geigertown Road, Box 301, Geigertown, PA 19523-0301.

HOSTELLING INTERNATIONAL — HARPERS FERRY LODGE perches on a bluff overlooking the Shenandoah and Potomac Rivers. Hike the nearby Appalachian Trail, or bike the C&O Canal Towpath. Be sure to stop off in the historic village of Harpers Ferry, site of John Brown's raid. Both AMTRAK and MARC offer regular train service to Washington, D.C. Cost: $11-14 per night. Information and reservations: 301-834-7652. Address: 19123 Sandy Hook Road, Knoxville, MD 21758-1330.

HOSTELLING INTERNATIONAL — IRONMASTER'S MANSION is located in beautiful Pine Grove Furnace State Park, which is crisscrossed by bicycle trails for both mountain bikes and road bikes, as well as streams for fishing and swimming. The original ironworks manufactured cannonballs used in the Revolutionary War. The 1829 Ironmaster's Mansion sheltered slaves traveling on the Underground Railroad. Cost: $12-15 per night. Information and reservations: 717-486-7575. Address: 1212 Pine Grove Road, Gardners, PA 17324-8830.

HOSTELLING INTERNATIONAL – MARSH CREEK STATE PARK is a stone farmhouse which overlooks a 500-acre lake, perfect for all watersports. Bicyclists can enjoy nearby back country roads, as well as the Struble Bike Trail. Amish farms, Longwood Botanical Gardens, Brandywine Battlefield and Valley Forge are within an easy drive. Cost: $10-13 per night. Information and reservations: 610-458-5881. Address: East Reeds Road, Box 376, Lyndell, PA 19354-0376.

HOSTELLING INTERNATIONAL — SANGRAAL-BY-THE-SEA offers visitors a friendly rural setting on 18 acres alongside the Chesapeake Bay, and just 30 miles from Colonial Williamsburg. Back roads and bike trails wind by natural streams and springs. For great fishing, crabbing, sailing or canoeing, just head for the pier! Cost: $15.50-18.50 per night. Information and reservations: 804-776-6500. Address: Carlton Road (Route 626), Box 187, Urbanna, VA 23175-0187.

HOSTELLING INTERNATIONAL – WASHINGTON, D.C. is just minutes away from all the attractions of the nation's capital. Walk to the White House, the monuments, the Capitol and the Smithsonian Museums. The hostel offers daily walking tours and other special events for guests. Cost: $18-21 per night. Information and reservations: 202-737-2333. Address: 1009 11th Street NW, Washington, DC 20001-4401.

C. CAR-FREE BIKE TOURING

This section provides information on getting your bike to what may seem like inaccessible places without the use of a car. It includes information on crossing the Chesapeake Bay, getting your bike on Metro, transporting bikes on trains and planes, and getting to and from the region's three airports with a bike.

Crossing the Chesapeake Bay Bridge

Many of the most spectacular rides in this atlas are on Maryland's historic Eastern Shore. Flat terrain, beautiful countryside and quaint villages make the peninsula a bicycling paradise.

Bicycling is prohibited on the Chesapeake Bay Bridge, the primary passage between Washington and Maryland's Eastern Shore. After much lobbying by local cyclists, however, the Bridge Authority has proposed subsidizing commercial carrier service for bikes and bikers without a car.

At the time of publication of this guide (1997), the subsidy is in effect informally while a formal policy is under review. Kane Limousine Service will carry bicyclists and their bikes across the bridge for $10 per rider. Call 24 hours in advance for reservations and directions for pickup. The office number, 410-263-8100, is answered 8 a.m. to 5 p.m., Monday through Friday. There is a 24-hour number as well: 410-643-1500.

The ferry from Point Lookout to Smith Island, connecting to the Smith Island to Crisfield ferry is an alternative for a multi-day trip.

Bikes on Metro

Trying to escape the city to start your ride? Get a Bike-on-Rail permit and let Washington's Metrorail whisk you beyond the city line! Washington's Bike-on-Rail program is an invaluable resource for all cyclists.

The Bike-on-Rail program was instituted after years of advocacy by the Washington Area Bicyclist Association. With a Bike-on-Rail permit, you and your bicycle may use Metrorail from 10 a.m. to 2 p.m. and after 7 p.m. on weekdays, and all day weekends and holidays (except Independence Day). You pay the normal fare. A maximum of four bicycles are allowed per train, and bicyclists can use only the first and last doors of the last subway car. Other rules also apply.

To obtain your Bike-on-Rail permit, you must take a short test on the program's rules and regulations. The test is offered at Metro headquarters (600 5th Street NW, in Washington; 202-962-1116) Monday through Friday, 7:30 a.m. to 11 a.m. and 12:30 p.m. to 2:30 p.m. The closest Metro station is Gallery Place. The test is also offered at the Ballston (703-528-3541), Crystal City (703-413-4287) and Rosslyn (703-525-1995) Transit Stores in Arlington, Va., and at the North Bethesda Transportation Center (301-770-8108) in Bethesda, Md. — these locations all require you to supply your own photo. Allow about 30 minutes. A permit costs $15 and is valid for three years.

Bikes on Trains

Amtrak currently offers only very limited service to bicyclists in the Washington area. The Vermonter, which runs once daily between Washington's Union Station and Vermont, is the only long-distance train in the Washington area that provides bicyclists with roll-on access (there are bike racks in the Vermonter's baggage car). Reservations are required, and it costs $10 to take your bike with you.

Otherwise, bikes must be boxed (Amtrak will provide a box for a fee, or you can provide your own) and can only travel as checked baggage in baggage cars. Not all Amtrak trains have baggage cars, so plan your trip carefully if you want to travel on the same train as your bike.

For more information about taking your bike on Amtrak or to make a reservation for the Vermonter, call 1-800-USA-RAIL. To ask Amtrak for expanded roll-on bicycle access, write: Tom Downs, President & CEO, Amtrak, 60 Massachusetts Avenue NE, Washington, DC 20002-4285.

Bikes on Planes

Most airlines charge approximately $50 to check a bicycle on a commercial flight within the United States. This charge has nothing to do with any size or weight restriction; it automatically applies to all bicycles. (Check with your individual airlines for their exact policies.)

To avoid these fees, join the League of American Bicyclists. As a League member, you can get free bike passes on six airlines (Continental, USAirways, Northwest, AmericaWest, TWA and Western Pacific) when you book your trip through their travel agent. Restrictions apply. For more information or to join the League, call 202-822-1333.

U.S. airlines generally require bicycles to be boxed. Boxes are available from the airlines and from bike shops. Airlines generally charge approximately $15 for a bike box and require the handlebars to be turned and the pedals to be removed (bring your own tools with you to the airport). Bike shop boxes are usually free (call ahead for availability) but smaller than airline bike boxes, thus requiring further bicycle disassembly. Bike shops will box a bicycle for you for a fee. An alternative to cardboard boxes is special bicycle luggage, which is highly protective but expensive.

Getting to and from D.C. Area Airports by Bike

Three airports serve the Washington metropolitan area. *National Airport* is by far the most convenient to the city. It is located across the Potomac River in Arlington, Va., within a few miles of downtown Washington. The Mount Vernon Trail traverses the airport (see Tour 5). The airport also has its own Metrorail station, served by the Yellow and Blue Lines, although you need a Bike-on-Rail permit to take your bicycle with you on Metrorail. Taxis and shuttles to downtown D.C. are plentiful at the airport.

Dulles International Airport is located about 20 miles west of the city in western Fairfax and eastern Loudoun Counties, Va. Bicycle access to Dulles is extremely limited. It is feasible to bicycle from the airport along the Dulles

Access Road (but be prepared for lots of traffic) to VA 28 (bicycles are not permitted past VA 28 on the Dulles Access Road). Take VA 28 (Sully Road) north to VA 846 (Sterling Boulevard), about two miles. Turn right on VA 846. It will intersect the W&OD Trail (Tour 6) in less than a mile. Turn right on the W&OD Trail and proceed to Washington. Alternatively, you can take a bus, limo, or taxi from the airport to the West Falls Church Metrorail station, which is near the W&OD Trail (see Tour 6). Airport Connection buses serve downtown Washington and will take boxed bicycles. Some airport shuttles will take boxed bicycles and provide door-to-door service, but these are more expensive than the bus.

Baltimore-Washington International Airport (BWI) is located just south of Baltimore, near Severn, Md. To get to Washington by bicycle from the BWI terminal, ride 0.5 miles along Elm Road to the traffic light at MD 170 (Aviation Boulevard). Turn right. In approximately 0.5 miles, turn left onto Camp Meade Road (Aviation Boulevard continues straight at this point). Turn left on Hammonds Ferry Road. At the intersection with West Nursery Road, pick up cues of the Washington to Baltimore Tour (Tour 25) beginning at mile 37.0. Follow cues to Baltimore, or reverse cues to Washington. There is an Amtrak station approximately one mile from BWI (see above for bike-on-train information); the Amtrak station should be accessible by the BWI Trail in the fall of 1997. Light rail service to Baltimore is also scheduled to begin in fall 1997. Bicycles are permitted on light rail. Taxis and shuttles are also available at the airport.

D. BICYCLING AND THE LAW

This section provides information concerning the applicability of traffic laws to bicyclists in the Washington area.

Bicycles are legally classified as vehicles in the District of Columbia, Maryland and Virginia, which means that bicyclists generally share the same rights and responsibilities as car drivers. Each jurisdiction additionally enforces special bicycling laws that recognize the bicycle's small size, vulnerability and limited speed. The laws are designed for the cyclists' safety, and, although sometimes inconvenient, always should be observed.

Metropolitan Washington area bicyclists should be familiar with the laws of the three jurisdictions, as well as the regulations of the National Capital Region of the National Park Service, which oversees many area parks. Some municipalities also have their own local bicycle ordinances. Even Capitol Hill has its own rules — and its own police department.

Maryland law prohibits bicyclists from riding on roads with speed limits above 50 mph (though shoulder riding is legal), on controlled access highways (with entrance ramps), in state-run tunnels, or over state-run bridges. Bicyclists have the right to use any other roadways unless expressly prohibited.

Maryland and *Virginia* require cyclists to ride as near to the right road edge as is safe, reasonable and practical, unless turning left or passing slower-moving traffic. *Virginia* makes exceptions for various hazards and narrow lanes.

The *District of Columbia* requires only that "slower-moving traffic keep right." The *National Capital Region* of the National Park Service has a similar regulation. The *District of Columbia* also prohibits unnecessary obstruction or impeding of traffic by bicyclists; *Maryland* and *Virginia* laws do not address this issue.

Special situations may exist when an off-road trail lies adjacent to a road. *Virginia* allows localities to enact ordinances for mandatory use of adjacent trails. *Maryland* requires bicyclists to use a bike lane or shoulder if it is paved to a "comparable surface to the road." The *District of Columbia* does not require the use of trails at all. In all of the tours in this atlas where roads adjoin trails, bicycling in the roadway is legal, except where the roadway is a limited access highway (e.g., the Mount Vernon Trail along the George Washington Memorial Parkway in Virginia).

Cycling on sidewalks is banned in *Maryland* unless permitted by local ordinance. *Virginia* takes the opposite approach, allowing the use of sidewalks unless forbidden by a locality. The *District of Columbia* allows bicycling on all sidewalks outside the downtown area (roughly defined as Georgetown to the west, Capitol Hill to the east, the waterfront to the south and Dupont Circle and Union Station to the north). When on a sidewalk or in a crosswalk in the *District of Columbia* or *Virginia*, bicyclists have the same rights and duties as pedestrians. Wherever you bicycle on a sidewalk, extend every courtesy to pedestrians, and give an audible warning before passing.

Maryland allows two bicyclists to ride abreast of each other so long as traffic is not impeded. The *District of Columbia* allows riding abreast if "persons are not endangered." *Virginia* and the *National Capital Region* of the National Park Service forbid riding abreast.

In many localities, residents must register their bicycles, usually with the police. For more information on registration, contact the police department or bicycle coordinator in your community.

A growing number of jurisdictions have enacted legislation requiring the use of bicycle helmets. Typically, fines collected from offenders provide helmets to low-income families.

Equipment

In the *District of Columbia* and *Maryland*, bicycles must be equipped with a bell or other device capable of giving a signal audible for a distance of 100 feet. *Virginia* has no statewide law, but localities may have such an ordinance.

For night riding, the *District of Columbia, Maryland* and *Virginia* require use of a lamp emitting a white light visible for 500 feet to the front, while the *National Capital Region* of the National Park Service requires simply a "white light." The *District of Columbia* and *Virginia* also require that bicycles used at night have a red reflector or a red light visible from the rear. *Maryland* and the *National Capital Region* of the National Park Service require only a reflector. *Maryland* and *Virginia* laws require that lights must be attached to the bicycle, technically prohibiting battery-operated arm or leg lights.

Requirements for riding with lights sometimes extend into daylight hours. In *Maryland*, lights must be used when persons and vehicles "are not clearly discernible at a distance of 1,000 feet." Therefore, lights and reflectors are not required on some well-lit streets at night, but are required during dark daytime hours. The *National Capital Region* of the National Park Service similarly requires use of lights during periods of low visibility.

For a brochure on local laws pertaining to bicyclists, send a self-addressed stamped envelope to WABA. You also can read ordinances and state codes in local libraries.

Accidents

If you are involved in an accident on your bicycle, you must stop, identify yourself, and render aid to anyone injured. If death, injury, or substantial property damage has occurred, you must notify the police immediately. These laws apply to car drivers as well as bicyclists.

You can "be involved" in an accident without having physical contact with a motor vehicle or pedestrian. For instance, if a motorist passes you and collides with an oncoming car, you are legally involved.

If you are involved in an accident that results in death, injury, or substantial property damage, you should notify your homeowner and/or automobile insurance company. Failure to provide notice may give your insurance company the right to refuse to pay a claim. If you are injured by a car collision while bicycling, an automobile insurance policy may cover some medical expenses and wage losses.

A bicyclist who violates a law and causes an accident can be sued, and may be required by a court to compensate the injured person. Hence, liability insurance is desirable. Most homeowner or tenant insurance provides liability protection for bicyclists. Automobile insurance policies generally do not provide such protection.

Obeying the law does not insure your safety. You should strive to adopt a philosophy of "defensive cycling," anticipating difficult situations and yielding the road as safety requires.

Acknowledgments

The editors and publishers gratefully thank everyone who helped to make this book a reality. Many people checked rides, suggested routes, read drafts, took photographs, and otherwise provided information and good advice. Our thanks go to Heather Andersen, Tim Arnold, Ruddy Aukschun, Megan Bevan, Susan Blanchard, Camilla Buchanan, Gary Buff, Ken Buja, John Campanile, John Carey, Andy Carruthers, Mimi Castaldi, Eric Ciccoretti, Mary Clarke, Brad Convis, Chris Craig, Harry Davis, Mark Eakloff, Zoe Edelstein, Helen Epps, Kippi Fagerlund, Andrea Ferster, Jonathan Fleming, Quindi Franco, Dave Frankel, Bob Friedman, Willa Friedman, Andrew Gallo, Jim Gent, James Gentner, Maripage Grubic, Peter Harnik, Cindy Harrington, Darryl Hathaway, Tim Hayes, Valerie Hayes, Russ Hedge, Ron Hicks, Aviva Hord, Ed Hord, Viv Hynes, Elaine Johnston, Ellen Jones, David Kay, Ed Kearney, Jennifer Longsworth, Agnes Loo, John Malcolm, Larry McClemons, Sue McClemons, Karen Menczer, Jeannie Mozier, Allen Muchnick, David Muhlbaum, Mike Mulligan, James Menzies, Jim Nash, Lauren Nichols, Gary Nooger, Rick Nunno, Anu Oinas, Colin Patching, Charles Pekow, John Pescatore, Barry Polisar, Abigail Porter, Mary Reynolds, Tom Roberts, Amy Robins, Charlie Rowe, Bill Ryerson, Ben Sandel, Neil Sandler, Dan Schaller, Jane Schnell, Ian Schoen, Bill Silverman, Stephen Smith, Jack Stansbury, Koraleen Stavish, Diane Stokes, Ruth Stornetta, Randy Swart, Leslie Tierstein, Lori Urban, Ritch Viola, Tamara Washington, Larry West and Melissa Yanowitz.

This fifth edition of the *Greater Washington Area Bicycle Atlas* also owes much to its earlier editions, which date back more than two decades to 1974, and to the editors of those editions.

JIM MCCARTHY, who didn't understand what he was getting into when he volunteered for this project, is a member of the Washington Area Bicyclist Association and husband of Ellen Jones, WABA's Executive Director. A bicycle commuter and weekend cyclist, he has been touring the Washington area by bike for nearly 20 years.

SHARON GANG is an avid bicycle tourist, having traveled extensively throughout the United States. As a free-lance journalist, she published tales of some of her adventures in *Vermont Life*, *Adventure Cyclist*, *Spokes*, *Mid-Atlantic Outdoor Traveler*, and *The Washington Post*. A D.C. native, she is currently exploring the hills and back roads of Seattle, Washington, where she moved in 1996.

MARTHA TABOR is a full-time visual artist working in the mediums of photography, printmaking and sculpture. She is a member of WABA and lives in Washington, D.C.

Index

A

B

C

G

H

M

N

Q

R

S

T

U

V

W

XYZ

Eight good reasons to join Hostelling International.

1. **Access to nearly 5,000 hostels in over 70 countries.**
Whether vacationing in Europe or biking to Harpers Ferry, your hostel membership is the key to clean, friendly, inexpensive accommodations.

2. **Free copy of the *Hostelling North America* handbook.**
Packed with information about 225 US and Canadian hostels, this handbook will help you get the most of your travels from Key West to Saskatchewan.

3. **Big discounts at any Hostelling International Travel Center.**
Discover a wide range of guidebooks and maps, backpacks and bags, travel accessories and other gear — all at special member prices.

4. **Super savings on airfares and the best advice on railpasses.**
Call either of our travel centers for bargains on tickets around the globe, as well as the European railpass that best matches your itinerary.

5. **Free workshops and travel programs.**
Explore the world through the Tall Tales Travel Club. Learn how to do it cheaply at a Budget Travel Workshop.

6. **Terrific volunteer opportunities.**
Meet and mix with visitors from overseas by leading walking tours, or escorting groups to embassy concerts and other special events.

7. **Enjoyable evenings of international culture.**
Savor ethnic dinners or learn about foreign countries at travel slide shows and panel discussions about international issues.

8. **International Travel Day.**
Plan your worldly wandering at the region's premiere travel expo, featuring top travel writers, workshops, exhibitors and travel information from 50 countries.

HOSTELLING
INTERNATIONAL

We invented budget travel.

For membership information, see reverse side.

HOSTELLING INTERNATIONAL

We invented budget travel.

Membership Application

Name_____

Address _____

_____

City_____ State _____ Zip _____

Daytime Area Code & Phone _____

Birth Date: Month_____ Year_____

Please check the appropriate membership category:

☐ Adult (18-54) ....$25   ☐ Supporting* $50

☐ Youth (under 18) ....$10   ☐ Sustaining* $100

☐ Senior Citizen (over 54).......$15   ☐ Life $250

☐ Family (w/ children under 18) $35   Contribution* .... $_____

Any amount over your annual membership fee is tax deductible.

Postage & Handling............$2.50

TOTAL .... $_____

Join by mail:
by sending this form to "Dept. M" at the Washington address below.

☐ Check enclosed
☐ Visa/MC

CC No._____

Signature_____   Expiration_____

Join in person at either of our travel centers:

1108 K Street NW 2nd Floor
Washington, DC 20005
202/783-4943

17 West Mulberry Street
Baltimore, MD 21201
410/576-8880

SUPPORT WABA
HELP IMPROVE BICYCLING IN THE WASHINGTON AREA

What is WABA?

The Washington Area Bicyclist Association is a non-profit educational organization dedicated to improving bicycling conditions in the Washington metropolitan region. The nation's oldest regional bicycle advocacy group, WABA has been a respected and effective force for area cyclists since 1972.

- 🚲 We serve as a valuable bicycling information resource for members, government, the media and the public.

- 🚲 We sponsor the National Capital Bicycle Tour, Earth Day Bike-In, Effective Cycling classes, and commuter mentoring.

- 🚲 We work for better bicycle accommodations on roads, bridges and transit.

- 🚲 We get bikeways and trails built, improved and maintained.

- 🚲 We press for bicycle commuter amenities at work sites and suitable bicycle parking at all destinations.

- 🚲 We testify before federal, state and local government bodies on bicycling concerns.

- 🚲 We coordinate and support local and regional coalitions and individuals working on specific bicycling projects.

What We Can Do For You

Bicycling in a busy metropolitan area can mean more than the risk of a flat tire. You may need training in how to ride in traffic. And there are always improvements you would like to see on your favorite trails and roads. WABA can help you with these membership benefits:

- 🚲 Discounts on bikes, accessories and repairs at 40 area bike shops.

- 🚲 Access to a wealth of information on bicycle safety, laws, events, maps and publications.

- 🚲 *Ride On!*, a monthly newsletter covering the latest news about bicycling in the area, articles on current issues and proposals, a calendar of upcoming events, and notices about WABA activities.

- 🚲 The opportunity to volunteer to participate in bicycling issues in your region.

- 🚲 Personalized bicycle commuting and routing assistance.

To join, please complete the membership application on the next page.

WABA Membership Application

Name
_____

Address
_____

City _____ State ____ Zip+4 ____

Additional Names (family memberships only)
_____

Phone: home _____ work _____

E-mail (only if you prefer this form of communication for notices)

WABA needs volunteers! Please indicate below if you are interested in assisting in any of the following categories:

__Advocacy   __Mailing parties
__Commuter Mentor   __Graphic Art
__Safety and Education   __Photography
__Events   __Other Skills

One Year Memberships   **Two Year Memberships**
___$15 Low income
       or Student
___$25 Individual   ___$35 Individual
___$35 Family   ___$55 Family
___$75 Sustaining
___$150 Patron
___$400 Life

___Other Contribution $_____

Memberships expire on the 15th of the month one/two year(s) from application. Dues and contributions are tax deductible. Please add $5 **per year** and check here for first class receipt of the newsletter:____

TOTAL ENCLOSED:_____

Mail application to: *Washington Area Bicyclist Association*
                         1511 K Street NW #1015
                         Washington, DC 20005
                         Phone: 202-628-2500
                         Fax: 202-628-4141
                         E-mail: waba@waba.org
                         Website www.waba.org